Updated Student's Study Guide and Solutions Manual

Lori Rosenthal

Austin Community College

to accompany

Using and Understanding Mathematics

A Quantitative Reasoning Approach

Third Edition

Jeffrey Bennett

University of Colorado at Boulder

William Briggs

University of Colorado at Denver

Boston San Francisco New York
London Toronto Sydney Tokyo Singapore Madrid
Mexico City Munich Paris Cape Town Hong Kong Montreal

Reproduced by Pearson Addison-Wesley from electronic files supplied by the author.

Publishing as Pearson Addison-Wesley, 75 Arlington Street, Boston, MA 02116

ISBN 0-321-34328-X

1 2 3 4 5 6 BB 08 07 06 05 04

Introduction

Welcome to the *Study Guide and Solutions Manual* for *Using and Understanding Mathematics*. Hopefully, with the help of this book, your course in quantitative reasoning will be both enjoyable and successful. The goal of this guide is not to add to your workload for the course, but to give you a set of concise notes that will make your studying as effective as possible. If you work with this guide as you read and do exercises, you should get the most from the course.

This guide is organized according to the units in the textbook. For each unit you will find the following features:

Overview

This section provides a brief survey of the unit, its major points and its goals. This feature is not a substitute for reading the text!

Key Words and Phrases

This section is simply a list of the important words and phrases used in the unit. You can use this section for review, study, and self-testing. You should be able to explain or define all of the terms on this list.

Key Concepts and Skills

In this section you will find a summary of the most important concepts in each unit. These concepts may be general ideas (for example, the distinction between deductive and inductive arguments) or basic skills (for example, creating the equation of a straight line). This section should also be helpful for review, study, and self-testing.

Important Review Boxes

If a unit has one or more Review Boxes, they are listed. These boxes are quite important for providing background skills or knowledge needed for the unit.

Solutions to (Most) Odd Problems

Following all of the unit summaries, the second half of this Guide provides full solutions to most of the odd-numbered problems in the textbook. Mathematics is not a spectator sport! Reading the solutions is never a substitute for working the problems. *You are strongly advised to work the problems first and then check the solutions.*

How to Succeed In This Course

Using *This* Book

Before we get into more general strategies for studying, here are a few guidelines that will help you use *this* book most effectively.

- Before doing any assigned problems, read assigned material *twice*:
  - On the first pass, read quickly to gain a feel for the material and concepts presented.
  - On the second pass, read the material in more depth, and work through the examples carefully.
- During the second reading, take notes that will help you when you go back to study later. In particular:
  - *Use the margins!* The wide margins in this textbook are designed to give you plenty of room for making notes as you study.
  - Don't highlight — underline! Using a pen or pencil to underline material requires greater care than highlighting, and therefore helps to keep you alert as you study.
- After you complete the reading, and again when studying for exams, make sure you can answer the *review questions* at the end of each unit.
- You'll learn best by *doing*, so work plenty of the end-of-unit exercises. Don't be reluctant to work more than the exercises that your instructor assigns.

Budgeting Your Time

A general rule of thumb for college courses is that you should expect to study about 2 to 3 hours per week *outside* class for each unit of credit. For example, a student taking 15 credit hours should spend 30 to 45 hours each week studying outside of class. Combined with time in class, this works out to a total of 45 to 60 hours per week — not much more than the time required of a typical job. If you find that you are spending fewer hours than these guidelines suggest, you can probably improve your grade by studying more. If you are spending more hours than these guidelines suggest, you may be studying inefficiently; in that case, you should talk to your instructor about how to study more effectively for a mathematics class.

General Strategies for Studying

- Don't miss class. Listening to lectures and participating in discussions is much more effective than reading someone else's notes. Active participation will help you retain what you are learning.
- Budget your time effectively. An hour or two each day is more effective, and far less painful, than studying all night before homework is due or before exams.
- If a concept gives you trouble, do additional reading or problem solving beyond what has been assigned. If you still have trouble, *ask for help*: you surely can find friends, colleagues, or teachers who will be glad to help you learn. Never be reluctant to ask questions or ask for help in this

course. If you have a question or problem, it is extremely unlikely that you will be alone!

- Working together with friends can be valuable; you improve your own understanding when discussing concepts with others. However, be sure that you learn *with* your friends and do not become dependent on them.

Preparing for Exams

- Rework exercises and other assignments; try additional exercises to be sure you understand the concepts. Study your assignments, quizzes, and exams from earlier in the semester.
- Study your notes from lectures and discussions. Pay attention to what your instructor expects you to know for an exam.
- Reread the relevant sections in the textbook, paying special attention to notes you have made in the margins.
- Study individually before joining a study group with friends. Study groups are effective only if *every* individual comes prepared to contribute.
- Try to relax before and during the exam. If you have studied effectively, you are capable of doing well. Staying relaxed will help you think clearly.

Finally, good luck! We wish you an enjoyable and rewarding experience with quantitative reasoning.

1 Thinking Critically

Overview

Before discussing Chapter 1, we urge you to take a few minutes to read the prologue to the textbook. This short chapter sets the stage for the entire book. It presents the idea of quantitative reasoning and discusses the importance of interdisciplinary thinking. It gives a high altitude picture of mathematics and how it impacts many other subjects that you will encounter either in other courses or in your career. Finally, it gives some advice on using the book and studying for your course. It's worth a quick reading. Now on to Chapter 1.

In teaching this course to many students of over many years, we know that often the most serious weakness that students bring to the course is not poor mathematical skills, but poor reasoning skills. Often it's not multiplying two numbers that creates problems, but deciding *when* to multiply! For this reason, the book opens with a chapter that contains virtually no mathematics. The emphasis of the chapter is critical thinking and logical skills.

In this chapter you will encounter some introductory logic, but don't worry; we don't get carried away with symbolic logic and heavy-duty truth tables. In fact, much of this chapter may be familiar to you from previous courses in logic or philosophy.

Unit 1A Recognizing Fallacies

Unit 1A opens the chapter by explaining that a logical **argument** (as opposed to an everyday argument) is a set of facts or assumptions, called **premises**, that lead to a **conclusion**. A **fallacy** is an argument that is either deceptive or wrong. This unit explores common fallacies that you might encounter in advertising or (bad) news reports. We present ten different so-called informal fallacies, some of which may seem quite obvious, others of which may be quite subtle. Critical reading and thinking will help you avoid becoming a victim of these fallacies!

Key Words and Phrases

logic	argument	premise
conclusion	fallacy	appeal to popularity
false cause	appeal to ignorance	hasty generalization
limited choice	appeal to emotion	personal attack
circular reasoning	diversion	straw man

Key Concepts and Skills

- identify the premise and conclusion of an argument.
- recognize informal fallacies in advertisements and news report.

Unit 1B Propositions and Truth Values

Overview

In this unit formal logic is introduced in a somewhat casual way. We start with **propositions** — statements that make a claim that can be true or false. Then we look at the **connectors** that can be used with propositions to make more complex propositions. The connectors that you will encounter are

- *not* (negation)
- *or* (disjunction)
- *and* (conjunction)
- *if ... then* (implications).

Whereas many logic books make heavy use of symbolic logic and truth tables, we will use truth tables primarily for fairly simple propositions that involve one, two, or three connectors. So our excursion into symbolic logic will be limited and designed to provide only an introductory glimpse.

The *if ... then* connector is quite important in both logic and everyday speech (for example, *if I pass this course, then I will graduate*). For this reason, we spend a little time discussing other forms of the proposition *if P, then Q*. These other forms are the

- **converse** (*if Q, then P*),
- **inverse** (*if not P, then not Q*), and
- **contrapositive** (*if not Q, then not P*).

This particular discussion may seem a bit technical, but it's also extremely practical. For example, suppose it's true that *if I read the book, then I will pass the course*. Does it follow that *if I don't read the book, then I won't pass the course*? You will see!

Key Words and Phrases

proposition	truth table	negation
conjunction	disjunction	conditional
antecedent	consequent	converse
inverse	contrapositive	logical equivalence

Key Concepts and Skills

- understand negation, conjunction, disjunction, and conditionals and their truth tables.

- use truth tables to evaluate the truth of compound propositions that use two or more connectors.
- analyze various forms of *if ... then* propositions.

Unit 1C Sets and Venn Diagrams

Overview

You may have encountered Venn diagrams before now as a way to illustrate the relationships between collections of objects, or **sets**. In this unit, we review some of the most basic properties of sets and then discuss how Venn diagrams can be used to work with sets. Throughout the unit, the emphasis is on practical applications of sets and Venn diagrams. One of the important applications of Venn diagrams is to illustrate what are called **categorical propositions** of logic. We will study four basic categorical propositions. Given a **subject set** *S* and a **predicate set** *P*, they may be related in the following ways:

- All *S* are *P* (for example, all whales are mammals)
- No *S* are *P* (for example, no fish are mammals)
- Some *S* are *P* (for example, some doctors are women)
- Some *S* are not *P* (for example, some teachers are not men).

As we will see, each form of categorical proposition has a specific Venn diagram. Equally important, the negation of each categorical proposition is one of the other propositions in the list above. Specifically, we have the following relations between the four propositions and their negations.

Proposition	Negation
All *S* are *P*	Some *S* are not *P*
No *S* are *P*	Some *S* are *P*
Some *S* are *P*	No *S* are *P*
Some *S* are not *P*	All *S* are *P*

The unit concludes with a nice collection of other uses of Venn diagrams. As you will see, Venn diagrams with two or more circles can be used to organize all sorts of information.

Key Words and Phrases

set	Venn diagram	subset
disjoint sets	overlapping sets	categorical propositions

Key Concepts and Skills

- use set notation.
- construct Venn diagrams for categorical propositions.

- put propositions in standard form.
- negate categorical propositions.
- construct Venn diagrams for three or more sets.

Important Review Box

- A Brief Review of Sets of Numbers

Unit 1D Analyzing Arguments

Overview

The propositions that we studied in the previous unit can be combined in various ways to form arguments. Of primary importance is the distinction between **deductive** and **inductive** arguments. Deductive arguments generally proceed from general premises to a more specific conclusion. As we will see, in a deductive argument all of the premises are needed to reach the conclusion. By contrast, inductive arguments generally proceed from specific premises to a general conclusion; in an inductive argument the premises independently support the conclusion.

To analyze inductive arguments, we ask about the **strength** or **weakness** of the argument. Determining the strength of an inductive argument is often a subjective judgment, and so there are no systematic methods to apply.

Most of the unit is spent analyzing three-line deductive arguments using Venn diagrams. They can consist of the four types of categorical propositions or they may involve conditional propositions (studied in Unit 1C). Of fundamental importance in this business is the distinction between valid and invalid arguments. An argument is **valid** if, based on the Venn diagram analysis, it is logically solid and consistent. An argument that fails the Venn diagram analysis must contain a fallacy and is **invalid**. Validity has nothing to do with the truth of the premises or conclusion; it is a measure of the logical structure of the argument.

Having shown that an argument is valid, we can then ask if it is sound. A **sound** argument is valid *and* has true premises; a sound argument must lead to a true conclusion. Soundness is the highest test of a deductive argument.

Fallacies can arise in deductive arguments in many ways. Perhaps the most common fallacies occur in arguments that involve conditional (*if...then*) propositions. These fallacies appear in the everyday arguments of advertising and news reports. There are four different forms of conditional arguments; two are valid and two are invalid:

- affirming the antecedent (valid)
- affirming the consequent (invalid)
- denying the antecedent (invalid)
- denying the consequent (valid).

The unit closes with examples of how inductive and deductive arguments are used in mathematics.

Key Words and Phrases

deductive	inductive	strength/weakness
valid/invalid	sound	affirming the antecedent
affirming the consequent	denying the antecedent	denying the consequent
Pythagorean theorem		

Key Concepts and Skills

- know the distinction between deductive and inductive arguments.
- determine the strength of inductive arguments.
- assess the validity of three-line deductive arguments consisting of categorical propositions, using Venn diagrams.
- assess the validity of three-line deductive arguments involving conditional propositions, using Venn diagrams.
- identify fallacies that arise in conditional arguments.
- understand various combinations of valid/invalid and sound/unsound that can occur in deductive arguments.
- determine the soundness of three-line deductive arguments.

Unit 1E Critical Thinking in Everyday Life

Overview

Critical thinking is an approach to problem solving and decision-making that involves careful reading (or listening), sharp thinking, logical analysis, good visualization, and healthy skepticism. In this chapter, we present several guidelines design to sharpen critical thinking skills as they apply to practical problems. The following guidelines are all accompanied by one or more specific examples.

- Read or listen carefully
- Look for hidden assumptions
- Identify the real issue
- Use visual aids (pictures, diagrams, tables)
- Understand all the options
- Watch for fine print and misinformation
- Are other conclusions possible?

Key Concepts and Skills

- apply the guidelines of the unit to practical decisions and problems

2 Approaches to Problem Solving

Overview

The first chapter of the book was devoted to *qualitative* issues — topics that don't require extensive use of numbers and computation. In this chapter (and the remainder of the book) we turn to *quantitative* matters. Perhaps it's not surprising that we begin our study of quantitative topics with problem solving. The first two units of the chapter deal with a very basic and important problem solving technique, the use of units. The last unit of the chapter presents various problem-solving strategies. It is a valuable chapter whose lessons run through the rest of the book.

Unit 2A The Problem-Solving Power of Units

Overview

Nearly every number that you encounter in the real world is a measure of *something*: 6 billion *people*, 5280 *feet*, 5 trillion *dollars*, 26 *cubic feet*. The quantities that go with numbers are called **units**. And the message of this unit of the book is that using units can simplify problem solving immensely. Indeed the use of units is one of the most basic problem solving tools.

We begin by considering the most basic **simple units** for the fundamental types of measurement. Here are a few examples of simple units.

- length — inches, feet, meters
- weight — pounds, grams
- capacity — quarts, gallons, liters
- time — seconds, hours.

From these simple units, we can build endless **compound units**.

The rest of the unit is spent illustrating a wide variety of such compound units. Among the many you will meet and work with are units of

- units of area such as square feet and square yards
- units of volume such as cubic inches and cubic feet
- units of speed such as miles per hour
- units of price such as dollars per pound
- units of gas mileage such as miles per gallon.

One of the realities of life is that there are many units for the same quantity. For example, we can measure lengths in inches, centimeters, feet, meters, miles, or kilometers. For example, we measure rooms in square feet, but have to buy carpet in square yards. Thus one of the necessities of problem solving is being able to convert from one unit to another consistent unit. The key to doing conversions between units is to realize that there are three equivalent ways to express a conversion factor. For example, we can say 1 foot = 12 inches, or we can say 1 foot *per* 12 inches, or we can say 12 inches *per* foot. Mathematically, we can write

$$1 \text{ foot} = 12 \text{ inches} \quad \text{or} \quad \frac{1 \text{ foot}}{12 \text{ inches}} \quad \text{or} \quad \frac{12 \text{ inches}}{1 \text{ foot}}.$$

These three forms of the same conversion factor are absolutely equivalent. The key to a happy life with units is choosing the appropriate form of the conversion factor for a given situation.

Additional problem solving skills can then be built on these fundamental skills. You will see and learn how to make a chain of conversions factors to solve more complex problems. For example, the time required to count a billion dollars at the rate of one dollar per second is

$$\$1{,}000{,}000{,}000 \times \frac{1 \text{ sec}}{\$1} \times \frac{1 \text{ min}}{60 \text{ sec}} \times \frac{1 \text{ hr}}{60 \text{ min}} \times \frac{1 \text{ day}}{24 \text{ hr}} \times \frac{1 \text{ yr}}{365 \text{ days}} = 31.7 \text{ years.}$$

The fact that the units cancel and give an answer in *years* tells you that the problem has been set up correctly.

Finally, we look at a very practical type of unit conversion problem, those associated with currency. If you travel to France you learn that 1 franc is equal to about 18 cents. From this fact, you might need to answer questions such as

- which is larger, 1 franc or 1 dollar?
- how many francs in a dollar?
- how many dollars in a franc?
- how many dollars in a 23.45 francs?
- if apples cost 23 francs per kilogram, what is the price in dollars per pound?

Here are a few final words of advice: Never was the motto *practice makes perfect* more true than with problem solving and units. You should work all assigned exercises, and then some, in order to master these techniques. And unless your instructor tells you otherwise, there is no need to memorize hundreds of conversion factors. It's helpful to know a few essential conversion factors off the top of your head. As for the rest, it's easiest just to know how to find them quickly in the book.

Key Words and Phrases

simple units	compound units	area
volume	conversion factor	

Key Concepts and Skills

- convert from one simple unit to another; for example, from inches to yards.

- convert from one unit of area to another unit of area; for example, from square inches to square yards.
- convert from one unit of volume to another unit of area; for example, from cubic inches to cubic yards.
- solve problems involving chains of conversion factors; for example, finding the number of seconds in a year.
- convert from one unit of currency to another; for example, from dollars to pesos.

Important Review Box

- A Brief Review of Working with Fractions

Unit 2B Standardized Units: More Problem-Solving Power

Overview

In this unit we continue the study of units and conversion factors, but now explore the two standard systems of units: The U.S. Customary System of Measurement (or USCS system, which is used primarily in the Unites States) and the metric system (which is used everywhere else in the world).

We first proceed systematically and survey the USCS units for length, weight, and capacity. Tables 2.2, 2.3, and 2.4 contain many conversion factors, but you should focus on *using* these conversion factors, not memorizing them! Having seen the complications of the USCS system, the metric system should come as a welcome relief. Next we present the metric units for length, weight and capacity. As you will see, the system is based on powers of ten and standard prefixes (Table 2.5), which makes conversions between units relatively simple.

Unfortunately, for people living in the United States, conversions between the metric system and the USCS system are necessary. (If you would like to avoid doing such exercises, then you should work on getting the United States to go metric!) Table 2.6 has a few of the essential conversion factors between the metric and USCS systems. You may want to write other useful conversion factors in the margin near this table.

Finally, we explore two more categories of units. **Energy** (what makes things move or heat up) and **power** (the rate at which energy is used) are incredibly important concepts in understanding the world around us. Uses of energy and power units are presented in matters such as utility bills, diet, and the environment. The other category of units is **density** and **concentration**. In measuring population density, the capacity of computer discs, levels of pollution, and blood alcohol content, these units are indispensable.

Armed with all of these units and conversion factors (and don't forget currency conversion factors as well), we can do even more elaborate problem solving; this is the goal of the remainder of the unit and the problems at the end of the unit.

Key Words and Phrases

USCS system	metric system	meter
gram	liter	second
metric prefixes	Celsius	Fahrenheit
Kelvin	energy	power
kilowatt-hour	watt	density
concentration	population density	

Key Concepts and Skills

- given the required conversion factor, convert between two consistent USCS units; for example, rods to miles.
- multiply and divide powers of ten.
- know basic metric units and commonly used prefixes.
- given the required conversion factor, convert between two consistent metric units; for example, millimeters to kilometers.
- given the required conversion factor, convert between a USCS unit and a consistent metric unit; for example, ounces to liters.
- convert between temperatures in the three standard systems.
- solve problems using chains of conversion factors involving USCS units, metric units, and currency units.
- understand and apply units of energy and power.
- understand and apply units of density to materials, population, and information.
- understand and apply units of concentration to pollution, and blood alcohol content.

Important Review Box

- A Brief Review of Powers of Ten

Unit 2C Problem Solving Guidelines and Hints

Overview

Having seen very specific examples of problem solving in the previous two units, we now present some strategies for problem solving in general. *There is no simple and universal formula for solving all problems*! Only continual (and hopefully enjoyable) practice can led one towards mastery in problem solving. This unit is designed to provide you some of that practice.

The unit opens with a very well known four-step process for approaching problem solving. As you will see, this process is not a magic formula, but rather a set of guidelines. They four basic steps are

- understand the problem,
- devise a strategy,
- carry out the strategy, and
- look back, check, interpret and explain your solution.

The remainder of the unit is a list of eight strategic hints for problem solving. Here are the strategic hints:

- there may be more than one answer.
- there may be more than one strategy.
- use appropriate tools.
- consider simpler, similar problems.
- consider equivalent problems with simpler solutions.
- approximations can be useful.
- try alternative patterns of thought.
- don't spin your wheels.

Most of the unit consists of examples in which the four-step process and these strategic hints are put to use. Study these problems and solutions, and try to see how the techniques might be used in other problems that you might encounter.

Key Concepts and Skills

- carry out the four-step problem solving process.
- identify and use the eight strategic problem solving hints.

---

3 Numbers in the Real World

Overview

In this chapter we explore how numbers are used in real and relevant problems. The first unit deals with percentages and is arguably one of the most practical and important units of the book. As you know, many real world numbers are incredibly large (the federal debt or the storage capacity of a computer disk) or very small (the diameter of a cancer cell or the wavelength of an x-ray); so in the next unit we introduce scientific notation to deal with large and small numbers. The next unit discusses another reality of numbers in the real world: they are often approximate or subject to errors. The news is filled with reference to index numbers; for example, the consumer price index. Such index numbers are critical to an understanding of the news, so they are the subject of the next unit. Finally, the last unit is a fascinating exploration of how numbers deceive us. All in all, it's a very practical and useful chapter.

Unit 3A Uses and Abuses of Percentages

Overview

If you read a news article, a financial statement, or an economic report, you will see that one of the most common ways to communicate quantitative information is with percentages. In this unit, we will explore the many ways that percentages are used — and abused. Percentages are used for three basic purposes:

- as fractions (for example, 45% of the voters favored the incumbent),
- to describe change (for example, taxes increased by 10%), and
- for comparison (for example, women live 3% longer than men).

In this unit, we examine each of these uses of percentages in considerable detail with plenty of examples taken from the news and from real situations. The use of percentages as fractions is probably familiar. The use of percentages to describe change relies on the notions of **absolute change** and **relative** (or **percentage change**). When some quantity changes from a previous value to a new value, we can define its changes in either of two ways:

$$\text{absolute change} = \text{new value} - \text{previous value}$$

$$\text{relative change} = \frac{\text{absolute change}}{\text{previous value}} = \frac{\text{new value} - \text{previous value}}{\text{previous value}}.$$

The use of percentages for comparison relies on the notions of **absolute difference** and **relative** (or **percentage difference**). To make comparisons between two quantities, we must identify the **compared quantity** (the quantity that we are comparing) and the **reference quantity** (the quantity that we are comparing to). For example, if we ask how much larger is one meter than one yard, *one meter* is the compared quantity and *one yard* is the reference quantity. Then we can calculate two kinds of difference:

$$\textbf{absolute difference} = \text{compared quantity} - \text{reference quantity}$$

$$\textbf{relative difference} = \frac{\text{absolute difference}}{\text{reference quantity}} = \frac{\text{compared quantity} - \text{reference quantity}}{\text{reference quantity}}$$

A powerful rule for interpreting statements involving percentages is what we call the **of versus more than rule**. It says that if the compared quantity is *P% more than* the reference quantity, then it is (100 + *P*)% *of* the reference quantity. For example, if Bess' salary is 30% more than Bob's salary, then Bess' salary is 130% of Bob's salary. Similarly, if Jill's height is 30% *less than* Jack's height, then Jill's height is 70% of Jack's height.

All of these ideas are assembled in this unit to solve a variety of practical problems. Our experience in teaching this subject is that the greatest difficulty is understanding the problem and translating it into mathematical terms. It is important to read the problem carefully, draw a picture if necessary, decide how percentages are used in the problem (as a fraction, for change, or for comparison), and to write a mathematical sentence that describes the situation. It is important to study the examples in the unit and work plenty of practice problems.

The unit closes with several examples of ways that percentages are abused. Be sure you can identify problems in which the previous value shifts and problems in which the quantity of interest is itself a percentage.

Key Words and Phrases

absolute change	relative change	percentage change
reference quantity	compared quantity	absolute difference
relative difference	percentage difference	of versus more than rule

Key Concepts and Skills

- identity and solve problems that use percentages as fractions.
- identity and solve problems that use percentages to describe change.
- identity and solve problems that use percentages for comparison.
- apply the *of versus more than rule* to practical problems.
- identify fallacies and errors in statements involving percentages.

Important Review Boxes

- A Brief Review of Percentages
- A Brief Review of What is a Ratio?

Unit 3B Putting Numbers in Perspective

Overview

Numbers in the world around us are often very large or very small. In order to write large and small numbers compactly, without using a lot of zeros, we use **scientific notation**. This is the main new mathematical idea in this unit. If you haven't used scientific notation before, you will want to practice writing numbers in scientific notation, and multiplying and dividing numbers in scientific notation.

We next spend some time showing how to make rough calculations using estimation. Often we can use approximate values of quantities and arrive at useful **order of magnitude** answers.

All of us suffer from number numbness: large and small numbers eventually lose all meaning. For example, most of us have no sense of how large $5 trillion (the federal debt) or 6 billion (the world's population) really are. Therefore, just as important as *writing* large and small numbers is *visualizing* large and small numbers. We look at some fascinating methods, such as **scaling**, for giving large and small numbers meaning. The goal is often to associate numbers with a striking visual image. For example, if the Earth is the size of a ball-point pen tip, the Sun would be a grapefruit 15 meters away.

Key Words and Phrases

scientific notation	order of magnitude	scaling
scale ratio	light-year	

Key Concepts and Skills

- write numbers in scientific notation.
- multiply and divide numbers in scientific notation.
- use estimates to compute order of magnitude answers.
- use scaling methods for visualizing large and small numbers.

Important Review Boxes

- A Brief Review of Working with Scientific Notation

Unit 3C Dealing With Uncertainty

Overview

While they may appear totally reliable, the numbers we see in the news or in reports often are quite uncertain and prone to errors. This unit is reminds us of this fact in many different ways, as we consider the sources of errors and the measurement of uncertainty in numbers.

The precision of a number can be described by the number of **significant digits** it has. Significant digits are those digits in a number that we can assume to be reliable, although, this is where care must be used in reading numbers. It's usually easy to determine the number of significant digits in a number; there are a few subtle cases that are listed in the summary box in the unit.

Errors enter problems and calculation in two ways: Errors that arise in unpredictable and unavoidable ways are called **random errors**. On the other hand, **systematic errors** arise due to a problem in the system that affects all measurements in the same way; these errors can often be avoided.

We next discuss **absolute errors** and **relative errors**. It is important to note the analogy between absolute/relative errors and absolute/relative difference (discussed in Unit 3A).

The next observation in the unit concerns the difference between **accuracy** and **precision**. A pharmacist's scale that can weigh fractions of an ounce has much more *precision* that a butcher's scale that can measure only in pounds. Thus precision refers to how precisely a quantity can be measured or how precisely a number is reported.

On the other hand, the *accuracy* of a measurement refers to how close it is to the exact value (which we often don't know). Suppose a marble weighs 4.5 ounces. If one scale reports a weight of 4.4 ounces and another scale reports a weight of 4.7 ounces, the first measurement is more accurate; both measurements have the same precision — to the nearest tenth of an ounce.

A few technicalities arise when it comes to doing arithmetic with approximate numbers. There are two rules that tell us how much precision should be assigned to the sum, difference, product, or quotient of two approximate numbers.

- when adding or subtracting two approximate numbers, the result should be rounded to the same precision as the *least precise* number in the problem.
- when multiplying or dividing two approximate numbers, the result should be rounded to the same number of significant digits as the number in the problem with the *fewest significant digits*.

Key Words and Phrases

significant digits	random errors	systematic errors
absolute error	relative error	accuracy
precision		

Key Concepts and Skills

- determine the number of significant digits in a given number.
- distinguish between random errors and systematic errors.
- compute absolute and relative errors.
- understand the difference between accuracy and precision.
- determine the precision of the sum or difference of two approximate numbers.
- determine the precision of the product or quotient of two approximate numbers.

Important Review Boxes

- A Brief Review of Rounding

Unit 3D Dealing With Uncertainty

Overview

Suppose you want to compare the price of gasoline today with its price 25 years ago. Simply comparing the prices now and then does not give a realistic comparison, because the price of just about everything increased during those 25 years. In this unit, we study the use of index numbers to make such comparisons more realistic. Among the most familiar index number is the **Consumer Price Index** (CPI), which essentially measures the cost of living and its changes due to **inflation**. However, there are many other index numbers, some of which will be explored in this unit.

Key Words and Phrases

index number	gasoline price index	Consumer Price Index
inflation	rate of inflation	health care quality index
precision		

Key Concepts and Skills

- compute index numbers and use them to make comparisons.
- use the CPI to compare prices.
- adjust prices for inflation.

Unit 3E How Numbers Deceive: Polygraphs, Mammograms, and More

Overview

The topics in this unit may seem a bit unrelated, but they are connected by the common theme of how numbers can be deceptive. The unit begins with a curious phenomenon known as **Simpson's paradox**. It can occur in many different ways, but it always arises when quantities are averaged and some crucial information is missing. The examples illustrate the effect in many ways and should be studied carefully.

We next turn to surprisingly deceptive results that occurs when using percentages in what are called *two-by-two tables* (such as Table 3.8). These tables are used to describe two different outcomes (for example, cured and not cured) for two different groups of people (for example, treatment and no treatment). Situations such as this give rise to the terms **false positive**, **false negative**, **true positive**, **and true negative**. Several practical examples are given as they apply to medical tests, lie detectors and drug tests. This is a very practical unit that contains some very subtle ideas.

Key Words and Phrases

Simpson's paradox	false positive	false negative
true positive	true negative	

Key Concepts and Skills

- identify and explain Simpson's paradox.
- compute percentages in tables and interpret them correctly.
- understand the subtleties in interpreting medical, drug, and polygraph tests.

---

4 Financial Management

Overview

One of the most immediate ways in which mathematics affects every person's everyday life is through finances: bank accounts, credit cards, loans, and investments. In this chapter we take an in-depth look at personal financial matters. In addition, we will explore the financial affair of the United States as we look at the federal budget. As you will see there are many relevant topics in this chapter and plenty of good mathematics.

Unit 4A The Power of Compounding

Overview

The phenomenon of **compounding** plays a fundamental role in all of finance, both on the investment side of the coin (earning money) and on the loan side (borrowing money). The unit opens by considering simple and compound interest problems as they arise in banking. Compound interest problems rely on four pieces of information:

- **initial deposit**, which we call *P*,
- **annual percentage interest rate**, which we call *APR*,
- **number of compoundings per year**, which we call *n,* and
- **number of years** the account is held, which we call *Y*.

You will see that there are precise formulas that tell you how much a bank account increases in value if you know these four pieces of information. These formulas (and others in the chapter) can get rather complicated and must be evaluated on a calculator. Be sure you study the highlighted boxes that show you how to use your calculator on these formulas; needless to say, practice helps immensely!

An important distinction must be made between the *APR* and the **annual percentage yield** (*APY*) of a bank account. If an account uses compounding at more than once a year, then the balance will increase by *more* than the *APR* in one year (due to the power of compounding). The amount by which the balance in the account actually increases in a year is the *APY*.

As you will see, the more often compounding takes place during the year, the more the balance increases. The limiting case occurs when compounding takes place every instant, or **continuously**. With continuous compounding, you get the maximum return on your money (for a fixed *APR*). The continuous compounding formula involves the mathematical constant *e,* which is approximately 2.71828. You should become familiar with how to compute with *e* on your particular calculator.

The unit concludes with a very practical problem. The usual compound interest formulas tell you how much money you will have in your account after Y years with a given initial deposit *today*. But what if you know you would like to have, say $30,000, in 20 years? How much should you deposit *today* in order to reach this goal? This is an example of a **present value** problem value, and it's quite important for planning purposes.

Key Words and Phrases

simple interest	principal	compound interest
annual percentage rate (APR)	compound interest formula	annual percentage yield (APY)
continuous compounding	present value	

Key Concepts and Skills

- determine the balance in an account with simple interest with a given initial deposit and interest rate.
- determine the balance in an account with compounding with a given initial deposit, *APR*, number of compoundings, and number of years.
- determine the balance in an account with continuous compounding with a given initial deposit, *APR*, and number of years.
- understand the difference between *APR* and *APY,* and be able to compute the *APY* for an account.
- determine the present value for an account that will produce a given balance after a specified number of years.

Important Review Boxes

- A Brief Review of Three Basic Rules of Algebra

Unit 4B Savings Plans and Investments

Overview

An **annuity** is a special kind of savings plan in which deposits are made regularly, perhaps every month or every year. People who are creating a college fund or building a retirement plan usually use an annuity. An annuity account increases in value due to compounding (as in regular bank accounts as studied in the previous unit) and due to the regular deposits. Not surprisingly, the mathematics of annuity plans follows naturally from the compound interest formulas of the previous unit.

There is just one basic formula that needs to be mastered in order to work with annuities. The formula requires all of the input needed for the compound interest formula of the previous unit (initial deposit, APR, number of compoundings, and number of years), *plus* the amount of the regular deposits.

To keep matters simple (but still realistic) we assume that the regular deposits are made as often as interest is compounded. There is no doubt that the savings plan formula is complicated. Be sure to study the *Using Your Calculator* box to learn how your calculator can be used to evaluate the formula.

Just as with a bank account, it is practical to ask present value questions with savings plans. If you know how much money you would like to have at a future time (perhaps the time of retirement), then how much should you deposit, say monthly, between now and then in order to reach that goal? You will see some practical examples of solving present value problems.

Having discussed the mathematics of investments, the unit concludes with a comprehensive summary of various types of investment plans. Some key considerations in choosing investment plans are **liquidity** (how easily your money can be withdrawn), **risk** (how safe your money is), and **return** (the amount that you earn on your investment). Liquidity is fairly easy to determine, risk is less easy to assess, and for return there is a fairly simple formula that gives the annual return on an investment.

We examine four general types of investments in light of these three factors:

- small company stocks,
- large company stocks,
- corporate bonds, and
- Treasury bills.

These four types of investment have very different characteristics in terms of liquidity, risk, and return.

An essential part of investing money is keeping track of how well your investments are doing. Many people follow their investments using the financial pages of the newspapers. For this reason, we spend some time discussing how to read the financial pages for stocks, bonds, and mutual funds. Bonds in particular have some special terminology (such as **face value**, **coupon rate**, and **discount**) and a special formula for calculating the **current yield** on a bond.

Key Words and Phrases

savings plan	annuity	savings plan formula
stocks	bonds	cash
mutual fund	liquidity	risk
return	total return	annual returns
portfolio	corporation	shares
market price	dividends	PE ratio
percent yield	face value	coupon rate
maturity date	discount	points

load current yield

Key Concepts and Skills

- determine the value of a savings plan given the initial deposit, APR, number of compoundings, number of years, and the amount of the regular deposits
- determine the present value for an savings plan that will yield a given balance after a specified number of years.
- understand the terms liquidity, risk, and return as they apply to various forms of investment.
- determine the annual yield on an investment given the total return.
- understand the terms used to report stocks in the financial pages of a newspaper.
- understand the terms used to report bonds in the financial pages of a newspaper.
- understand the terms used to report mutual funds in the financial pages of a newspaper.
- compute the current yield of a bond.

Important Review Boxes

- A Brief Review of Algebra with Powers and Roots

Unit 4C Loan Payments, Credit Cards, and Mortgages

Overview

While most people have bank accounts or investments that earn money, the sad reality is that most people also have debts due to loans of one kind or another. In this unit we will explore the most common kinds of loans: short-term loans (such as automobile loans), loans on credit cards, and **mortgages** (or house loans).

One basic formula governs all loan problems; it is called the **loan payment formula**. Given

- the amount of the loan (called the **principal**),
- the interest rate on the loan (still called the *APR*),
- the number of payment periods per year (usually taken to be 12 for monthly payments), and
- the term of the loan (the number of years over which it will be paid back),

the loan payment formula tells you the amount of the regular payments on the loan. Once again, the loan payment formula is rather complicated, so be sure to study the *Using Your Calculator* box.

The entire unit is devoted to using the loan payment formula for various practical problems. There are a lot of strategic questions involved in choosing a loan. Often you must choose between a loan with a high interest rate and a short term and a loan with a lower interest rate but a longer term. Which is the best choice? You will see several examples of such decisions.

The biggest loan that many people will every use is a house loan or mortgage. Since mortgages involve such large amounts of money over long periods of time, the decision you make in choosing a mortgage are critical. We explore some of the options and strategies involved with mortgages. Specifically, we explain the differences and advantages of fixed-rate mortgages as opposed to adjustable rate mortgages. We also discuss issues of prepayments, refinancing, points, and closing costs. All in all, you will find this to be quite a practical unit, one whose lessons you probably will need someday!

Key Words and Phrases

loan principal	installment loan	loan payment formula
mortgage	down payment	fixed rate mortgage
adjustable rate mortgage	closing costs	points
prepayment penalties	refinance	

Key Concepts and Skills

- know the terminology associated with loans.
- determine the loan payment given the principal, the APR, the number of payment periods, and the term of the loan.
- analyze two loan options to determine which is best for a given situation.
- be familiar with the practical issues associated with a home mortgage, such as points, closing costs, and fixed rate vs. adjustable rate loans.

Unit 4D Income Taxes

Overview

Another aspect of most peoples' financial lives is income taxes. The mathematics of income taxes is not difficult. However there are a lot of concepts and terminology involved with the subject. This unit is designed to give you a fairly thorough survey of income taxes, enough for you to make sense of complex tax forms and make critical decisions.

The first step in determining the amount of income tax you owe is to calculate your **taxable income**. From your **gross income** (the total of all your income), you subtract deductions and exemptions to arrive at your taxable income. Having computed your taxable income, the next step is to determine the tax itself. The U.S. tax system uses tax brackets or **marginal tax rates**: the percentage of your taxable income that you pay in taxes depends on your tax bracket. It also depends on your **filing status**, whether you are filing as a single person, a married person, or a head of household. This is also an appropriate place to discuss the **marriage penalty**.

Two other forms of income tax are **social security taxes** and **medicare taxes** (collectively called FICA taxes). These taxes apply to income from wages (not investments), and for self-employed people, these taxes must be paid in full by the taxpayer. The rules that govern these taxes are discussed with examples.

Of great political and personal interest are the taxes assessed on **capital gains**, profits made from selling property or stocks. We will examine the (new) laws for capital gains and give several examples that illustrate the laws. Also of practical value are the tax implications of **tax-deferred savings plans** that many people use for retirement pensions and the **mortgage interest tax deduction,** which is a large tax benefit for people holding mortgages.

In this unit you will find some relief from the big formulas and long calculations of previous units in this chapter. This chapter is very conceptual and it presents a lot of new terminology and practical information.

Key Words and Phrases

gross income	adjusted gross income	deductions
exemptions	dependents	standard deduction
itemized deduction	taxable income	tax credits
progressive income tax	marginal tax rates	filing status
social security tax	medicare tax	capital gain
ordinary income	short-term capital gain	long-term capital gain
tax-deferred savings plan	mortgage interest deduction	marriage penalty

Key Concepts and Skills

- understand the basic terminology associated with income tax.
- compute taxable income from gross income given deductions and exemptions.
- use marginal tax rates to compute the tax on a given taxable income.
- compute the social security and Medicare taxes on a given income.
- understand and determine taxes on capital gains.
- incorporate tax-deferred savings plans and mortgage interest deductions into a tax calculation.

Unit 4E Understanding the Federal Budget

Overview

Several times in this book, particularly in problems about large numbers, we have referred to the federal budget or the federal debt. There is no question that the federal budget is a source of truly huge numbers – numbers so large that most people, including politicians, don't even have a sense of their size.

In this chapter, we give a brief survey of the essentials of the federal budget. While the details can be confusing, the general principles of the budget are straightforward. The government has **receipts** or **income** (primarily from taxes) and it is has **outlays** or **expenses** (that cover everything from defense to education to social security). In a given year, if outlays exceed receipts, then the government has a **deficit**. On the other hand, if receipts exceed expenses, then the government has a **surplus**. If the government has a deficit then it must borrow money and in the process goes into **debt**. The devastating effect of going into debt is that **interest** must be paid on the borrowed money. This interest payment itself becomes an expense category in the budget. The U.S. government typically spends 15-20% of its budget on interest on the debt. If the government has many consecutive deficit years (as has been the case in the United States), then the debt continues to grow and cannot be paid off until there are surplus years.

In this unit we clarify the ideas of deficit and debt by looking at the budget of an imaginary small business which. We then consider the federal budget for the last five years and see how the major spending categories have contributed to a deficit in each year. With many deficit years, it also becomes clear how the debt has grown to its current level of about $5 trillion.

A few paragraphs are spent explaining a subtle point in federal budget reports. If you look closely at the federal budget summaries in this unit, you will see that the increase in the debt from one year to the next is *not* equal to the deficit for the current year, as one might expect. The explanation lies in the distinction between the **publicly held debt** and **gross debt**, which is explained in the text.

A balanced budget can be achieved either by increasing receipts or decreasing outlays or both. However, not all outlays can be reduced: **mandatory** expenses must be paid and **entitlements** are very difficult to cut. This leaves only **discretionary** expenses that are eligible for cuts.

The federal budget, together with its deficits, surpluses, and debts, effects everyone in many ways. Hopefully this unit will give you a basic understanding of this important issue.

Key Words and Phrases

receipts	outlays	net income
deficit	surplus	debt

mandatory outlays	entitlements	discretionary outlays
publicly held debt	gross debt	

Key Concepts and Skills

- explain the terms receipts, outlays, surplus, and deficit.
- given a budget for a company or government compute surplus or deficit.
- understand how debt arises in a budget and propagates from year to year.
- explain the difference between publicly held debt and gross debt.

---

5 Statistical Reasoning

Overview

Much of the quantitative information that flows over us every day is in the form of data that are gathered through surveys and other statistical studies. When a person, business, or organization wants to know something, often the first (and only) idea that comes to mind is "collect data." From news reports to scientific research, from political polls to TV viewer surveys, we are surrounded by statistics. How are these numbers gathered? Are the conclusions based on those numbers reliable? And most important of all, should you believe the results of a statistical study? Should you change you life based on the results of a statistical study?

These are the questions that we will *begin* to answer in this chapter. The emphasis of this chapter is on qualitative issues, and there will not be a lot of computation involved. We will resume the study of statistical problems in Chapter 6 when we look at the quantitative side of statistics. If you master these two chapters, you will have a good foundation in statistical studies — enough to allow you to read the news critically and to take a complete course in statistics.

Unit 5A Fundamentals of Statistics

Overview

The goal of this unit is to learn how a statistical study should (and should *not*) be done. Of utmost importance is the distinction between the **population**, the group of people or objects that you would like to learn about, and the **sample**, the group of people and objects that you actually measure or survey. As you will see, there are basically two aspects to any statistical study:

- collecting data from the people or objects in the sample, and
- drawing conclusions about the entire population based on the information gathered from the sample.

There are many ways that either of these steps can go wrong. Most of this chapter will deal with the first step, which is often called **sampling**. This step is crucial; if a sample is not chosen so that it is representative of the entire population, the conclusions of the study cannot be reliable.

Four different sampling methods will be discussed:

- simple random sampling
- systematic sampling
- convenience sampling
- stratified sampling

It is also important to distinguish between two basic types of statistical studies. An **observational study** is one in which participants (people or objects) are questioned, observed, or measured, but in no way manipulated. By contrast, in an **experiment**, the participants *are* manipulated in some way, perhaps by dividing them into a **treatment group** and a **control group**. A subtle borderline situation is a **case-control study**, in which participants naturally form two or more groups by choice (for example, people who choose to smoke and not to smoke). While a case-control study looks like an experiment, it is actually an observational study.

Other features of statistical studies that should be noticed are the **placebo effect** (when people who *think* they received a treatment respond as if they received the treatment, even though they did not), **single blinding** (when participants do not know whether or not they receive a treatment), and **double blinding** (when neither researchers nor participants know who received a treatment).

You often hear statements like, "The President's approval rating is 54% with a margin of error of 5%." Because results of surveys are often given in this way, we will also look briefly the notions of **confidence interval** and **margin of error**. Although these ideas are rather technical, it is important to understand how to interpret them. In Chapter 6, we will see how confidence intervals and margins or error are actually determined.

Key Words and Phrases

sample	population	raw data
sample statistics	population parameters	representative sample
simple random sampling	systematic sampling	convenience sampling
stratified sampling	bias	observational study
experiment	treatment group	control group
placebo	placebo effect	single blind experiment
double-blind experiment	case control study	cases

controls margin of error confidence interval

Key Concepts and Skills

- understand the distinction between a sample and the population.
- know the five basic steps of a statistical study.
- be able to form a representative sample by various sampling methods.
- understand the difference between an observational study, an experiment, and a case-control study.
- understand the placebo effect, and single and double blinding.
- interpret margins of error and confidence intervals.

Unit 5B Should You Believe a Statistical Study?

Overview

Suppose you read that 68% of all TV viewers watched the NCAA basketball final game or that 1 in 5 people in the world do not have access to fresh drinking water, or that a preelection poll says that the Republican candidate leads by 5 percentage points. In this unit, we address the basic question: how do you know whether to believe the claims of these statistical studies?

The unit takes the form of a list of eight guidelines for evaluating a statistical study. Each guideline is accompanied by examples and analyses. It may not be possible to assess a particular study in light of *all* eight guidelines, but the more of these guidelines that a study satisfies, the more confident you can be about the conclusions of the study. Just for completeness, we'll list the eight guidelines here.

1. Identify the goal, type and population of the study.
2. Consider the source.
3. Look for bias in the sample.
4. Look for problems in *defining* or *measuring* the quantities of interest.
5. Watch for confounding variables.
6. Consider its setting and wording in surveys.
7. Check that results are presented fairly.
8. Stand back and consider the conclusions.

Key Words and Phrases

bias variables selection bias

participation bias

Key Concepts and Skills

- understand the eight guidelines for evaluating a statistical study, and be able to carry them out on a particular study.

Unit 5C Statistical Table and Graphs

Overview

We often think of data and statistics as long lists of numbers, and indeed they start in that form. But these numbers don't become meaningful until they are summarized in some digestible form; and one of the best ways to represent long lists of numbers is with a picture. In this and the next unit, we will explore the many ways in which quantitative information can be displayed. This unit focuses on the basic types of graphs, ones that can often be drawn with a pencil and paper. The next unit highlights the more exotic types of graphs which are more difficult to produce, but equally common in news and research reports.

Often the best first step in summarizing data is to make a **frequency table** that shows how often each category in a study appears (for example, the number of students receiving grades of A, B, C, D, and F on an exam). Such a table can also show the **relative frequency** and the **cumulative frequency** for each category.

The type of display used for a set of data also depends on the type of data that are collected. We distinguish between **qualitative data** (non-numerical categories that have no natural order) and **quantitative data** (numerical values that are ordered).

Here is a summary of the types of graphs that will be considered in this unit.

- **Bar graphs** are used to show how some numerical quantity (for example, population) varies from one category to another (for example, for several different countries). The categories are usually qualitative and can be shown in any order.
- **Pie charts** are used to show the fraction (or percentage) of a population that falls into various categories. The categories are usually qualitative and can be shown in any order. For example, a pie chart could be used to show the fraction of a class has brown, black, blond, and red hair.
- **Histograms** are bar graphs in which the categories are quantitative, and thus have a natural order. Histograms often show how many objects or people are in various categories. For example, a histogram would be used to show the number of people in a town that fall into age categories 0–9, 10–19, 20–29, and so on.
- **Line charts** serve the same purpose as histograms, but instead of using bars to indicate the number of objects or people in each category, they use dots connected by lines.

- **Time-series diagrams** are usually histograms of line charts that show how a quantity changes in time. For example, the day-to-day changes in the stock market would be displayed as a time-series diagram.

We might point out that there seems to be no standard definition of histograms and bar graphs. We have tried to choose a distinction that is common in many books: a histogram is any graph that uses bars, while a histogram is a particular kind of bar graph that is used for ordered quantitative data.

Key Words and Phrases

bar graph	pie chart	histogram
line chart	time-series diagram	scatter plot

Key Concepts and Skills

- construct a frequency table for a set of table showing frequencies, relative frequencies, and cumulative frequencies.
- determine an appropriate kind of display for a given set of data.
- display an appropriate set of data with a bar graph by finding the correct height of the bars.
- display an appropriate set of data with a pie chart by finding the correct angles for the sectors of the pie.
- display an appropriate set of data with a histogram by finding the correct height of the bars.
- display an appropriate set of data with a line chart by finding the correct location of points on the line chart.
- display an appropriate set of data with a time-series diagram by finding the correct location of points on the diagram.
- display an appropriate set of data with a scatter plot by finding the correct location of points on the plot.

Unit 5D Graphics in the Media

Overview

Whereas the previous unit dealt with graphs that are relatively easy to produce yourself, this unit will survey more complicated displays that frequently appear in the media. The goal in this unit is not to actually produce these more sophisticated graphs; often a powerful software packages is needed to create them. Rather the emphasis will be on interpreting these displays of quantitative information.

Here is a summary of the types of graphs that we will consider in this unit.

- **Multiple bar graphs** are used to show how *two or more* quantities (for example, population and birth rate) vary from one category to another (for example, for several different countries). Multiple bar graphs are really two or more bar graphs combined with each other; they include multiple histograms.

- **Stack plots** are used to display several quantities simultaneously, often showing how they all change in time. For example, a stack plot could be used to show how the incidence of several diseases has changed in time.
- **Geographical plots**, such contour plots and weather maps, give a two-dimensional picture of how a quantity varies over a geographical region. Such displays are also used to show the distribution of a disease over a geographical region.
- **Three-dimensional** graphs take many different forms, but they are all used to show how three different quantities (or variables) are related to each other.

As graphical displays become more complex, there is more opportunity for confusion and deception. The unit closes by discussing several ways in which you can be misled by such displays. Although graphs can be beautiful and effective, they must be interpreted with caution!

Key Words and Phrases

multiple bar graph	stack plot	three-dimensional graphics
contour plots	exponential scale	pictograph
perceptual distortions	percent change graphs	

Key Concepts and Skills

- interpret multiple bar graphs and histograms.
- interpret stack plots.
- interpret three-dimensional graphics.
- interpret contour plots.
- detect deceptive pie charts.
- interpret percent change graphs.
- interpret exponential scales.
- detect deceptive pictographs or other displays of data.

Unit 5E Correlation and Causality

Overview

This unit deals with the critical task of determining whether one event *causes* another event. The process often begins by looking for **correlations** between two variables; a correlation exists when higher values of one variable are consistently associated with higher (or lower) values of the second variable. For example, body weight is correlated with height, because in general, greater body weights mean greater heights. Correlations can be detected by making a **scatter diagram** of the two variables in question.

There are three possible explanations for a correlation between two variables. It may be due to

- a coincidence,
- a common underlying cause, or
- a genuine cause and effect relation.

Of the three possibilities, the most interesting and the most difficult to establish is the last one: when can we be sure that one event caused another?

The unit presents six methods (attributed to the philosopher John Stuart Mill) for establishing cause and effect relations:

1. Look for situations in which the effect is correlated with the suspected cause even while other factors vary.

2. Among groups that differ only in the presence or absence of the suspected cause, check that the effect is similarly present or absent.

3. Look for evidence that larger amounts of the suspected cause produce larger amounts of the effect.

4. If the effect might be produced by other potential causes (besides the suspected cause), make sure that the effect still remains after accounting for these other potential causes.

5. If possible, test the suspected cause with an experiment. If the experiment cannot be performed with humans for ethical reasons, consider doing the experiment with animals, cell cultures, or computer models.

6. Try to determine the physical mechanism by which the suspected cause produces the effect.

Because causality is important in legal cases, we also look at the legal standards for establishing causality. They are crucial in determining the guilt or innocence of defendants. They are

- possible cause,
- probable cause, and
- cause beyond reasonable doubt.

The unit also presents three (real) case studies in which identifying a cause and effect relation led to a discovery or the solving of a mystery.

Key Words and Phrases

correlation	scatter diagram	positive correlation
negative correlation	coincidence	underlying cause
causality	probable cause	possible cause

cause beyond reasonable doubt

Key Concepts and Skills

- construct a scatter diagram for two variables.
- identify positive, negative, and no correlation between two variables.
- understand the three explanations for a correlation.
- apply the six methods for determining causality.
- understand the three legal levels of confidence in causality.

---

6 Putting Statistics to Work

Overview

We now continue our study of statistics, having already introduced some of the qualitative aspects in Chapter 5. The treatment of statistics in this chapter is more quantitative and involves some numerical calculations. In Unit 6A we present several methods for characterizing data sets, including the calculation of the mean, median, and mode. The next unit continues in the same vein by discussing measures of variation in a data set. In Unit 6C, we introduce the normal distribution which lies at the heart of many statistical methods. The final unit discusses the powerful process known as *statistical inference* – drawing reliable conclusions about a population based on data taken from a sample of that population.

Unit 6A Characterizing a Data Distribution

Overview

Typical data sets often contain hundreds or thousands of numbers; so one goal is to summarize data sets in compact and meaningful ways. In this unit we explore methods used to describe and summarize data beyond the frequency tables discussed in the previous chapter.

For a very concise summary of a set of data, it is common to compute their **mean**, **median**, and/or **mode**. These one-number summaries are defined as follows:

- The *mean* of a data set is calculated by the formula

$$\text{mean} = \frac{\text{sum of all values}}{\text{total number of values}}.$$

- The *median* is the middle score in the data set. Note that there will be two “middle” values if a data set has an even number of data points; if the two middle values are different, the median lies halfway between them.

- The *mode* is the most common score in a data set. A data set may have more than one mode, or no mode.

Having determined where the "center" of the data set lies, it is next useful to describe the shape of the data: are the data values symmetric? Are they weighted to the right or left? These questions can be answered qualitatively by finding whether the data values are **positively** or **negatively skewed**.

Key Words and Phrases

distribution	mean	median
mode	single-peaked	bimodal
symmetric	outliers	positively skewed
negatively skewed		

Key Concepts and Skills

- compute the mean, median, mode of a set of data.
- understand the effect of outliers on mean and median.
- be aware of possible sources of confusion about averages.
- determine the qualitative shape of a data set and identify whether it is skewed.

Unit 6B Measures of Variation

Overview

We continue the theme of the previous unit by exploring additional ways to summarize a distribution of data in compact ways. In this unit, we look at ways to describe the *spread* or **variation** of a set of data. The simplest measure of variation is called the **range**, the difference between the maximum and minimum data values. We can improve on the range by computing the **upper** and **lower quartiles**, and the maximum and minimum data values to make a **five-number summary** for the distribution. A **boxplot** is a picture of the five-number summary and provides a good snapshot of the distribution.

The variation is best captured in a single number by computing the **standard deviation** of a distribution. This calculation can become laborious for large data sets, and is often done with calculators or computer software. But you should know how to set up that standard deviation calculation using a table, as shown in Table 6.2. A useful approximation to the standard deviation is given by the **range rule of thumb**.

Key Words and Phrases

range
five-number summary
upper quartile
lower quartile
box plot
deviation
standard deviation

Key Concepts and Skills

- compute the range of a data distribution.
- find the lower and upper quartiles of a data distribution.
- construct the five-number summary and a boxplot for a data distribution.
- compute and interpret the standard deviation of a small data set.

Unit 5C The Normal Distribution

Overview

This unit is about the normal distribution, which plays an important role in all of statistics. This unit lays the groundwork for the following unit in which we learn how draw conclusions about an entire population when we have data from a relatively small sample of that population. This process of inferring something about the population based on a sample is often called **inferential statistics**.

We begin by introducing the **normal distribution**, a whole family of symmetric distributions that are characterized by their mean and their standard deviation. Many variables, such as test scores, heights, weights, and other physical characteristics, follow a normal distribution closely. One of the most important results about the normal distribution is the **68-95-99.7 Rule:**

- About 68% (actually 68.3%) of the data points fall within 1 standard deviation of the mean.
- About 95% (actually 95.4%) of the data points fall within 2 standard deviations of the mean.
- About 99.7% of the data points fall within 3 standard deviations of the mean.

Thus if we know that a variable is distributed normally and we know its mean and standard deviation, we can say a lot about where a particular data value lies in the distribution. Working with the normal distribution is made much easier with the use of **standard scores** (or ***z*-scores**) and **percentiles**. The standard score simply measures how many standard deviations a particular data value is above or below the mean. Once the standard score is known, the percentile can be found using Table 6.3 (which appears in all statistics books). Similarly, given a percentile, the corresponding standard score can be found.

Key Words and Phrases

normal distribution 68-95-99.7 rule percentile

standard score

Key Concepts and Skills

- identify normal distributions and know how they arise.
- draw a normal distribution curve with a given mean and standard deviation.
- use the 68-95-99.7 Rule to analyze a normal distribution.
- convert standard scores to percentiles and vice versa.

Unit 6D Statistical Inference

This unit explains in a fairly qualitative way one of the most important aspects of statistics: the process by which information from a sample can be used to make reliable claims about the entire population from which the sample is taken. This is a technical topic, but it is so important that it's worth understanding, at least in general terms.

The unit begins with an explanation of **statistical significance**: a set of observations or measurements is said to be statistically significant if it is unlikely to have occurred by chance. For example, if we toss a fair coin 100 times and see 52 heads, we would not be surprised, and might attribute the outcome to chance. However, if we observed 80 heads in 100 tosses of a fair coin, it would be difficult to attribute this outcome to chance; we would say this outcome is statistically significant.

We can be a bit more precise if we use idea probability in an intuitive way:

- if the probability of an observed outcome occurring by chance is 1 in 20 (0.05) or less, the outcome is significant at the **0.05 level of significance.**
- if the probability of an observed outcome occurring by chance is 1 in 100 (0.01) or less, the outcome is significant at the **0.01 level of significance**.

The discussion next returns to **margins of error** and **confidence intervals**. The problem of interest is very common for opinion polls and surveys. Suppose you want to know the proportion (or percentage) of people in a population who hold a particular opinion or have some trait. The usual practice is to select a sample and determine what proportion (or percentage) of people in the sample hold that particular opinion or have that trait; this is called the **sample statistic**. Knowing the sample statistic, what can you conclude about the entire population?

You will see in the unit (with plenty of explanation and examples) that if the sample has n individuals, then the proportion of interest for the population lies within $1/\sqrt{n}$ of the sample statistic – with 95% certainty. The quantity $1/\sqrt{n}$ is called the **margin of error** and the interval that extends $1/\sqrt{n}$ on either side of the sample statistic is called the **95% confidence interval**. For example, if in a randomly selected sample of n = 10,000 people, 45% have blond hair, then the margin of error is $1/\sqrt{10{,}000} = 0.01 = 1\%$ and the margin of error is 45% – 1% to 45% + 1% or 44% to 46%. We can conclude with 95% certainty that between 44% and 46% of the entire population has blond hair. This is one of the most basic results of inferential statistics. It allows us to say something about an entire population based on what we learn from a sample.

The last topic in the unit is hypothesis testing, which is the procedure for determining whether a claim about a population, based on observations of a sample, is valid. The claims we will study involve either a population mean (for example, the mean weight of all college women is 115 pounds) or a population proportion (for example, 54% of all college students eat pizza at least once a week). The hypothesis test involves two hypotheses: The **null hypothesis** claims a specific value for a population parameter. (It is often the value expected in the case of no special effect.) It takes the form:

null hypothesis: population parameter = claimed value

The **alternative hypothesis** is the claim that is accepted if the null hypothesis is false.

There are two possible outcomes of a hypothesis test:

- rejecting the null hypothesis, in which case we have evidence that supports the alternative hypothesis.
- not rejecting the null hypothesis, in which case we lack sufficient evidence to support the alternative hypothesis.

How do we decide whether or not to reject the null hypothesis? Here's where the subject gets a bit technical to carry out in detail. But we can say it in words:

- If the chance of a sample result at least as extreme as the observed result is less than 1 in 100 (or 0.01), the test is significant at the 0.01 level. The test offers strong evidence for rejecting the null hypothesis (and accepting the alternative hypothesis).
- If the chance of a sample result at least as extreme as the observed result is less than 1 in 20 (or 0.05), the test is significant at the 0.05 level. The test offers moderate evidence for rejecting the null hypothesis.
- If the chance of a sample result at least as extreme as the observed result is greater than 1 in 20, the test is not significant. The test does not provide sufficient grounds for rejecting the null hypothesis.

While this subject is challenging, the text does offer several good examples and analogies to clarify this important topic.

Key Words and Phrases

statistical significance	sampling	confidence interval

	distribution	
margin of error	null hypothesis	alternative hypothesis
significance at the 0.05 level	significance at the 0.01 level	

Key Concepts and Skills

- explain the meaning of statistical significance.
- construct and interpret a confidence interval given a margin or error.
- describe the basic purpose and aspects of a hypothesis test.
- construct a null and alternative hypothesis for a given situation.
- given the relevant probability, decide whether or not to reject a null hypothesis.

---

7 Probability: Living With the Odds

Overview

Probability is involved in nearly every decision we make. Often it is used on a subjective or intuitive level; but occasionally we try to be more precise. As you will see in this chapter, probability is one of the most applicable branches of mathematics. Before we are done with the chapter, we will be able to apply probability to lotteries, gambling, life insurance problems and air traffic safety. It is a fascinating chapter, full of mathematics and real-life problems.

Unit 7A Fundamentals of Probability

Overview

We all have an intuitive sense of what a probability is and that sense is useful. A probability is a number between zero and one. If the probability of an event is zero, then it cannot happen; if the probability of an event is one, then it is certain to happen; and if the probability is somewhere is in between zero and one, it gives a measure of how likely the event is to happen.

We can approach probabilities in three different ways:

- a **theoretical probability** uses mathematical methods to find the probability of an event occurring.
- an **empirical probability** is determined with experiments or by data collection .
- a **subjective probability** is based on intuition.

This unit will focus on theoretical probability calculations; it will mention empirical probabilities, and we will leave subjective probabilities for another course!

If you wanted to find the probability that a fair die will show a 5 when rolled once, you might reason that there are six possible outcomes of a single roll and a success (rolling a 5) is one of those six outcomes. So you might reason that the probability of rolling a 5 is 1/6. You would be correct! This thinking is the basic procedure for computing theoretical probabilities:

Step 1: Count the total number of possible outcomes of an event.
Step 2: Count the number of outcomes that represent **success** — that is, the number of outcomes that represent the sought after result.
Step 3: Determine the probability of success by dividing the number of successes by the total number of possible outcomes:

$$\text{probability of success} = \frac{\text{number of outcomes that represent success}}{\text{total number of possible outcomes}}$$

This procedure can be used to compute probabilities in many different situations, as you will see in the examples of the text.

Another important fact that will be used often is that if the probability of an event occurring is p, then the probability that it does *not* occur is $1 - p$. For example, the probability of rolling a fair die and getting a five is 1/6; therefore the probability of rolling *anything but* a five is $1 - 1/6 = 5/6$.

Suppose you flip three coins and are interested in the number of heads that appear. In this case, there are four possible events: three heads, two heads, one head, and three tails. We will show how to find the probability of all of the events. The collection of the probabilities of *all* possible events is called a **probability distribution**.

There are many situations in which it's impossible to determine theoretical probabilities. In these situations, we can't use mathematical methods, but we have records or data to work with. Such an approach leads to empirical probabilities. For example, we often talk about a 100-year flood, which means that based on historical records, a flood of this magnitude occurs once every 100 years. So the empirical probability of such a flood occurring in any given year is 1/100. We discuss empirical probabilities because they are used so often in practice.

Finally, we take a few pages to clarify the confusion that can arise over the use of the word *odds*. The odds *for* an event *A* are found by dividing the probability of an event occurring by the probability of the event *not* occurring. For example, the odds of tossing a fair coin and getting a head are 1, often said *1 to 1*. Unfortunately, the term *odds* has an even slightly different meaning when used in gambling. In that case, it is the amount a winning bet will pay for every dollar that you bet. Needless to say, care must be used when dealing with odds (and gambling!).

Key Words and Phrases

event	outcome	theoretical probability
empirical probability	subjective probability	probability distribution
odds		

Key Concepts and Skills

- distinguish between theoretical probability, empirical probability, and subjective probability.
- use the three-step process to determine simple theoretical probabilities.
- find probability distributions for coin and dice experiments.
- determine empirical probabilities from data or historical records.
- find the probability of an event *not* occurring.
- find the odds for an event from its probability.

Important Review Boxes

- A Brief Review of the Multiplication Principle

Unit 7B Combining Probabilities

Overview

In the previous unit, we studied methods for finding the probability of individual events. However, many interesting situations actually consist of multiple events. For example, what is the probability of tossing ten heads in a row with a fair coin? Or what is the probability of drawing a jack or a heart from a standard deck of cards? We will answer these and many other practical questions in this unit.

The unit presents five different techniques that involve multiple events. As always, it's important to know *how* to apply these techniques and *when* to apply them. The five situations covered by these methods are:

- independent AND events
- dependent AND events
- either/or mutually exclusive events (non-overlapping)
- either/or non-mutually exclusive events (overlapping)
- *at least once* events.

The term **AND event** refers to two or more events *all* happening. For example, what is the probability of rolling two fair dice and seeing a six on *both* dice (a six *and* a six)? Or what is the probability of drawing four cards from a standard deck and getting an ace each time? The important distinction with AND events is whether they are **independent** or **dependent**. If one event does not affect the others (for example, in rolling two dice, the outcome of one die does not affect the outcome of the other die), then we have independent events. The rule that applies for two independent events is

$$P(A \textit{ and } B) = P(A) \times P(B).$$

This principle can be extended to any number of independent events. For example, the AND probability of A *and* B *and* C is

$$P(A \textit{ and } B \textit{ and } C) = P(A) \times P(B) \times P(C).$$

If the events are not independent, then a bit more care is needed. For example, if you draw two cards from a deck, but don't replace the first card before drawing the second, then the outcome of the second card depends on the outcome of the first card. The rule that applies in this case for two dependent events is

$$P(A \textit{ and } B) = P(A) \times P(B \text{ given } A).$$

With **either/or events**, we are interested in the probability of *either* event A *or* event B occurring. The important distinction with either/or events is whether the events in question are mutually exclusive. If the occurrence of the first event prevents the occurrence of the second event, then the events are **mutually exclusive** or **non-overlapping**. For example, drawing a heart and drawing a diamond from a deck of cards are mutually exclusive events because if one event occurs (say, drawing a heart), then the other event (drawing a diamond) cannot occur. The rule that applies in this case with two mutually exclusive events is

$$P(A \textit{ or } B) = P(A) + P(B).$$

This principle can be extended to any number of mutually exclusive events. For example, the probability that either event A *or* event B *or* event C occurs is

$$P(A \textit{ or } B \textit{ or } C) = P(A) + P(B) + P(C).$$

If events are **non-mutually exclusive** or **overlapping** (for example, going into a room of people and meeting a woman *or* a Democrat), then a modification of the above rule must be used. The rule that applies in this case is

$$P(A \textit{ or } B) = P(A) + P(B) - P(A \textit{ and } B).$$

In general, for AND probabilities we multiply probabilities and for either/or probabilities we multiply probabilities. However, modifications must be made in the cases of dependent or non-mutually exclusive events.

Finally, a very important situation is one in which we ask about the probability of an event happening *at least once*. For example, if you buy ten lottery tickets, what is the probability of *at least* one ticket being a winner? If you roll a die ten times, what is the probability of rolling *at least* one six? The rule that gives the probability of an event A occurring *at least once* in n trials is

$$P(\text{A at least once in } n \text{ trials}) = 1 - P(\text{A does not occur in } n \text{ trials})$$
$$= 1 - P(\textit{not } \text{A})^n.$$

The unit has explanations of these rules and many examples to show how they are used. And be sure you also give yourself plenty of time to practice!

Key Words and Phrases

AND probability	independent events	dependent events
either/or probability	mutually exclusive	non-mutually exclusive
at least once rule		

Key Concepts and Skills

- identify AND probabilities and either/or probabilities.
- distinguish between independent events and dependent events.
- distinguish between mutually exclusive events and non-mutually exclusive events.
- identify *at least once* situations.
- know when and how to apply the five probability rules given in the unit.

Unit 7C The Law of Large Numbers

Overview

This unit is designed to strengthen your intuition about probabilities and to point out some common misconceptions about probabilities. It also deals with the important concept of expected value, which has many important applications.

We start by discussing the **law of large numbers**. We know that the probability of tossing a head with a fair coin is 1/2. This does not mean that if you toss a coin twice that you will always get one head and one tail. It does not mean that if you toss a coin ten times that you will always get five heads and five tails. What we *can* say is that the more often you toss the coin, the closer the fraction of heads is to the fraction of tails. This is an example of the law of averages.

The important concept in this chapter is **expected value**. Consider a situation in which there are several different outcomes. Each outcome has a known probability and a known **payoff** (which could be positive or negative). For example, a lottery may have a \$10 prize, a \$100 prize, a \$1000, and a grand prize of \$1,000,000. These are the payoffs of the four outcomes, and each outcome has a certain probability. If you play this lottery many times, how much do you expect to win or lose in the long run? The answer is given by the expected value.

There is a general rule for computing expected values. In a situation with just two outcomes, the expected value is given by

$$\text{expected value} = \begin{pmatrix}\text{value of}\\ \text{event 1}\end{pmatrix} \times \begin{pmatrix}\text{probability of}\\ \text{event 1}\end{pmatrix} + \begin{pmatrix}\text{value of}\\ \text{event 2}\end{pmatrix} \times \begin{pmatrix}\text{probability of}\\ \text{event 2}\end{pmatrix}.$$

The unit presents several other applications of expected value as it arises in life insurance policies, lotteries, and the **house edge** in casino gambling. There are some important practical lessons to be earned here.

The law of averages is related to the outlook called the **gambler's fallacy**. Gamblers often feel that if they get behind or start losing money, then their luck will change and their chances will improve. The fact is that probabilities do not change just because someone is losing. Once behind, it is likely that you will stay behind or get even further behind.

Key Words and Phrases

law of averages	expected value	payoff
gambler's fallacy	house edge	

Key Concepts and Skills

- explain the law of averages.
- explain the gambler's fallacy.
- compute the expected value in situations with two or more outcomes.
- understand the house edge and compute it in specific situations.

Unit 7D Assessing Risk

Overview

This unit is a nice collection of topics, all related in some way to probability. The first topic is estimating risk. You often hear statements such as "you are more likely to get struck by lightning than die in an airplane crash." How are such statements concocted? And to what extent are they true? We will explore how such comparisons of risk are made, particularly as they apply to **vital statistics** — data about births and deaths.

You will see that these problems are examples of empirical probability. If we know the number of deaths due to, say, heart disease, we can estimate the probability of a person dying from heart disease. If we know the number of deaths due to automobile accidents, we can estimate the chances of a person dying in an automobile accident. With these two facts, it is possible to compare the risks of automobiles and heart disease. Clearly, risk analysis and decision-making are closely related.

Related to vital statistics are the subjects or **mortality** and **life expectancy**. We will look at graphs of death rate and life expectancy as they change with age. The interpretation of these graphs reveals a few surprises. Why should life expectancy actually increase with age? Does the death rate increase steadily with age? Needless to say, these graphs have many implications.

Key Words and Phrases

accident rate	death rate	vital statistics
life expectancy	mortality	

Key Concepts and Skills

- determine the probability of an event given the number of people who experience the event.
- understand different measures of risk.
- compare the risks of two events or two causes of death.
- interpret life expectancy and mortality tables.

Unit 7E Counting and Probability

Overview

We all know how to count *individual* objects or people, but there are many other types of counting problems that arise when we want to count *groups* of objects or people. That is the subject of this chapter. There are four basic counting methods presented in this chapter:

- selections from two or more groups (multiplication principle)
- arrangements with repetition
- permutations
- combinations.

In this unit, we will learn not only how to apply these methods, but equally important, how to determine *when* to use each method.

Selection from two or more groups occurs when we have several different groups of objects and we need select one item from each group. For example, in a restaurant, you might have four choices for an appetizer (first group), six choices for a main course (second group), and five choices for a dessert (third choice). How many different meals could you select?

Problems of this sort can be solved using a table, a tree, or (the easiest of all) the **multiplication principle** (see Review Box in Unit 7A). You will see that the total number arrangements of items from two or more groups is

(number of items in first group) × (number of items in second group) × (number of items in third group) × ···· × (number of items in last group).

In the above example, there would $4 \times 6 \times 5 = 120$ different possible meals that you could order.

Arrangements with repetition occur when you select items from a single group and items may be used more than once. Often the items in problems of this kind are letters or numerals. For example, how many different three-digit area codes can be formed from the numerals 0 through 9? There are 10 ways to choose the first numeral and, because repetition is allowed, there are 10 ways to choose the second numeral, and 10 ways to choose the third numeral. This amounts to a total of $10 \times 10 \times 10 = 1000$ different three-digit area codes. The general rule is that

> if we make r selections (for example, the three digits of the area code) from a group of n items (for example, the numerals 0–9), n^r different arrangements are possible.

Permutations also involve selecting items from a single group with one important difference — repetition is not allowed. Furthermore, in counting permutations, the order of the arrangements matters; that is, we count ABCD and DCBA as two different arrangements. To summarize, permutations require

- selection from a single group,
- repetition is not allowed, and
- order matters.

In the unit, we work slowly through several examples towards the general formula for counting permutations. We need a bit of mathematical notation along the way, so we introduce the **factorial** function.

$$n! = n \times (n-1) \times (n-2) \times \ldots \times 2 \times 1.$$

You might resist learning and using factorials, but they will make your life much easier! Just a little practice is all it takes.

With factorials in hand, we can write a general formula for counting permutations.

> If we make r selections from a group of n items, the number of possible permutations is
>
> $${}_nP_r = \frac{n!}{(n-r)!},$$
>
> where ${}_nP_r$ is read as "the number of permutations of n items taken r at a time."

Combinations are much like permutations with one difference — order does not matter; that is, we count ABCD and DCBA as the *same* arrangement. The requirements for combinations are

- selection from a single group,
- repetition is not allowed, and
- order does *not* matters.

The number of combinations of n objects taken r at a time is the same as the number of permutations, except that we have to correct for the overcounting that the permutation formula does (because permutations care about order and combinations don't). This subtle point is explained in the text. The result is the combinations formula.

If we make r selections from a group of n items, the number of possible *combinations*, in which order does not matter, is

$$_nC_r = \frac{_nP_r}{r!} = \frac{n!}{(n-r)! \times r!}$$

where $_nC_r$ is read as "the number of combinations of n items taken r at a time."

The key to mastering these methods is knowing not only *how* to use a particular method, but *when* to use it. There are plenty of practice exercises at the end of the unit; you should work as many as possible. Another hint is to learn the capabilities of your calculator. You will need a calculator that at least does exponentiation (n^r). Many calculators compute factorials directly with a special factorial key. Some calculators have keys for permutations and combination. You will save yourself considerable work if you let your calculator do as much work as possible.

The unit concludes with a brief look at the subject of **coincidence**. Should you really be surprised when you win a raffle drawing at a basketball game? Should you really be surprised that after an evening of playing cards you are dealt a 13-card hand with ten hearts? Many so-called coincidences are bound to happen to someone, but we are always surprised when they happen to us.

We discuss the famous birthday problem and show that if there are 25 people in a room, then there is better than a 50% chance that two people have the same birthday. We also explore the phenomenon of **streaks**, particularly in sports, when a player repeats a certain success for many consecutive games. Should you really be surprised?

Key Words and Phrases

selection from two or more groups	multiplication principle	arrangements with repetition
permutation	combination	coincidence

Key Concepts and Skills

- describe the four different counting methods discussed in the unit.
- determine which of the four methods applies in a given counting problem.
- use factorials confidently.
- apply each of the four methods on appropriate problems.
- understand why not all coincidences should be surprising.

8 Exponential Astonishment

Overview

If you had to learn just one lesson from a quantitative reasoning course, it might well be the difference between exponential growth, which is the subject of this chapter, and linear growth, which is the subject of Chapter 9. Exponential growth and decay impact our everyday lives in many ways, but most people are not aware of its presence or its power. In this chapter you will learn how everything from bank accounts to populations to radioactive waste are governed by exponential models. In practical terms, this is an immensely important chapter.

Unit 8A Growth: Linear vs. Exponential

Overview

The difference between linear and exponential growth is stated on the first page of the chapter.

- *Linear growth* occurs when a quantity grows by the same *absolute* amount in each unit of time.
- *Exponential growth* occurs when a quantity grows by the same *relative* amount — that is, by the same *percentage* — in each unit of time.

Notice how these facts are related to the ideas of absolute and relative change studied in Unit 3A. It would be a good idea to contemplate these two statements and try to understand what they really mean. Hopefully this unit will also help!

This unit introduces the ideas surrounding exponential growth in a very basic way. We use three parables (*From Hero to Headless*, *The Magic Penny*, and *Bacteria in a Bottle*) that illustrate quite dramatically the power of exponential growth. The goal is to develop some intuition about exponential growth and understand doubling processes.

The lessons of the unit are summarized in the highlight box at the end of the unit:

- Exponential growth is characterized by repeated doublings. With each doubling the amount of increase is approximately equal to the *sum* of all preceding doublings.
- Exponential growth cannot continue indefinitely. After only a relatively small number of doublings, exponentially growing quantities reach impossible proportions.

Key Words and Phrases

linear growth   exponential growth   doublings

Key Concepts and Skills

- explain the difference between linear and exponential growth.
- identify whether a given growth pattern is linear or exponential.
- understand the implications of a doubling process.

Unit 8B Doubling Time and Half-Life

Overview

Exponential growth is characterized by a constant **doubling time**. If a quantity (for example, a population or a bank account) is growing exponentially, then it doubles its size during a fixed period of time, and it continues to double its size over that same period of time forever. For example, if a tumor, growing exponentially, has a doubling time of two months, then it doubles its number of cells during the first two months, and doubles that number again during the next two months, and continues to double *every* two months. Knowing the doubling time essentially defines the growth pattern for all times.

We denote the doubling time T_{double}. If we know T_{double} for a particular quantity that grows exponentially, then over a period of t time units, the quantity will increase by a factor of

$$2^{t/T_{\text{double}}}.$$

If we know the doubling time and the initial value of a particular quantity that grows exponentially, then we can find its value at all later times. The new values at later times are given by

$$\text{new value} = \text{initial value} \times 2^{t/T_{\text{double}}}.$$

If we know that a quantity grows with a constant percentage growth rate (for example, 5% per year), then we know it grows exponentially and that it has a constant doubling time. This suggests that there should be a connection between the percentage growth rate, which we call P, and the doubling time. We use a specific example of an exponentially growing population to present a widely used formula that relates percentage growth rate to doubling time. It is called the **Approximate Doubling Time Formula** or the **Rule of 70**. It says that

$$T_{\text{double}} \approx \frac{70}{P}.$$

This formula is an approximation and works best when the percentage growth rate is small (say, less that 10%). For example, if a bank account grows at 4% per year, it will double it value in approximately 70/4 = 17.5 years.

Everything we learned about exponential growth has a parallel with exponential decay. For example, if a quantity decays exponentially at a rate of 5% per month, it *decreases* by 5% during the first month, and by 5% during the second month, and continues to decrease by 5% every month. A quantity that decays exponentially has a constant **half-life** – the period of time over which it decreases its size by 50% or one-half.

We denote the doubling time T_{half}. If we know T_{half} for a particular quantity that decays exponentially, then over a period of t time units, the quantity will decrease by a factor of

$$\frac{1}{2}^{t/T_{\text{half}}}$$

If we know the half-life and the initial value of a particular quantity that decays exponentially, then we can find its value at all later times. The new values at later times are given by

$$\text{new value} = \text{initial value} \times \frac{1}{2}^{t/T_{\text{half}}}.$$

The **Approximate Half-Life Formula** also applies to exponentially decaying quantities. If a quantity decreases by $P\%$ per unit time, the then half-life is given by

$$T_{1/2} \approx \frac{70}{P}.$$

As with the Approximate Doubling Time Formula, this half-life formula is approximate and works best when P is small (say, less than 10%).

You might wonder if there are exact formulas for finding the doubling time or half-life from the percentage growth or decay rates. For those who are curious, the unit closes with the *exact* doubling time and half-life formulas. These formulas are a bit more complicated and require the use of logarithms. They are exact for all percentage growth and decay rates, not just small ones.

Key Words and Phrases

doubling time	percentage growth rate	approximate doubling time formula
Rule of 70	half-life	percentage decay rate
approximate half-life formula	exact doubling time formula	exact half-life formula

Key Concepts and Skills

- identify the percentage growth rate from the description of an exponential growth process.
- find the doubling time from percentage growth rate.
- find the percentage growth rate from doubling time.
- determine the value of an exponentially growing quantity given the doubling time and initial value.
- identify the percentage decay rate from the description of an exponential decay process.
- find the half-life from percentage decay rate.
- find the percentage decay rate from half-life.
- determine the value of an exponentially decay quantity given the half-life and initial value.

Unit 8C Real Population Growth

Overview

In the previous units of this chapter, we have seen that exponential growth models allow only for rapid and continual growth. While this sort of growth is realistic for some populations (for example, bacteria, tumor cells, or small populations of animals), it cannot continue forever. Eventually lack of space or resources must limit growth.

In this short unit we look briefly at more realistic approaches to population modeling. We begin by discussing how the overall growth rate really consists of **birth rates** and **death rates** (and immigration rates). We then introduce the important concept of **carrying capacity** — the maximum number of individuals that the environment can sustain. Any realistic population model must account for the carrying capacity.

The next observation is that as a population grows, its percentage growth rate cannot remain constant, as it does in an exponential growth model. The **logistic growth model** uses a growth rate that actually decreases as the population grows, and reaches zero when the population reaches the carrying capacity. A type of population growth, called **overshoot and collapse** is also presented as an alternative, but realistic population model. The unit closes with a discussion of estimating the carrying capacity of the Earth.

Key Words and Phrases

birth rate	death rate	carrying capacity
logistic growth model	collapse	overshoot

Key Concepts and Skills

- determine the exponential growth rate from birth and death rates.

- understand the limitations of exponential growth models.
- understand the assumptions and effects of a logistic growth model.
- determine growth rates for a logistic model.
- describe overshoot and collapse models.

---

9 Modeling Our World

Overview

Just as a map or a globe is a model of the Earth and a set of floor plans is a model of a building, we can also create mathematical models that represent real-world problems and situations. In fact, it might be argued that one of the fundamental goals of mathematics is to create mathematical models.

In this chapter, we introduce perhaps the most basic tool of mathematical modeling: functions. In fact, we have already encountered modeling and functions prior to this chapter: the financial formulas of Chapter 4 are examples are functions, and the exponential formulas of Chapter 8 are examples of mathematical models. The presentation of functions in this chapter may be different than those you have seen elsewhere. We start at the beginning and develop the idea of a function in a practical and visual way. Hopefully, in this way, whether you are seeing functions for the first time or not, you will become comfortable with this essential mathematical concept.

Unit 9A Functions: Building Blocks of Mathematical Models

Overview

This unit is brief and has a single purpose. Using words, a few definitions, pictures, and tables, the goal is to give a very qualitative idea of a **function**. There is no mysterious notation, no x's and y's, just an intuitive introduction to functions.

A function is a relationship between two quantities or **variables**. A function could describe how your height increases in time or how the temperature decreases with altitude. We call the variables the **independent variable** and the **dependent variable**. The terminology arises because we usually think of the dependent variable *changing with respect to* the independent variable; that is, if we make a change in the independent variable, it produces a change in the dependent variable.

There are three different ways to visualize or represent a function:

- with a data table of values of the two variables,
- with a graph (picture), and
- with an equation or formula.

In the remainder of this unit, we explore the first two ways of representing functions. The first approach (a data table) is straightforward and probably familiar. So we focus on graphing functions. The use of equations will be studied in the next unit.

Two concepts are important in graphing functions.

- The **domain** of a function is the set of values that both make sense and are of interest for the *independent variable*.
- The **range** of a function consists of the values of the *dependent variable* that correspond to the values in the domain.

If you can identify the domain and range of a function, then you have saved yourself a lot of work. You need to make the graph only for those values of the independent variable in the domain and for those values of the dependent variable in the range. Having defined the domain and range, we present several examples of functions and their graphs.

Key Words and Phrases

mathematical model	function	variable
independent variable	dependent variable	graph
coordinate plane	axis	origin
coordinates	quadrants	domain
range		

Key Concepts and Skills

- find the domain and range of a function given in table form.
- use the domain and range of a function to scale the axes of a graph of the function.
- know when it makes sense to “fill in” between the points of a graph.
- use the four-step process to create a graph of a function given a data table.

Important Review Boxes

- A Brief Review of The Coordinate Plane

Unit 9B Linear Modeling

Overview

From the previous unit, you probably appreciate that graphs of functions can take many different forms. In this unit we study one very special, but widely used, family of functions — those functions whose graphs are straight lines. Not surprisingly, these functions are called **linear functions**.

The most important property of a linear function is its **rate of change**. If the graph of two variables is a straight line, it means that a fixed change in one variable always produces the *same* change in the other variable. The rate at which the dependent variable changes with respect to the independent variable is called the rate of change of the function. For linear functions, the rate of change is constant and it is equal to the **slope** of the straight-line graph. These two fundamental properties of linear functions are summarized in the following rules.

$$\text{slope of a linear graph} = \frac{\text{vertical } \textit{rise}}{\text{horizontal } \textit{run}}$$

$$\text{rate of change} = \text{slope} = \frac{\text{change in } \textit{dependent variable} \text{ from } P_1 \text{ to } P_2}{\text{change in } \textit{independent variable} \text{ from } P_1 \text{ to } P_2}.$$

Having established the equivalence of the slope and the rate of change, we introduce the rule for calculating the change in the dependent variable. This rule simply says that if we know the rate of change of a linear function and we are given a change in the independent variable, then we can determine the corresponding change in the dependent variable:

Change in dependent variable = (rate of change) × (change in independent variable).

The rate of change rule is really just a stepping-stone to the final goal of the unit — to write a general equation for a linear function. After a detailed example to motivate the idea of a linear equation, we present the general form of a linear equation. It looks like this:

dependent variable = initial value + (rate of change × *independent variable*)

Up to this point we use words for the variable names. But you will soon see that this practice gets cumbersome. So for the sake of economy, we can use single letter names for variables. For example, instead of writing *time*, we just use *t*; and instead of writing *number of chips*, we could use *N*. Don't let the use of letters confuse you; it just makes working with linear equations easier.

After several examples of creating and using linear equations, we come to one last topic. A linear equation is a model or a compact description of a particular situation. Once we have it, it can be used for prediction or to answer other useful questions. We want to be able to answer questions such as:

- when the independent variable has a certain value, what is the corresponding value of the dependent variable?
- when the dependent variable has a certain value, what is the corresponding value of the independent variable?

This brings us to the necessity of *solving* linear equations when we are given a particular value of either the dependent variable or the independent variable. Two simple rules are all we need to solve any linear equation for either variable:

- we can always add or subtract the same quantity from both sides of an equation.
- We can always multiply or divide both sides of an equation by a (nonzero) quantity.

Several examples conclude this action-packed unit. There is a lot of material in this unit and it is best to work at it slowly and allow plenty of time for reading and for practice.

Key Words and Phrases

linear function	linear graph	rate of change
slope	change in dependent variable	initial value
general equation for a linear function		

Key Concepts and Skills

- determine the slope of a straight line given two points on the line.
- determine the rate of change of a linear function, either from a description of the function or from two points associated with the function.
- compute the change in the dependent variable given the rate of change and a change in the independent variable.
- find the equation of a linear function given the rate of change and the initial value.
- evaluate a linear function for the dependent variable given a value of the independent variable.
- solve a linear function for the independent variable given a value of the dependent variable.
- create a linear function from information about its rate of change and initial value.

Unit 9C Exponential Modeling

Overview

Having learned about the fundamentals of exponential growth and decay in Chapter 8, we can put these ideas to work to create models. Just as we used linear functions to model real world situations, we will now use exponential functions to model situations in which exponential growth or decay occur. We begin by introducing the general **exponential function**

$$Q = Q_0 \times (1 + r)^t,$$

where t represents time. This law requires an initial value Q_0 and a growth or decay rate r. Notice that if r is positive, then Q grows in time and if r is negative, then Q decays in time. Also important is that the units used for r and t must be the same (for example, if t has units of *days*, then r has units of 1/*days*). Once a specific exponential function is found, it can be used to predict the value of Q at all future times.

Be sure to study the highlight box entitled *Forms of the Exponential Function.* It shows that there are really several forms for the exponential function depending on whether you are given a growth rate, a doubling time, or a half-life.

With these exponential functions at hand, the rest of the unit is devoted to various applications. We look at how population growth, economic inflation, oil consumption, pollution, and drugs in the blood can all be modeled using these laws. Of particular importance is the technique called **radioactive dating**, which also relies on the exponential decay law. If these examples don't convince you of the widespread presence of exponential growth and decay, you will find even more applications in the problems!

Key Words and Phrases

exponential function   growth or decay rate   radioactive dating

Key Concepts and Skills

- given either a growth rate or a doubling time, use the appropriate form of the exponential function to model an exponentially growing quantity.
- given either a decay rate or a half-life, use the appropriate form of the exponential function to model an exponentially decaying quantity.
- be familiar with forms of the exponential function that use the doubling time or half-life.
- understand radioactive dating and know how to determine the age of a material that contains a radioactive element.

Important Review Boxes

- A Brief Review of Algebra with Logarithms

---

10 Modeling with Geometry

If you like geometry, you will probably like this chapter. If you didn't, this chapter may show you some things you had not thought about before and may be able to use. The first chapter is a review of some fundamental concepts from high school geometry. You may already know these things, but many of us will need the review.

The last two sections have applications many of you have not seen before. While the ideas in 10B are not particularly difficult, they are particularly useful in many walks of life. Applications to astronomy, road construction, and how tall to make a house under certain building restrictions are typical of the way simple geometry can be used to solve problems.

The last chapter will be quite new for many of you. You may have heard about fractals and even seen one, but now you will know how to make your own, among other things.

Unit 10A Fundamentals of Geometry

Overview

Because much of this chapter is based on ideas and concepts from geometry, it makes sense to do some review. If much of this unit is familiar, just sit back and enjoy it!

The unit begins by defining and giving examples of the basic concepts of geometry: **points**, **lines**, **planes**, and **angles**. We then move on to familiar two-dimensional objects (also called plane objects). The most basic objects are **circles** and **regular polygons** such as **triangles**, **squares**, **rectangles**, **pentagons**, and **hexagons**. A few formulas are given along the way. You should know or be able to find quickly formulas for the

- area of a circle,
- circumference of a circle,
- area of a triangle, and
- area of a **parallelogram** (which include squares and rectangles).

We give several practical examples of the uses of these formulas.

The next subject is solid objects in three dimensions. You will want to be familiar with the table that has formulas for the

- surface area and volume of a **rectangular prism** (box),
- surface area and volume of a **cylinder** (soda can),
- surface area and volume of a **sphere**.

We give several examples of these formulas applied to practical problems.

The unit closes with a very useful and far-reaching section on scaling laws. We first discuss scale models, such as maps or architectural models. If we take an object and increase all of its dimensions by a factor of, say 10, then the **scale factor** is 10. The important result of this section is that

- areas scale with the *square* of the scale factor, and
- volumes scale with the *cube* the scale factor.

So if you were to enlarge yourself by a scale factor of two, your surface area would increase by a factor of $2^2 = 4$, and your volume (and weight) would increase by a factor of $2^3 = 8$.

These scaling laws explain a lot of interesting biological and physical phenomena. By considering the **surface area to volume ratio**, we can answer questions such as, why does crushed ice keep your drink colder than large ice cubes? Why can flies walk on ceilings? Why does the Moon have no volcanoes?

Key Words and Phrases

geometry	Euclidean geometry	point
line	plane	dimension
angle	vertex	right angle
straight angle	acute angle	obtuse angle
perpendicular	parallel	radius
diameter	polygon	regular polygon
circumference	perimeter	parallelogram
rectangular prism	cube	cylinder
sphere	scale factor	scaling laws
surface to volume ratio		

Key Concepts and Skills

- define and give examples of point, line, and plane.
- convert angle measurements to fractions of a circle and vice versa.
- determine the perimeter and area of common plane objects (circle, triangle, square, rectangle, parallelogram).
- determine the surface area and volume of common three-dimensional objects (cube, rectangular prism, cylinder, sphere).
- use geometrical ideas and formulas to solve practical problems.

- **understand scaling laws and surface area to volume ratio arguments.**

Unit 10 Problem Solving with Geometry

Overview

Much of this chapter is based on ideas and concepts from geometry, but it involves applications which may be new to you. The unit begins by defining and giving examples of the basic concept of angles and how to measure them.

The first application uses the perhaps familiar notion of **latitude** and **longitude**. As you may recall, this way of measuring the earth gives coordinates for locations with respect to the **prime meridian** and the **equator**. Knowing latitude and longitude, one can easily calculate the distance between two locations on the same meridian.

For the next application, we need a relationship between **angular size, physical size** and **distance** to an object. Using this relationship, one can calculate any one of the three from the other two. For example, one can estimate the diameter of the moon (its physical size) knowing the distance to it and its angular size.

The next application involves the notions of **pitch**, **grade**, and **slope.** They are basically the same thing, but one is usually preferred in a given context. For example, one speaks of the "pitch of a roof" or the "grade of a road."

Almost no discussion of geometry and measurement is complete without mentioning the **Pythagorean Theorem** and **similar triangles**. The first gives a relationship between the lengths of the sides in a right triangle. The second gives a relationship between the sides of two triangles whose angles are all equal. This relationship is $\frac{a'}{a}=\frac{b'}{b}=\frac{c'}{c}$ where a, b, and c are the lengths of the sides in one triangle corresponding to the lengths a', b', and c' in a similar triangle. A nice application of similar right triangles is the calculation of heights from ground measurements such as the solar access problem of example 8.

The last unit has to do with **optimal shapes**. As it turns out

- squares are optimal rectangles in that they maximize area while minimizing perimeter
- cubes are optimal prisms in that they maximize volume while minimizing surface area.

Key Words and Phrases

latitude	longitude	prime meridian
equator	angular size	physical size
pitch	grade	slope
Pythagorean Theorem	similar triangles	optimal shape

Key Concepts and Skills

- use latitude to find distance between two locations with same longitude

- use any two of angular size, physical size, and distance to an object to find the third
- find the slope from pitch or grade and/or find a distance or height from them
- find a distance using Pythagorean Theorem; also calculate are of right triangle
- identify similar triangles and use to solve measurement problems

---

Unit 10C Fractal Geometry

Overview

In this unit we explore perhaps the most recent mathematical development in this book. **Fractal geometry** arises with the observation that classical geometry (invented by the ancient Greeks and studied by all of us in high school) works very well for regular objects such as circles and square. But many objects in the real world, particularly natural forms, are far more complex and are not described well by classical geometry. Fractal geometry was proposed, in part, to describe the complicated forms we find in nature.

We begin by looking at what happens when we measure the length of a line segment. If we continually magnify the line we don't see anything new. This means that if we measure the length of a line segment, we get the same length regardless of the length of the ruler. Similarly, if we measure the area of a square, we get the same area regardless of how small the ruler might be. And if we measure the volume of a cube, we get the same volume regardless of how small the ruler is. This leads to the conclusion that a line is a one-dimensional object, a square is a two-dimensional object, and a cube is a three-dimensional object.

Here is how we define the **dimension** of an object. We imagine successively reducing the length of our ruler by a **reduction factor** R. Each time we reduce the length of the ruler, we observe by what factor the number of **elements** increases. For regular objects, we find that

- For a one-dimensional object (e.g., a line segment), $N = R^1$.
- For a two-dimensional object (e.g., a square), $N = R^2$.
- For a three-dimensional object (e.g., a cube), $N = R^3$.

In each case, we see that $N = R^D$, and D is the **dimension** of the object.

For irregular objects, we result may be quite different. If we carry out the same measurement process, we may find that the relationship between R and N has the form $N = R^D$, but D is no longer a whole number. If D is not a whole number, the object is called a **fractal**.

With this definition in hand, we look at some examples of fractal objects, notably the **snowflake curve,** the **Cantor set,** the **Sierpinski triangle**, and the **Sierpinski sponge**. We also discuss how to measure the fractal dimension of realistic objects such as coastlines. We close with the most famous fractal of all, the **Mandelbrot set**.

Key Words and Phrases

fractal geometry	element	reduction factor
fractal dimension	snowflake curve	snowflake island
self-similar	Sierpinski triangle	Sierpinski sponge
Cantor set	Mandelbrot set	

Key Concepts and Skills

- understand the meaning of dimension for regular objects (line, square, and cube).
- understand the meaning of dimension for fractal objects.
- determine the dimension of simple fractal objects.

---

11 Mathematics and the Arts

Overview

In this chapter we explore some very different applications of mathematics, namely music and the fine arts. As you will see, the connections between mathematics and the arts go back to antiquity. First, we devote one unit to music, one unit to classical painting, one unit to proportion as it appears in art and nature. This chapter should provide you with a new perspective and change of pace!

Unit 11A Mathematics and Music

Overview

The ties between mathematics and music go back to the ancient Greeks in about 500 B.C. The followers of Pythagoras discovered some of the basic laws that underlie our understanding of music today. They realized that the **pitch** of a musical note created by a plucked string is determined by the **frequency** of the string — how many times the string vibrates each second. They also discovered that if the length of a string is halved, the frequency doubles, and the pitch goes up by an **octave**. With these few facts we can explain a lot.

In a standard scale that you might play on a piano or a guitar, one octave consists of 12 tones or **half-steps** (for example, the white and black keys between middle C and the next higher C). Here is the basic question we address: If we know the frequency of the first note of the scale, can we find the frequency of all 12 notes of the scale?

We show that to move up the scale a half step, we must *multiply* the frequency of the current tone by a fixed number. We give a brief argument showing that the magic number that generates the entire scale by multiplication is $f =$ 1.055946 ... or the twelfth root of 2. It turns out the notes of the scale follow an exponential growth law, as discussed in Chapter 9.

The ancient Greeks understood that when two notes have a pleasing sound when played together (**consonant tones**), then the ratio of their frequencies must be the ratio of two small numbers, such as 3/2 or 4/3. We investigate how these ratios of small numbers compare to the exact frequencies generated by the magic number f.

The unit closes with a few observations about the modern connections between music and mathematics: digital music, compact disks, and synthesizers.

Key Words and Phrases

sound wave	pitch	frequency
cycles per second	fundamental frequency	overtones
octave	scale	half-step
consonant tones	analog	digital

Key Concepts and Skills

- understand the relation between frequency and pitch.
- determine the frequency of notes separated by an octave.
- determine the frequency of notes on a 12-tone scale, given the frequency of the first note.
- understand the Greek's explanation for consonant tones in terms of ratios of small integers.
- understand the difference between analog and digital music.

Unit 11B Perspective and Symmetry

Overview

It wasn't until the Renaissance (14th and 15th century) that painters attempted to draw three-dimensional objects realistically on a flat two-dimensional canvas. It took many years for these painters to perfect this technique, but in the end, they made a science of **perspective** drawing. In this unit we trace the development of perspective drawing and explore some of its mathematical necessities.

The key concept in perspective drawing is the **principal vanishing point**. It can be summarized as follows: If you are an artist standing behind a canvas, painting a real scene, then all lines that are parallel in the real scene and perpendicular to the canvas, must meet in a single point in the painting — this is the principal vanishing point. All other sets of parallel lines in the real scene (that are *not* perpendicular to the canvas) meet in their own vanishing points. All of the vanishing points (principal and otherwise) lie along a single line called the **horizon line**.

Another fundamental property of paintings and other objects of art is **symmetry**. Symmetry can mean many different things, but it often refers to a sense of balance. We define three different kinds of symmetry:

- **reflection symmetry**: an object can be "flipped" across a particular line and it remains unchanged (for example, the letter H).
- **rotation symmetry**: an object can be rotated through a particular angle and it remains unchanged (for example, the letter O).
- **translation symmetry**: an object or a pattern can be shifted, say to the right or the left, and it remains unchanged (for example, the pattern ....XXXXXX.... extended in both directions).

We investigate these symmetries in both geometrical objects and in actual paintings.

Symmetry arises in beautiful ways in **tilings** — patterns in which one or a few simple objects are used repeated to fill an region of the plane. We give several examples of how triangles and quadrilaterals can be translated and reflected to produce wonderful patterns. And you can try some tilings in the problems, too!

Key Words and Phrases

vanishing point	principal vanishing point	horizon line
symmetry	reflection symmetry	rotation symmetry
translation symmetry	tiling	

Key Concepts and Skills

- understand the role of the principal vanishing point in perspective drawing.
- draw simple objects in perspective using vanishing points.
- identify symmetries in simple objects.
- draw simple objects with given symmetries.

- create tilings from triangles or quadrilaterals using translations and reflections.

Unit 11C Proportion and the Golden Ratio

Overview

In this unit, we explore another fundamental aspect of art; that is proportion. As you will see, issues of proportion arise not only in the art created by humans, but in natural forms as well. The subject has a lot to do with aesthetics, our innate sense of what is beautiful. And one of earliest statements about proportion and beauty goes back to the ancient Greeks who introduced the golden ratio.

The first instance of the golden ratio arises in dividing a line segment. What division of a line segment has the most visual appeal and balance? More specifically, suppose that the line segment has a length of $L + 1$ units and we want to divide it into two pieces of length L and 1. How should we choose L? The Greeks answered that the best division is the one that makes

$$\frac{\text{length of long piece}}{\text{length of short piece}} = \frac{\text{length of entire piece}}{\text{length of long piece}},$$

that is, the ratio of the length of the long piece to the length of the short piece is the same as the ratio of the length of the long piece to the length of the whole segment. We can also write this as

$$\frac{L}{1} = \frac{L+1}{L}.$$

We show that the value of L that makes this happen is the special (irrational) number

$$\phi = \frac{1+\sqrt{5}}{2} = 1.61803\ldots$$

This number is called the **golden ratio** or **golden section**.

From the golden ratio, we can define a **golden rectangle**. Any rectangle with sides in the ration of ϕ is called a golden rectangle. Both the golden ratio and the golden rectangle arise throughout the history of art. Great architectural works (for example, the Greek Parthenon) have dimensions close to those of the golden rectangle (although some claim that these examples are coincidences). Many common objects such as post cards and cereal boxes also have dimensions of golden rectangles. We also look at some examples of how the golden rectangle appears in nature.

There is one final connection that is too intriguing to ignore. We introduce the **Fibonacci sequence**, which was first used as a population model in the 13th century. Each term of the sequence is formed by adding the two previous terms:

$$1, 1, 2, 3, 5, 8, 13, 21, 34, ...$$

We show how this sequence is related, perhaps unexpectedly, to the golden ratio. And the circle is closed by observing that the Fibonacci sequence also appears in the artwork of nature. This is a unit with several seemingly unrelated ideas that eventually become linked in a beautiful way.

Key Words and Phrases

proportion	golden ratio	golden rectangle
logarithmic spiral	symmetry	Fibonacci sequence

Key Concepts and Skills

- understand the golden ratio as a proportion and divide a line segment according to the golden ratio.
- construct and identify golden rectangles.
- generate the Fibonacci sequence and find the ratio of successive terms.
- understand the connection between the golden ratio and the Fibonacci sequence.

---

12 Mathematics and Politics

Overview

This chapter explores the surprisingly crucial role that mathematics plays in political matters. The first two units deal with elections. We will see that in elections with more than two candidates, there are several ways to determine a winner, and they may not agree. In fact, it can be shown that there is no single voting method that meets certain fairness conditions. The last unit is devoted to another political process, namely apportionment. How do we determine the number of representatives that each state sends to Congress? Again, there are several methods that can be used, and they do not always agree!

Unit 12A Voting: Does the Majority Always Rule?

Overview

In this and the following unit we investigate mathematical problems associated with voting. This may sound like an unusual application of mathematics, but voting problems have been studied for several centuries and it has long been known that curious things can happen in voting systems. We will study such curious things in these two units.

The discussion begins with elections between two candidates. Throughout these units a candidate can be interpreted as a choice between two or more alternatives. For example, a candidate may be a person running for office or a brand of bagels in a taste test. With only two candidates, the rules are straightforward: the **majority** rules. This means that the candidate with the most votes (which must be more than 50% of the vote) wins the election.

However, even with majority rule, there are some interesting situations that can arise. We first look at presidential elections in which the winner is chosen, not by the **popular vote**, but by the **electoral vote**. Historically, there have been U.S. presidential elections in which a candidate won the popular vote, but lost the election.

We then look at variations on majority rule that often involve **super majorities**. For example, many votes in the U.S. government require more than a 50% majority: it takes a 2/3 super majority in both houses of Congress, followed by a 3/4 super majority vote of the states to amend the U.S. Constitution. More than a 50% majority of a jury is required to reach a verdict in a criminal trial.

Things get interesting when we turn to elections with three or more candidates. Often such elections are based on a **preference schedule** in which each voter ranks the candidates in order of preference. For example, the following preference schedule shows the outcome of an election among five candidates that we call A, B, C, D, and E.

First	A	B	C	D	E	E
Second	D	E	B	C	B	C
Third	E	D	E	E	D	D
Fourth	C	C	D	B	C	B
Fifth	B	A	A	A	A	A
	18	**12**	**10**	**9**	**4**	**2**

There was a total of 55 voters and 18 voters ranked A first, D second, E third, C fourth, and B last. The other columns are interpreted in a similar way. The question is: how do we determine a winner of the election?

The remainder of the unit presents five methods to determine a winner to an election with a preference schedule.

- **plurality**: the candidate with the most votes wins (candidate A would win the above election).
- **top two runoff**: the top two candidates have a runoff in which the votes of the losing candidates are redistributed to the top two candidates (candidate B would win the above election).
- **sequential runoff**: the candidates with the fewest first place votes are successively eliminated one at a time, votes are redistributed, and

runoff elections are held at each stage (candidate C would win the above election).

- **point system** (or **Borda count**): with five candidates, five points are awarded for each first place vote, four points are awarded for each second place vote, and so on. The candidate with the most points wins (candidate D would win the above election).
- **pairwise comparison**: the winner between each pair of candidates is determined and the candidate with the most pairwise wins is the winner of the election (candidate E would win the above election).

You can probably already see the dilemma. We have proposed five reasonable methods for finding a winner and they all give different results for the above preference schedule! The unit closes inconclusively with this question unanswered. The next unit takes up the issue of fairness in voting systems and attempts to resolve the question.

Key Words and Phrases

majority rule	popular vote	electoral vote
super majority	preference schedule	plurality
top-two runoff	sequential runoff	point system
Borda count	pairwise comparisons	

Key Concepts and Skills

- understand the concept of majority rule and apply it in two-candidate elections.
- know the difference between popular vote and electoral vote.
- use super majority rules to determine the outcome of votes.
- create and interpret preference schedules.
- apply the methods of plurality, top-two runoff, sequential runoff, point system, and pairwise comparisons to determine the outcome of elections with preference schedules.

Unit 12B Theory of Voting

Overview

The previous unit closed with the observation that five reasonable methods for determining the winner of an election with three or more candidates can lead to five different winners. This unit attempts to resolve the dilemma, but as you will see, the resolution may be less than satisfying!

The analysis of voting methods involves what are known as **fairness criteria**. We will work with the following four criteria.

- **Criterion 1 (majority criterion):** If a candidate receives a majority of the first-place votes, that candidate should be the winner.
- **Criterion 2 (Condorcet criterion):** If a candidate is favored over every other candidate in pairwise races, then that candidate should be declared a winner.
- **Criterion 3 (monotonicity criterion):** Suppose that Candidate X is declared the winner of an election, and then a second election is held. If some voters rank X even higher in the second election (without changing the order of other candidates), then X should also win the second election.
- **Criterion 4 (independence of irrelevant alternatives criterion):** Suppose that Candidate X is declared the winner of an election, and then a second election is held. If voters do not change their preferences, but one or more of the losing candidates drops out, then X should also win the second election.

These criteria have been developed by researchers who study voting method; they are reasonable conditions that we would expect of any fair voting system. The first criterion, stating that a candidate with a majority of the votes should win, is the most natural. The second criterion is also quite straightforward: if a candidate has more votes than each of the other candidates taken individually, then that candidate should win the election. The third criterion just says that if some voters were to change their votes in favor of the winner of the election, then that candidate should still win the election. The last criterion says that if a losing candidate drops out of the election, the original winner should remain the winner.

Most of the unit is devoted to examining the five voting methods introduced in the previous unit to see whether they satisfy the four fairness criteria. You may be surprised at the results. None of the five methods always satisfies all of the fairness criteria! This is the message of a famous result in voting theory called **Arrow's Impossibility Theorem**. It says that there is no voting method that satisfies the four fairness criteria for all preference schedules.

We next look at a method called **approval voting** that has been proposed as an alternative way to handle elections with many candidates. It departs from the familiar one-person-one-vote idea that underlies all of the voting systems discussed so far.

The unit closes with some ideas about power blocks in voting. An example of this idea is the formation of **coalitions,** which is common not only in our own government, but even more so in foreign governments.

Key Words and Phrases

fairness criteria	Arrow's Impossibility Theorem	approval voting
voting power	coalition	

Key Concepts and Skills

- understand the four fairness criteria.
- apply the four fairness criteria to each of the five voting methods for a given preference schedule.
- understand the benefits and disadvantages of approval voting.
- analyze an election in terms of coalitions.

Unit 12C Apportionment: The House of Representatives and Beyond

Overview

The U.S. Constitution stipulates that each state should have representation in the House of Representatives proportional to its population. But it doesn't specify exactly how the number of representatives should be determined. The process of assigning representatives according to population, which has applications beyond the House of Representatives, is called **apportionment**.

Apportionment begins by computing a **standard divisor**, which is the average number of people in the population per representative. For example, if the total population is 100,000 and there are 100 representatives, then the standard divisor is 1000 people per representative. The next step is to compute the **standard quota** for each state, which is the number of representatives a state should have if fractional representatives were possible. For example, if a state has 5500 people, then with a standard divisor of 1000, that state should have 5500/1000 = 5.5 representatives. Now the dilemma of apportionment can be seen: it is not possible to have fractions of representatives!

The founding fathers proposed several methods to overcome this problem of fractional representatives. Here is a quick survey of the various methods that are considered in detail in the text:

- **Hamilton's method**: First, round the standard quota for each state *down* to form the **minimum quota** for that state; then give any remaining representatives to the states with the largest fraction of representatives.
- **Jefferson's method**: Choose a **modified divisor** such that when the new standard quotas are rounded *down* (to form a **modified quota**), all the representatives are used.
- **Webster's method**: Choose a **modified divisor** such that when the new standard quotas are rounded *according to the standard rounding rule* (to form a **modified quota**), all the representatives are used.
- **Hill-Huntington method**: Choose a **modified divisor** such that when the new standard quotas are rounded *according to a modified rounding rule* (to form a **modified quota**), all the representatives are used.

Notice that the methods appear quite similar, but involve slightly different rules for rounding. However, as the examples in the text show, the methods can produce different results. Many examples of are provided to show how these methods are carried out.

Which method is best? Two hundred years of American history has proved that none of the methods is perfect. Each method can exhibit at least one of several paradoxes or can violate certain reasonable expectations. To address this question of fairness, the unit explores and gives examples of the following situations:

- the **Alabama paradox**: when the total number of representatives increases, but at least one state actually loses representatives.
- the **population paradox**: when the population increases and under reapportionment a slow-growing state gains representatives at the expense of a fast-growing state.
- the **new states paradox**: when additional representatives are added to accommodate a new state and the apportionment of existing states changes.
- the **quota criterion**: under any apportionment, the number of representatives for any state should be one of the whole numbers nearest its standard quota (the standard quote rounded up or rounded down).

The apportionment problem is a bit like the voting problem, in that a perfect apportionment method cannot be found. This is the conclusion of the **Balinsky and Young theorem**.

Key Words and Phrases

apportionment	standard divisor	standard quota
Hamilton's method	Alabama paradox	population paradox
new states paradox	Jefferson's method	modified divisor
modified quota	quota criterion	Webster's method
Hill-Huntington method	geometric mean	Balinsky and Young theorem

Key Concepts and Skills

- understand the problem and the dilemma of apportionment.
- apply the four methods of the text to apportionment problems.
- identify the deficiencies of the four methods in terms of paradoxes and the quota criterion..

13 Mathematics and Business

Overview

In this chapter we will explore a different area of mathematics and many different kinds of applications. Discrete mathematics is the area of mathematics that deals with separate or individual items. The items might be people, objects, choices, or geographical locations. We have already seen some discrete mathematics in this book: the counting methods presented in Unit 7E are examples of discrete mathematics. This chapter will look at two more topics from discrete mathematics.

In Units 12A and B, we will look at applications of *network theory*. As you will see, a network is a mathematical model that illustrates how the various components of a system are interrelated. For example, the power lines that connect several communities or the trading relations between several countries can be displayed using a network. The applications of network theory are endless. The mathematics is quite different because it is visual and involves very little computation. In the last unit, we see how networks can be used to schedule large projects that involve many stages. These methods are used to achieve efficiency and cost-savings in many business applications.

Unit 13A Network Analysis

Overview

In this unit we introduce the idea of a **network** (also called a **graph**). A network is a collection of points (called **vertices**) connected by lines or **edges**. A nice example of a network arises in the 18th century **Konigsberg bridge problem** that led to the invention of network theory. We also give several more practical situations that lead to networks.

One of the fundamental network questions is whether it is possible to find a path that traverses every edge of the network exactly once and returns to the starting vertex. If such a path exists, it is called an **Euler circuit** (pronounced *oiler*, in honor of the mathematician who invented network theory). An Euler circuit would be of interest to an inspector, a meter reader, or a delivery person, who would like to do his/her job in the most efficient way. It turns out that there is a simple rule that determines whether a network has an Euler circuit.

> an Euler circuit exists for a network only if each vertex has an even number of edges attached to it.

Having determined whether a network has an Euler circuit doesn't tell you how to find it! So we also provide a rule, called the **burning bridges rule**, that tells you how to find an Euler circuit. The rule says that

> you may begin your circuit from any vertex in the network. However, as you choose edges to follow for your path, avoid using an edge that is the *only* connection to a part of the network that you have not already visited.

There is a lot of terminology associated with networks, some of which we introduce at this point. Here are a few important terms.

- a path within a network that begins and ends at the same vertex is a **circuit**.
- a network is **complete** if every vertex is connected to every other vertex.
- a **tree** is a network in which all of the vertices are connected, but there are no cycles (it looks like a tree with roots and branches).
- the **order** of a network is the number of vertices.
- the **degree** of a vertex is the number of edges connected to it (each vertex in a network could have a different order.

The last problem in this unit deals with networks in which every edge has a number or **weight** associated with it. The weights often represent distances or costs. A **spanning network** for such a network is a set of edges within the network that connects every vertex to every other vertex. In other words, if you walk along a spanning tree you can reach every vertex from every other vertex. A given network could have several different spanning networks, so an question of great importance is which, of many different spanning networks, has the minimum cost? This is called the **minimum cost spanning network** problem. (You might want to convince yourself that the minimum cost spanning network must be a tree).

We give some practical examples of minimum cost spanning tree problems and then provide an efficient method, called **Kruskal's algorithm**, for finding the minimum cost spanning tree of a network.

Key Words and Phrases

network	edge	vertex
Euler circuit	burning bridges rule	cycle
circuit	tree	order
degree	complete	spanning network
minimum cost spanning network	Kruskal's algorithm	

Key Concepts and Skills

- draw a network as a model of a given practical situation.
- determine if a given network has an Euler circuit and find one.
- understand the applications of Euler circuits.
- classify a network (in terms of cycles, tree, complete), identify the order of the network and the degree of each vertex.
- understand the applications of minimum cost spanning networks.
- apply Kruskal's algorithm to find the minimum cost spanning network.

Unit 13B The Traveling Salesman Problem

Overview

This unit is devoted to one of the most famous of all network problems. However the **traveling salesman problem** has many applications beyond its namesake. Consider a network in which the vertices might be the cities that a salesman must visit and the edges are the airline routes that connect them along with their distances. A very practical problem is to find the route of minimum length that visits every city exactly once and returns to the starting city. This is an example of a traveling salesman problem.

We begin the discussion by introducing a preliminary idea: a **Hamiltonian circuit** is a path through a network that visits every vertex exactly once and returns to the starting vertex. While a Hamiltonian circuit passes through every vertex, it may not traverse every edge (as an Euler circuit does). Not every network has a Hamiltonian circuit, and furthermore, it is very difficult to determine whether a general network has a Hamiltonian circuit. In fact, there is no simple rule (as there is with Euler circuits) that determines when a network has a Hamiltonian circuit.

There are a few cases in which it is possible to find Hamiltonian circuits easily. If a network is complete (every vertex is connected to every other vertex), then Hamiltonian circuits abound. In fact there are $(n-1)!/2$ Hamiltonian circuits in a complete network of order n. The number of Hamiltonian circuits increases explosively with the order of the network.

We must now imagine a network (which may or may not be complete) in which all of the edges have distances on them. To solve the traveling salesman problem for this network, we must find not just any Hamiltonian circuit, but the one with the least length. This turns out to be an incredibly difficult problem, especially for problems of practical interest in which there may be thousands of vertices in the network. We describe a method, called the **nearest neighbor method** that can be used to find nearly optimal traveling salesman solutions.

We close the unit with some general remarks about a branch of mathematics called **operations research** that includes problems such as the traveling salesman problem. Operations research often handles problems from business and management that involve finding the most efficient or least expensive way to carry out a task. Airlines and manufacturing companies use operations research every day to streamline their operations, and our lives are affected by this area of mathematics continuously.

Key Words and Phrases

traveling salesman problem	Hamiltonian circuit	nearest neighbor method
operations research		

Key Concepts and Skills

- understand the applications of Hamiltonian circuits.
- determine if a given circuit is a Hamiltonian circuit for a network.
- find the number of Hamiltonian circuits in a complete network.
- understand the applications of the traveling salesman problem.
- apply the nearest neighbor method to find a traveling salesman solution.

Unit 13C Scheduling Problems

Overview

In this unit we look at a very different use of networks that is just as practical as all the previous applications. Imagine a large project, such as building a house or planning a shopping center (or even landing a person on the Moon), that consists of many smaller tasks. Some of the smaller tasks can be done at the same time, but some must be done before or after others. For example, in a house building project, you must build the walls before you can paint the walls.

As you will see in this unit, a network can be used to schedule the smaller tasks and illustrate which tasks must precede other tasks. The network also shows the estimated time for the completion of each task. Once the scheduling network is created, several important questions can be asked. For example, we can determine the minimum time for completion of the project. The minimum completion time corresponds to the *longest* path through the network; this longest path is called the **critical path**. The critical path consists of all the **limiting tasks** for the project.

We can also determine when each task can be started and finished. The following four quantities are useful for this purpose:

- **earliest start time** for a task is the soonest that a task can be started after the beginning of the project.
- **earliest finish time** for a task is the soonest that a task can be finished after the beginning of the project.

- **latest start time** for a task is the latest that a task can be started after the beginning of the project and still have the project finish on time .
- **latest finish time** for a task is the latest that a task can be finished after the beginning of the project and still have the project finish on time .

A general rule is that you should start at the *beginning* of the project and work *forward* through the network to find the earliest start time and earliest finish time. You should start at the *end* of the project and work *backward* through the network to find the latest start time and latest finish time.

Finally, for each task we define the **slack time** as the difference between the latest start time and the earliest start time (or equivalently as the difference between the latest finish time and the earliest finish time). Tasks with a zero slack time are on the critical path. Tasks with a non-zero slack time are not on the critical path and can be delayed without affecting the outcome entire project. Knowing the slack times allows a project manager to decide which tasks must be completed on time and which tasks can be postponed.

The entire unit really consists of one detailed example that illustrates all of these points. After that, you will be ready to try some exercises on your own.

Key Words and Phrases

critical path	limiting task	earliest start time
earliest finish time	latest start time	latest finish time
slack time		

Key Concepts and Skills

- create and interpret a network as a schedule for a multi-stage project.
- find the critical path for a scheduling network.
- find the earliest start time, earliest finish time, latest start time, latest finish time, and slack times for all task in a scheduling network.

Unit 1A

Does It Make Sense?

5. Does not make sense. Arguments do not have to involve heated debate.
7. Makes sense. The premise and conclusion must be clearly identifiable in a logical argument.
9. Does not make sense. A fallacy is an error in reasoning-that is, in the construction of the argument supporting the conclusion-not an error in the conclusion itself. Indeed, it's often possible to create a solid argument (no fallacy) even for a conclusion that is clearly false.

Basic Skills and Concepts

Understanding Fallacies

11. a. *Premise*: Many polled support the proposal. *Conclusion*: The proposal is a good idea.
    b. Appeal to popularity. The fact that most people support an idea does not make it a good one.
13. a. *Premise*: No proof exists that global warming is harmful. *Conclusion*: No need to worry about global warming.
    b. Appeal to ignorance. The fact that something is not proven does not mean that it is not true.
15. a. *Premise*: Witness refused to testify. *Conclusion*: The witness is guilty.
    b. Limited choice. There may be other reasons why a witness refuses to testify. In fact, the Fifth Amendment does not require a person to give any reason at all for such a refusal.
17. a. *Premise*: The witness was convicted for dealing drugs. *Conclusion*: He is not trustworthy.
    b. Personal attack. This is a typical and often effective way of discrediting an opponent. The prior conviction is not relevant to the current issue.
19. a. *Premise*: There's too much air pollution. *Conclusion*: We should not build anymore highways.
    b. Diversion. The issue is whether or not to build more highways. Highways do not increase air pollution; they redistribute the flow of traffic.

Further Applications

Understanding Fallacies.

21. *Premise*: Following Reagan's defense buildup, the Soviet Union began the process of democratization that ultimately led to its breakup. *Conclusion*: Reagan is responsible for the changes that led to the demise of the Soviet Union. Without historical substantiation, this is a false cause fallacy.
23. *Premise*: The mother has used drugs in the past. *Conclusion*: The decision on the custody case depends on the mother's present drug use. Limited choice.
25. *Premise*: Mom smoked when she was my age. *Conclusion*: I won't heed her advice to stop smoking. This is a circumstantial case of a personal attack. The fact that another person smokes is irrelevant to one's own personal decision to smoke.
27. *Premise*: No one has ever proved that telepathy doesn't exist. *Conclusion*: I believe in telepathy. This is an appeal to ignorance: an absence of proof for one conclusion (telepathy does not exist) does not prove the opposite conclusion (telepathy does exist).
29. *Premise*: Senator Smith is one of the biggest recipients of campaign contributions from the National Rifle Association. *Conclusion*: Senator Smith's bill cannot help the cause of gun control. This is a case of personal attack: the fact that the Senator gets campaign funds from the NRA does not necessarily mean that he or she will only introduce bills that are to the NRA's liking. (One could also argue that it's a kind of "guilt by association," implying that on the one hand, there exist politicians who have received funds from the NRA, some of whom have gone on to support the NRA's position, and on the other, that Sen Smith is one of these politicians.

In this sense it's an implicit example of hasty generalization.)

31. *Premise*: The percentage of the population over 18 that smokes has decreased from 40% to about 20%. The percentage of overweight people has increased from 25% to 35%. *Conclusion*: Quitting smoking leads to overeating. This is false cause: just because there are now more overweight people and fewer smokers does not prove that quitting smoking causes overeating.
33. *Premise*: My little boy loves dolls and my little girl loves trucks. *Conclusion*: There's no truth to the claim that boys are more interested in mechanical toys while girls prefer maternal toys. This is an appeal to ignorance and hasty generalization.
35. *Premise*: Bush favors repealing the estate tax, which falls most heavily on the rich. *Conclusion*: Bush favors the rich, vote for Gore. This is a straw man argument.

Unit 1B

Does It Make Sense?

7. Does not make sense. A proposition must make a specific claim and cannot be a question.
9. Makes sense. In this case, the "or" is clearly exclusive, since a person can't be both dead and alive, but the statement is fine because he'll be one or the other.
11. Does not make sense. Truth tables show only how the truth of some statements depends on the truth values of their individual propositions; knowledge of the individual propositions is required.

Basic Skills and Concepts

Is It a Proposition?

13. This statement is a proposition. It has a subject and a predicate, and makes a claim that is capable of being true or false.
15. This statement is a proposition. It has a subject and a predicate, and makes a claim that is capable of being true or false.
17. This question is not a proposition, it makes no claim.

Negation.

19. Negation: London is not the capital of England. The original statement is true; its negation is false.
21. Negation: Caesar was not a Roman. The original proposition is true; its negation is false.

Multiple Negations.

23. The statement means that the city council supported the police chief, since they did not approve a vote against the police chief.
25. The statement means that Congress upheld the veto (i.e., opposed the bill), since it voted against a proposal that would have reversed the veto.
27. The statement means that the anti-discrimination policy is supported by the Constitution, since going against the policy is contrary to the spirit of the Constitution.

Truth Tables.

29. The columns for q and r contain all of the possible combinations of true and false values. The statement 'q and r' is true only if both q and r are true.

q	r	q and r
T	T	T
T	F	F
F	T	F
F	F	F

31. "Quebec is the capital of Canada" is false. "Moscow is the capital of Russia" is true. The conjunction is false.
33. "Ben is married" and "Ben is a bachelor" are the propositions, whose truth values cannot be assessed unless we know something about Ben. However, they cannot both be true, and so the conjunction is false.
35. "Grass is green" is true, as is "Skies are blue." The conjunction is true.

Truth Tables.

37. There are eight (2^3) possible combinations of true and false values for q, r, and s. The state-

ment 'q and r and s' is true only if all three parts are true.

q	r	s	q and r and s
T	T	T	T
T	T	F	F
T	F	T	F
F	T	T	F
T	F	F	F
F	T	F	F
F	F	T	F
F	F	F	F

Interpreting *Or*.

39. This is the exclusive Or; you cannot chose both.
41. This could be either Or, exclusive if you only intend to make one trip, inclusive if you'd consider both (which you'll certainly be able to afford!).
43. This is the exclusive Or if you assume that roads cannot be made of both asphalt and concrete. It's inclusive otherwise.

Truth Tables.

45. The columns for r and s contain all of the possible combinations of true and false values. The statement 'r or s' is false only if both r and s are false.

r	s	r or s
T	T	T
T	F	T
F	T	T
F	F	F

47. There are only two possible combinations of p and $\sim p$ because their truth values are always opposite. For example, p and $\sim p$ cannot both be true. The statement p and $\sim p$ is true only if both p and $\sim p$ are true. So this statement is always false.

p	$\sim p$	p and $\sim p$
T	F	F
F	T	F

49. There are eight (2^3) possible combinations. The statement 'p or q or r' can be false only if p, q, and r are all false.

p	q	r	p or q or r
T	T	T	T
T	T	F	T
T	F	T	T
F	T	T	T
T	F	F	T
F	T	F	T
F	F	T	T
F	F	F	F

***Or* Statements.**

51. "Seattle is the capital of the United States" is false, and "Paris is the capital of France" is true. The disjunction is true.
53. "Bill Clinton was a U.S. President" is true, and "Martin Luther King was a U.S. President" is false. The disjunction is true.
55. "$8 \times 4 = 32$" is true. "$7 \times 3 = 22$" is false. The disjunction is true.

Keyword Searches.

57. Search on "earthquakes" and "California."
59. Search on "Martin Luther King" and "assassination."

Truth Tables.

61. The statement 'if p, then r' can only be false if p is true and q is false.

p	r	if p, then r
T	T	T
T	F	F
F	T	T
F	F	T

***If... Then* Statements.**

63. The hypothesis is "San Francisco is in California," which is true. The conclusion is "San Francisco is in the Pacific Time Zone," which is also true. The implication is true.
65. The hypothesis is "Paris is the capital of China," which is false. The conclusion is "London is the capital of England," which is true. The implication is true.
67. The hypothesis is "Sparrows can fly," which is true. The conclusion is "Sparrows are birds," which is also true. The implication is true.
69. The hypothesis is "$2 + 2 = 5$," which is false. The conclusion is "Primates are not mammals," which is also false. The implication is true.

Rephrasing Conditionals.

71. "If a person is a resident of Miami, then that person is a resident of the United States." This implication is true, since all residents of Miami (Florida) are automatically residents of the U.S.

73. "If you are a musician, then you play the saxophone." This proposition is false: not all musicians play the saxophone.

75. "If you have prostate cancer, then you are a male." This proposition is true, since only males have a prostate gland.

Converse, Inverse, Contrapositive.

77. The converse is "If Marco lives in the United States, then he lives in Chicago," which is false. The inverse is "If Marco does not live in Chicago, then he does not live in the United States," which, being logically equivalent to the converse, has the same meaning, and is also false. The contrapositive is "If Marco does not live in the United States, then he does not live in Chicago," which is true, being logically equivalent to the original proposition.

79. The converse is "If I get wet, then I went swimming," which is false. The inverse is "If I don't go swimming, then I won't get wet," which, being logically equivalent to the converse, has the same meaning, and is also false. The contrapositive is "If I don't get wet, then I didn't go swimming," which is true, being logically equivalent to the original proposition.

81. The converse is "If there is gas in the tank, then the engine is running," which is false. The inverse is "If the engine is not running, then there is no gas in the tank," which, being logically equivalent to the converse, has the same meaning, and is also false. The contrapositive is "If there is no gas in the tank, then the engine is not running," which is true, being logically equivalent to the original proposition.

Famous Quotes.

83. There are two conditional statements here. The first is "If a young man has not wept, then he is a savage." The second is "If an old man will not laugh, then he is a fool."

85. "If a person has no vices, then that person has very few virtues."

Writing Conditional Phrases.

87. If Sue lives in Cleveland, then she lives in Ohio.

89. If Sue lives in Ohio, then she lives in Cleveland.

Library Search.

91. a. Under a title search for "Finnegan," the book should be on the list since the title is Finnegan's Wake.

b. A search for "Finnegan" and "Joyce" should produce a list with Finnegan's Wake and any other works by or about Joyce with "Finnegan" in the title.

c. A search for "Joyce" or "Yeats" would provide a list of all works by anybody with the names Joyce or Yeats; the list would include Finnegan's Wake.

d. Searching for "Joyce" and "James" would give a list with all works by James Joyce and any other author with both James and Joyce in the name; so Finnegan's Wake would be on the list.

e. Searching for "Joyce" and "Yeats" would not produce Finnegan's Wake because both Joyce and Yeats must appear in the title/author string.

f. This time one would get a list of all works by Joyce or Yeats with "Finnegan" in the title; this list would include Finnegan's Wake.

93. **Artificial Intelligence.** If a computer exhibits human-level intelligence, then it must have the requisite processing power.

Truth Tables and Logical Equivalence.

95. Comparing the two truth tables below, we see that the statements are logically equivalent.

p	q	p or q	$\sim (p$ or $q)$
T	T	T	F
T	F	T	F
F	T	T	F
F	F	F	T

p	q	$\sim p$	$\sim q$	$\sim p$ and $\sim q$
T	T	F	F	F
T	F	F	T	F
F	T	T	F	F
F	F	T	T	T

This has the same meaning as "neither," and together with the logical equivalence in Exercise 94, is known as De Morgan's Law.

97. Comparing the first truth table in Exercise 95 above with this one

p	q	$\sim p$	$\sim q$	$\sim p$ or $\sim q$
T	T	F	F	F
T	F	F	T	T
F	T	T	F	T
F	F	T	T	T

we see that "$\sim(p$ or $q)$" is not logically equivalent to "$\sim p$ or $\sim q$."

99. Comparing the two truth tables below, we see that "(p or q) and r" is logically equivalent to "(p and r) or (q and r)."

p	q	r	p or q	(p or q) and r
T	T	T	T	T
T	T	F	T	F
T	F	T	T	T
T	F	F	T	F
F	T	T	T	T
F	T	F	T	F
F	F	T	F	F
F	F	F	F	F

p	q	r	p and r	q and r	(p and r) or (q and r)
T	T	T	T	T	T
T	T	F	F	F	F
T	F	T	T	F	T
T	F	F	F	F	F
F	T	T	F	T	T
F	T	F	F	F	F
F	F	T	F	F	F
F	F	F	F	F	F

Unit 1C

Does It Make Sense?

7. Does not make sense. (Unless perhaps the electric company is owned by the phone company.)
9. Does not make sense. Irrational numbers are not counting numbers.
11. Does not make sense. The proposition does not have to be true to have a Venn diagram representation.

Basic Skills and Concepts

Classifying Numbers.

13. $2.3 = \frac{23}{10}$ is a rational number.
15. $-\frac{3}{2} = \frac{-3}{2}$ is a rational number.
17. 3 is a natural number.
19. -5 is an integer.
21. $100.1 = \frac{1001}{10}$ is a rational number.
23. $-6.1 = \frac{-61}{10}$ is a rational number.
25. $\sqrt{5}$ cannot be written as the ratio of two integers, so it is a real number.
27. 2005 is a natural number.

Set Notation.

29. {January, February, March, April, . . ., November, December}.
31. {Washington, Adams, Jefferson}.
33. {California, Colorado, Connecticut}.
35. {100, 101, 102, 103, . . . , 198, 199, 200}.

Venn Diagrams for Two Sets.

37. The sets *doctors* and *women* are overlapping sets, since it is possible for a person to be in one, both, or neither of these sets.

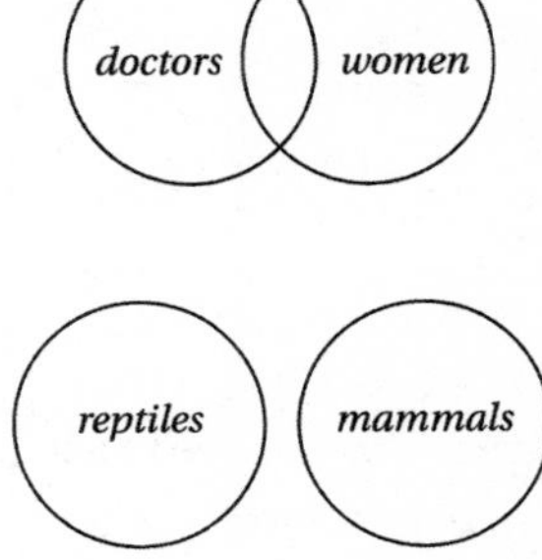

39. The set of *words* contains the set of *verbs*, since each verb is a word.

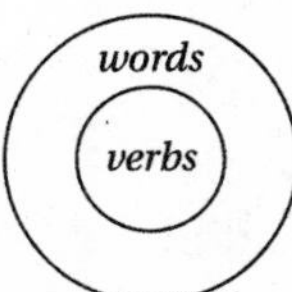

41. The set of *painters* intersects the set of *artists*, since some painters paint houses, not pictures.

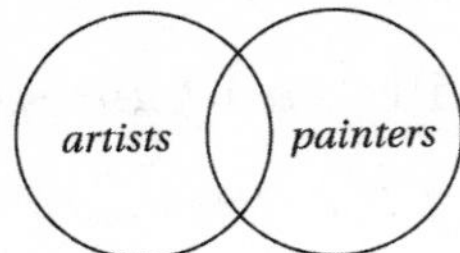

43. The sets *negative integers* and *natural numbers* are disjoint sets, since no number can be both negative and positive.

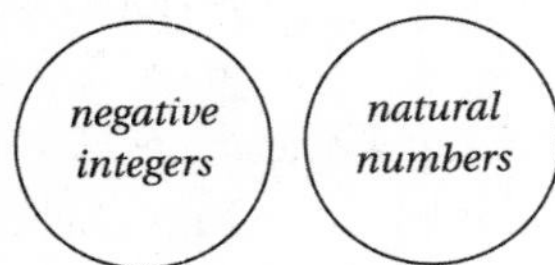

Categorical Propositions.

45. This is in standard form, with subject "bachelors" and predicate "men."

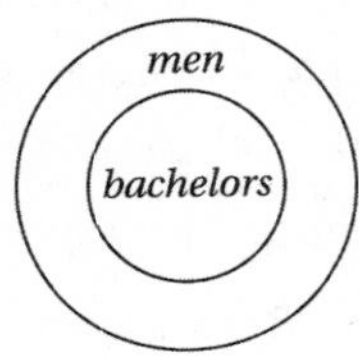

47. This is in standard form, with subject "U.S. presidents" and predicate "men."

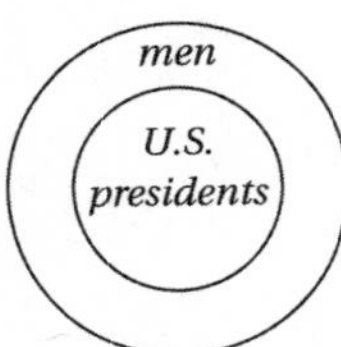

49. Standard form: "No fish are flying animals," with subject "fish" and predicate "flying animals."

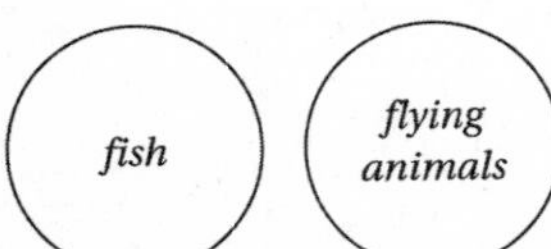

51. Standard form: "All nurses are people who know CPR," with subject "nurses" and predicate "people who know CPR."

Venn Diagrams for Three Sets.

53. Assuming that no pilots are dentists, we get:

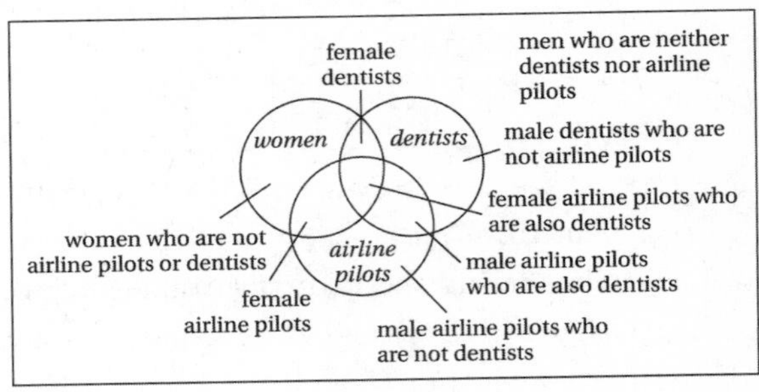

55. Assuming no songs are poetry and some poems and songs are unpublished, we get:

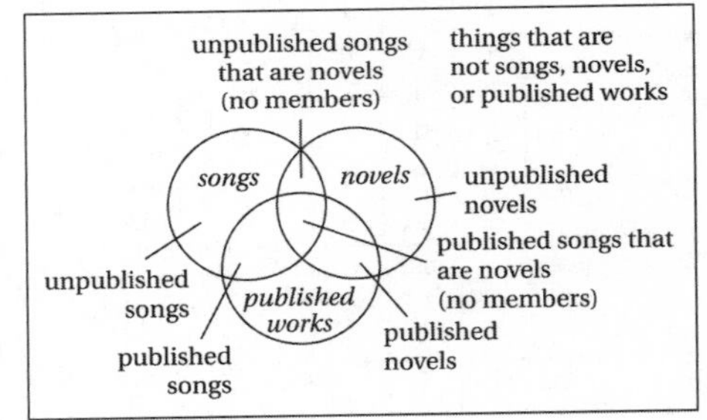

57.

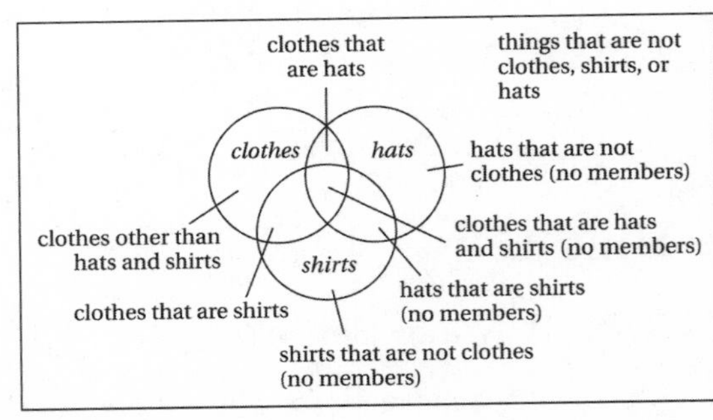

A Venn Diagram with Numbers.

59. a. There are $6 + 7 + 6 + 9 = 28$ people.

b. There are $6 + 9 = 15$ women.

c. There are $7 + 6 = 13$ men.

d. There are $7 + 6 = 13$ Republicans.

Venn Diagrams for Sets.

61. Two circles are needed, one for soccer and one for softball. Those who play neither will be represented outside of both circles.

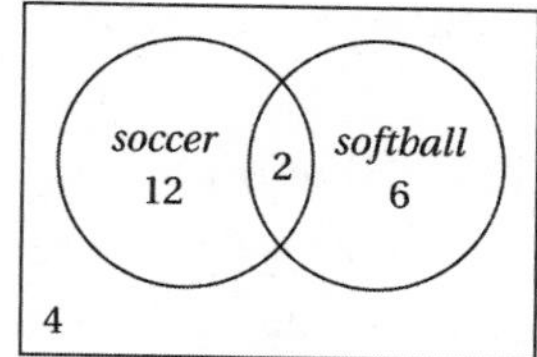

63. Only two circles are necessary, one for the drug treatment patients and one for improvement. A table of the data can also be helpful.

	improved	unimproved
placebo	6	12
drug treatment	9	3

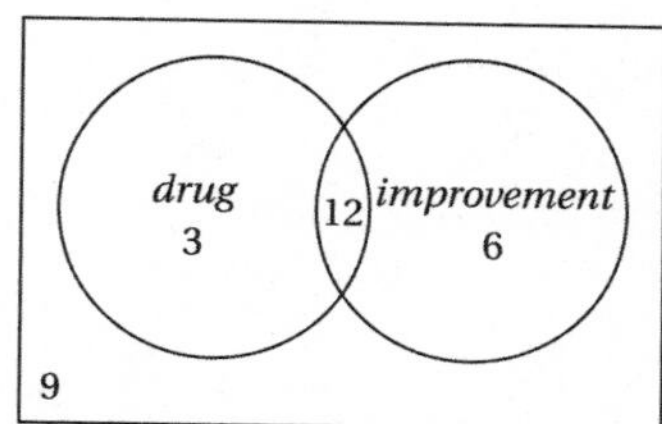

Further Applications

Venn Diagram Answers.

65. Since 16 students are taking at least math, and 9 are taking math only, then $16 - 9 = 7$ are taking math and biology. Since 23 are taking at least biology, then $23 - 7 = 16$ are taking biology only. Hence, $9 + 7 + 16 = 32$ are taking math or biology or both, and $43 - 32 = 11$ are taking neither.

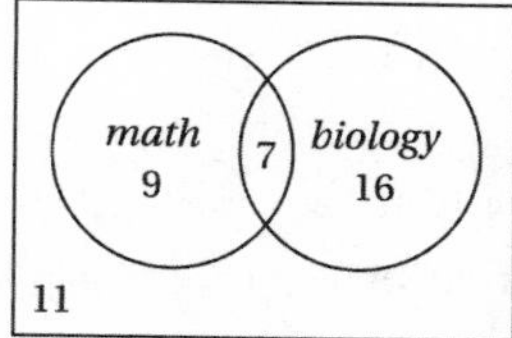

67. **Majors and Gender.** Using circles to represent women and biology, we get

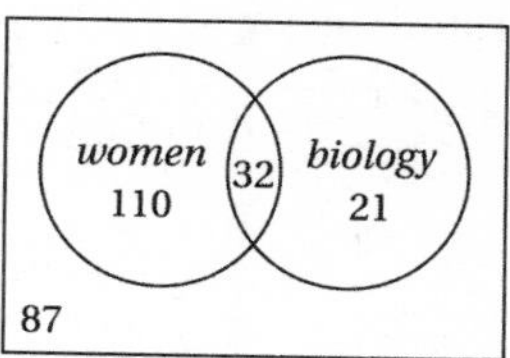

69. **Coffee and Gall Stones.** Using circles to represent coffee consumption and the incidence of gall stones, we get

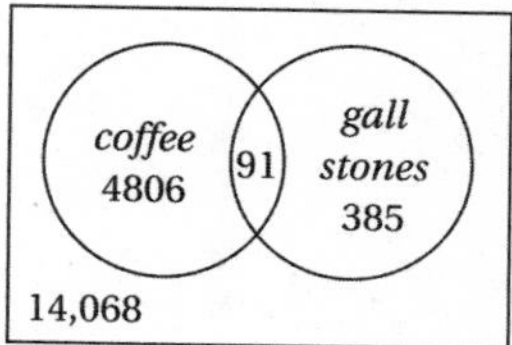

71. **Interpreting Sales.**

a. Using circles to represent the options chosen, we get

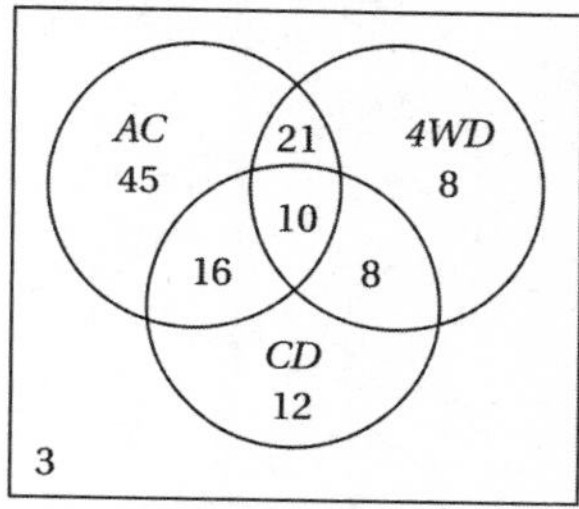

b. $10+21 = 31$ people chose AC and 4WD: the 10 buyers who went for all three options and 21 who opted for AC and 4WD only.

c. $45+16 = 61$ people chose AC but not 4WD: the 45 who went for AC only and the 16 who opted for AC and CP only.

d. Summing over all of the non-overlapping option categories, we find that $45 + 21 + 8 + 16 + 10 + 8 + 12 = 120$ people chose (at least one of) AC or 4WD or CP.

e. $21 + 16 + 8 = 45$ people chose exactly two options: the 21 who chose AC and 4WD only, the 16 who chose AC and CP only, and the 8 who chose CP and 4WD only.

More Than Three Sets.

73. While house pets may be dogs, cats, or canaries (and none of these overlap), not all dogs, cats, or canaries are house pets.

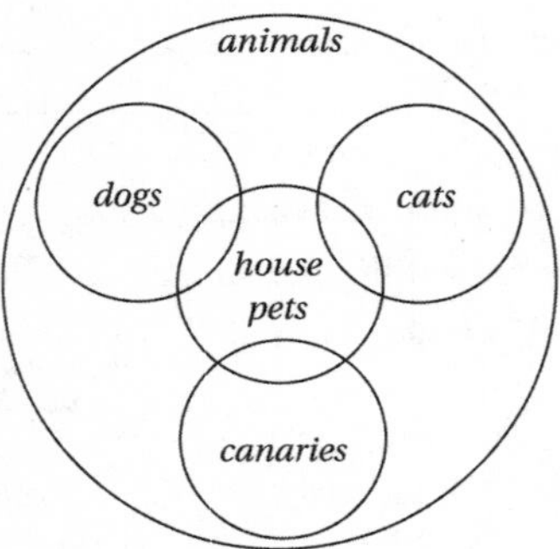

75. It may also be acceptable to overlap fruits and desserts.

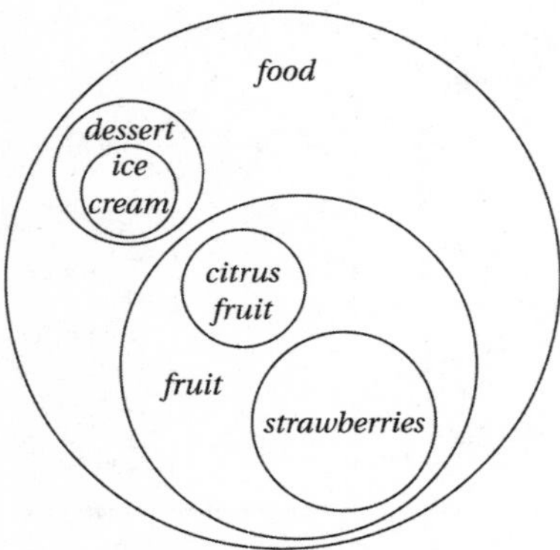

Organizing Propositions.

77. There could not be hairy fish. There could be hairy animals that swim. There could be mammals that walk on land. There could be hairy animals that walk on land.

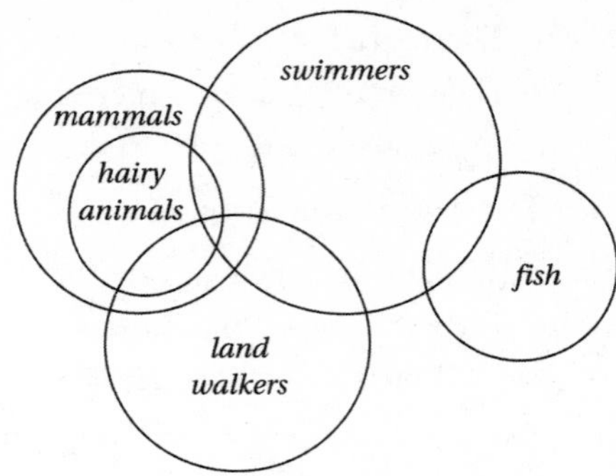

79. There could be conservative Democrats. There could be liberal Green Party members. There could not be liberal Republicans.

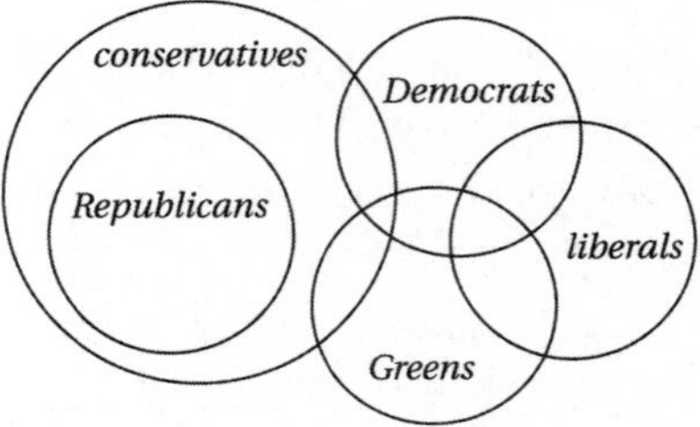

81. **Organizing Literature.**

a.

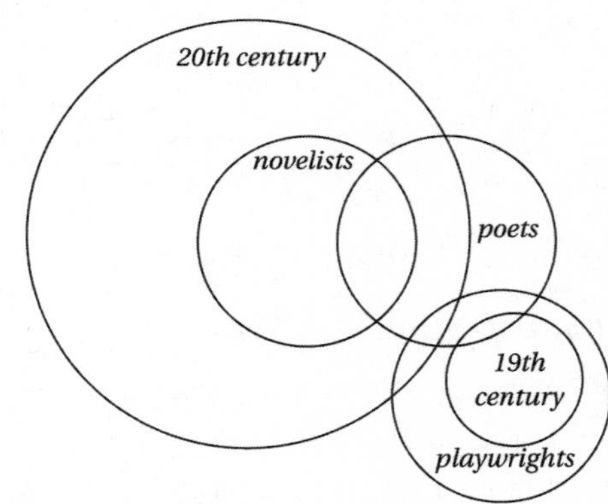

b. According to the Venn diagram 19th century writers lies entirely inside playwrights, which does not overlap novelists. Besides, a clearly stated condition is that all novelists were born in the 20th century.

c. You could have studied a 19th century poet, but only if they were also a playwright.

d. Yes, because 20th century writers overlaps the intersection of poets and playwrights.

83. **N Sets.**

a. Each buyer can be classified in one of $2 \times 2 \times 2 \times 2 = 16$ possible ways, in terms of whether they opted for or against (two choices) each of the four available options.

b. With three circles we get $2 \times 2 \times 2 = 8$ regions in our Venn diagram, which isn't enough for the purposes at hand. Even with four (or more) circles, it's not possible to show all 16 combinations of A, B, C and D.

c. Each buyer can be classified in one of $2 \times 2 \times 2 \times 2 \times 2 = 32$ possible ways, in terms of whether they opted for or against (two choices) each of the five available options.

d. Using this last result, notice that if we add option F, there will again be twice as many sets of options. A small table of results is helpful. The last line is a prediction based on the observed pattern.

Number of options	Number of sets of options
1	2
2	$4 = 2^2$
3	$4 * 2 = 8 = 2^3$
4	$8 * 2 = 16 = 2^4$
n	2^n

Unit 1D

Does It Make Sense?

9. Does not make sense. The speaker is making an inductive argument. Such arguments never constitute proof.
11. Makes sense. If she has a valid argument, and you accept her premises, she will have proved her argument.
13. Does not make sense. Many arguments which we use each day cannot be proven, yet are nonetheless useful. For example, "I should pay attention to class and do my homework to learn math." There is no conclusive proof that this will make you learn math.

Basic Skills and Concepts

Everyday Logic.

15. This is an inductive argument. Having seen the man regularly leaving the building creates a set of reinforcing experiences. Of course, the man may be there for some other reason.
17. The greatness of the first five novels has set a pattern which the speaker expects or hopes to be continued. This is inductive reasoning.
19. This is deductive. It can be phrased as a chain of conditional statements. "If they give free refills on coffee, they are OK. Fred's gives free refills, so Fred's is OK."
21. This is an inductive argument because it is based on four experiences.

Analyzing Inductive Arguments.

23. All of the premises are true, but the conclusion is obviously false. Given the great biological diversity of our planet, the argument (based on three observations) is weak.
25. The premises are true, but the plethora of counterexamples reveals the falsity of the conclusion.
27. Look at it this way. Assuming that the premises are true and you needed to do well in Algebra II, who would you take?

Deductive Arguments.

29. The argument includes the assertion "All islands are tropical lands," and is illustrated by the Venn diagram

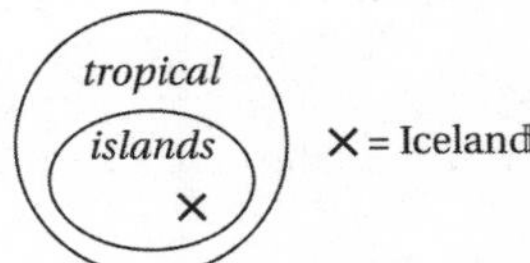

The argument is valid. The first premise is false, and the argument is not sound.

31. The argument includes the assertion "All salty foods are foods that cause high blood pressure (HBP)," and is illustrated by the Venn diagram

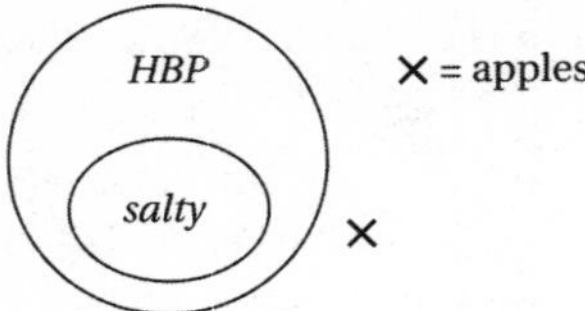

The argument is valid, and the premises could be true, in which case the argument is sound.

33. The argument includes the assertion "All states in the EST zone are states that are east of the Mississippi River," and is illustrated by the Venn diagram

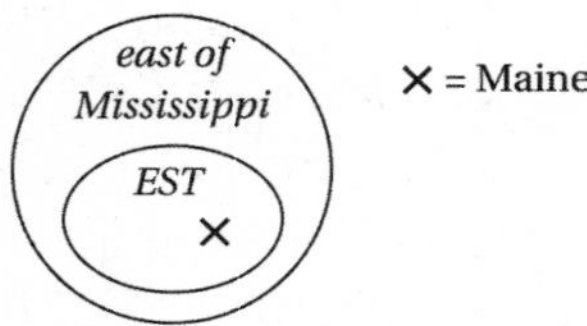

The argument is valid, the premises are true and the argument is sound.

35. The argument includes the assertion "All opera singers are people who can whistle a Mozart tune," and is illustrated by the Venn diagram

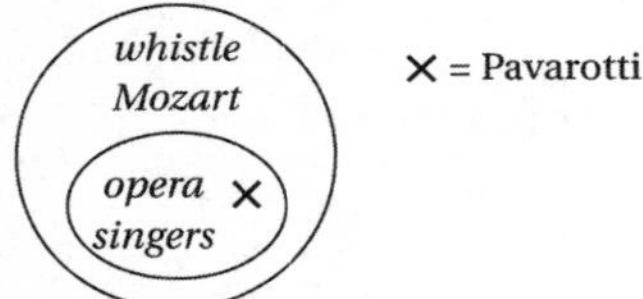

The argument is valid, and if the premises are true, then the argument is sound.

Conditional Deductive Arguments.

37. This is an example of affirming the hypothesis, and is illustrated by the Venn diagram

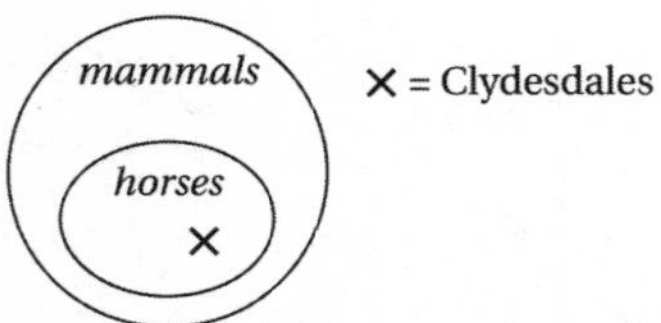

The argument is valid, the premises are true and the argument is sound.

39. This is an example of affirming the hypothesis, and is illustrated by the Venn diagram

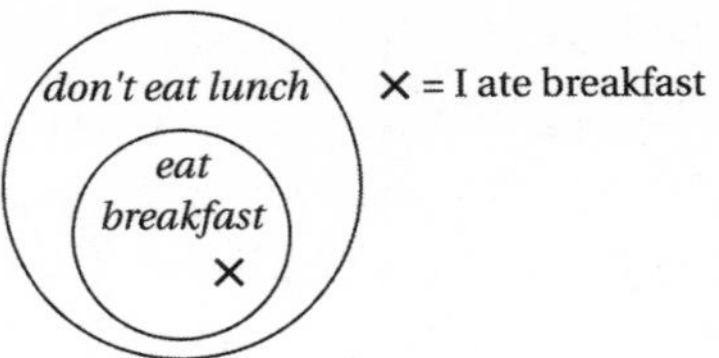

The argument is valid, and if the premises are true, then the argument is sound.

41. This is an example of denying the hypothesis, and is illustrated by the Venn diagram

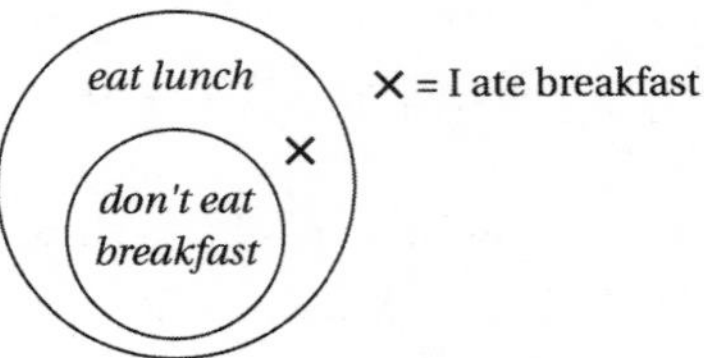

The argument is not valid, and regardless of the truth of the premises, it is not sound.

43. This argument includes the assertion "If interest rates decline, then the bond market improves," and is illustrated by the Venn diagram

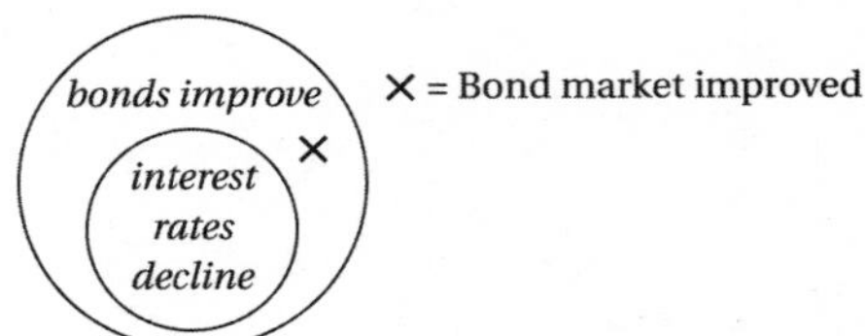

This is an example of affirming the conclusion, and the argument is not valid. Regardless of the truth of the premises, the argument is not sound.

Chains of Conditionals.

45. Each statement can be put in 'If...,then..' form by inserting the word 'then' after the comma. Let p = *you shop*, q = *I make dinner*, and r = *you take out the trash*. Then the argument has the form

Premise: If p, then q.

Premise: If q, then r.

Conclusion: If p, then r.

The argument is valid because there is a path from p to r.

47. The conditional form of the second premise is

"If there is more disposable income, then taxpayer spending will fuel the economy." The conditional form of the conclusion is "If taxes are cut, then the deficit will be larger." Let p = *taxes are cut*, q = *taxpayers will have more disposable income*, and r = *taxpayer spending will fuel the economy.* Then the argument has the form
Premise: If p, then q.
Premise: If q, then r.
Conclusion: If p, then r.
The argument is valid because there is a path from p to r. There is, of course, some debate about the premises.

Testing Mathematical Rules.

49. Try three examples.
   a. 3 + (-5) = -2 and -5 + 3 = -2
   b. $\frac{1}{2}+\frac{2}{3}=\frac{5}{6}$ $\frac{2}{3}+\frac{1}{2}=\frac{5}{6}$
   c. 7.8 + 9.42 = 17.22 and 9.42 + 7.8 = 17.22
   The statement appears to be true. This is the commutative law of addition.
51. Try one: $(2+3)^2 = 25$ but $2^2+3^2 = 4+9 = 13$. The statement is false. Indeed, exponents do not distribute over addition.

Further Applications

Validity and Soundness.

53. You need a well-constructed argument with true premises. Possible answer: All art students must take this class or statistics for their degree. Jamal is an art student. Jamal can take statistics for his degree.
55. In this case, you need a well-constructed argument with false premises. Possible answer: If you love me, then you'll do as I say. You haven't taken out the trash yet as I asked, so I guess you don't love me.
57. Possible answer: If all US presidents are men, and George Bush is a man, then George Bush is a US president.

Your Own Conditional Arguments.

59. Example of affirming the conclusion (invalid):
   Premise: If I am in Phoenix, then I am in Arizona.
   Premise: I am in Arizona.
   Conclusion: I am in Phoenix.
61. Example of denying the conclusion (valid):
   Premise: If I am in Phoenix, then I am in Arizona.
   Premise: I am not in Arizona.
   Conclusion: I am not in Phoenix.

Unit 1E

Does It Make Sense?

5. Makes sense. Not denying the claim means that they will pay, not Reed.
7. Does not make sense. Eighty minutes is less than an hour and a half (90 minutes).
9. Makes sense. The tires Michael bought have a better warranty; more time and more miles.

Basic Skills and Concepts

11. **Reading a ballot Initiative.**
   a. The state constitution is less strict than the U.S. Constitution.
   b. A yes vote would tighten (strengthen) laws against obscenity.
   c. False.
13. Possible answers: Owning a house is more desirable than renting. Interest rates are going to go up soon, hence, the urgency to act.
15. Possible answers. The United Nations is effective in teaching people to get along. The United Nations is either the best or the only way for people to get along.
17. We are looking for plausible, though unstated, assumptions. Possible answers. The speaker may be concerned that falling revenues will mean spending cuts in government programs. The speaker believes the tax cut is unfair and that everyone should benefit "equally" from government spending or tax cuts.
19. **IRS Guidelines.** a. No, Trip need not file a federal tax return because both his earned and unearned incomes were well below the thresholds mentioned in conditions (i) and (ii) of the

IRS guidelines, and he does not meet condition (iii) either.

b. No, Sally need not file a federal tax return because both her earned and unearned incomes were well below the thresholds mentioned in conditions (i) and (ii) of the IRS guidelines, and she does not meet condition (iii) either.

c. Yes, Monica must file a federal tax return because while her earned and unearned incomes were below the thresholds mentioned in conditions (i) and (ii) of the IRS guidelines, her total income of $\$3900 + \$300 = \$4200$ exceeds her earned income plus \$250 (which is $\$3900 + \$250 = \$4150$ here), so that she meets condition (iii).

d. No, Horace need not file a federal tax return. His earned and unearned incomes were below the thresholds mentioned in conditions (i) and (ii) of the IRS guidelines, and his total income of $\$4000 + \$200 = \$4200$ does not exceed his earned income plus \$250 (which is $\$4000 + \$250 = \$4250$ here), so that he does not meet condition (iii) either.

e. Yes, Delila must file a federal tax return because while her earned and unearned incomes were below the thresholds mentioned in conditions (i) and (ii) of the IRS guidelines, her total income of $\$4200 + \$200 = \$4400$ exceeds $\$4050 + \$250 = \$4300$ here, so that she meets condition (iii).

21. **What Is a Farmer?**

a. Solutions will vary.

b. Jack does not appear to qualify because he works 150 hours over a period of less than five weeks; the regulation may be stated incorrectly.

c. Jill does appear to qualify because she works 150 hours over a period of more than five weeks; the regulation may be stated incorrectly.

d. No, Ivan must also satisfy either (c) or (d) under provision (1).

e. Yes, Joan satisfies three of the conditions under provision (1).

23. **Choosing airline tickets.** Consider Plan A. If you go it costs \$1600, and if you cancel it costs \$400. With Plan B, if you go it costs \$2900, and if you cancel it costs nothing. If you go, Plan B costs \$1300 more. If you cancel, Plan A costs \$400 more.

25. **More Fine Print.** The deal does not state the "regular club prices," which could turn out to be much higher than the prices that would be paid in a store.

Further Applications

Ambiguity in the News.

27. The quote is ambiguous because it is unclear if there were 350 people on each jet, or on both jets combined. If this could be clarified, the ambiguity would be removed.

29. The quote is ambiguous because it is unclear if the \$83 billion refers to the gross domestic product or to 6% of the gross domestic product. If this could be clarified, the ambiguity would be removed.

31. **Comparing Candidates.**

a. They could be consistent; Alice does not specify the time period for her 253 cases.

b. They could be consistent if Alice prosecuted 127 cases more than five years ago, most of which resulted in conviction, and 126 cases in the last five years, only four of which resulted in a conviction (as Zack claimed). This seems an unlikely explanation.

c. Solutions will vary.

Decision Making.

33. Four individual sticks cost $4 \times 0.40 = \$1.60$. The package is the better choice.

35. If you go, plan (2) costs \$250 more. If you cancel, plan (1) costs \$75 more.

37. If you plan to fly 10 times (or a multiple of 10 times), then Plan A (\$3150) is better than Plan B (\$3250).

Critical Thinking.

38 - 46 If you are having trouble getting started, try asking these questions.

(a) Are there any fallacies in the argument?

(b) What are the premises and conclusions? Are there any unstated premises or conclusions?
(c) Is the argument valid? Is it sound?

47. **Poetry and Mathematics.** One interpretation is that the poet was 20 years old when he wrote the poem (*Twenty will not come again...*), and he expects to live to age 70 (*...of my threescore years and ten,*).

Unit 2A

Does It Make Sense?

7. Does not make sense. Miles are a measure of distance, not speed.
9. Does not make sense. Volume is measured in cubic, not squared units.
11. Does not make sense. Distance equals speed times time, d=st. To get time, divide distance by speed.

Basic Skills and Concepts

Working with Fractions.

13. a. $\frac{4}{3} \times \frac{1}{2} = \frac{2\times \cancel{2}}{3\times \cancel{2}} = \frac{2}{3}$.
    b. $\frac{4}{3} + \frac{1}{2} = \frac{8}{6} + \frac{3}{6} = \frac{8+3}{6} = \frac{11}{6}$.
    c. $\frac{4}{3} \div \frac{1}{2} = \frac{4}{3} \times \frac{2}{1} = \frac{4\times 2}{3\times 1} = \frac{8}{3}$.
    d. $\frac{4}{3} - \frac{1}{2} = \frac{8}{6} - \frac{3}{6} = \frac{8-3}{6} = \frac{5}{6}$.
    e. $\frac{7}{20} + \frac{3}{5} = \frac{7}{20} + \frac{12}{20} = \frac{19}{20}$.
    f. $\frac{12}{13} - \frac{1}{4} = \frac{48}{52} - \frac{13}{52} = \frac{48-13}{52} = \frac{35}{52}$.
    g. $\frac{\cancel{7}}{17} \times \frac{2}{\cancel{7}} = \frac{2}{17}$.
    h. $\frac{1}{3} + \frac{1}{5} = \frac{5}{15} + \frac{3}{15} = \frac{5+3}{15} = \frac{8}{15}$.
15. a. $0.3 = \frac{3}{10}$
    b. $0.124 = \frac{124}{1000} = \frac{31}{250}$
    c. $0.78 = \frac{78}{100} = \frac{39}{50}$
    d. $0.005 = \frac{5}{1000} = \frac{1}{200}$
    e. $1.84 = \frac{184}{100} = \frac{46}{25}$
    f. $3.009 = \frac{3009}{1000}$
    g. $0.0001 = \frac{1}{10000}$
    h. $0.1001 = \frac{1001}{10000}$.
17.
    a. $\frac{3}{2} = 1.5$ b. $\frac{4}{5} = 0.8$
    c. $\frac{1}{6} \approx 0.167$ d. $\frac{1}{7} \approx 0.143$
    e. $\frac{2}{9} \approx 0.222$ f. $\frac{7}{11} \approx 0.636$
    g. $\frac{88}{91} \approx 0.967$ h. $\frac{122}{30} \approx 4.067$

Identifying Units.

19. The price of apples will be in \$/lb, or dollars per pound.
21. The installation cost will be in \$/ft^2, namely in dollars per square foot.
23. The atmospheric pressure will be in lb/in^2, namely in pounds per square inch (commonly referred to as psi).
25. The gas mileage will be in mi/gal, namely in miles per gallon (commonly referred to as mpg).
27. The density will be in g/cm^3, namely in grams per cubic centimeter.

Unit Conversions.

29. To convert 18 yards to feet we use an appropriate conversion factor:

$$18 \text{ yd} \times \frac{3 \text{ ft}}{1 \text{ yd}} = 54 \text{ ft}.$$

31. To convert 7 miles to yards we use an appropriate conversion factor:

$$7 \text{ miles} \times \frac{1760 \text{ yd}}{\text{mile}} = 12,320 \text{ yd}.$$

33. To convert $\frac{1}{5}$ acre to square feet we use an appropriate conversion factor:

$$\frac{1}{5} \text{ acre} \times \frac{43,560 \text{ ft}^2}{1 \text{ acre}} = 8712 \text{ ft}^2.$$

35. To convert 3 miles to feet we use two conversion factors:

$$3 \text{ miles} \times \frac{1760 \text{ yd}}{1 \text{ mile}} \times \frac{3 \text{ ft}}{1 \text{ yd}} = 15,840 \text{ ft}.$$

37. To convert 4 weeks to minutes we use a chain of familiar conversion factors:

$$4 \text{ wk} \times \frac{7 \text{ day}}{1 \text{ wk}} \times \frac{24 \text{ hr}}{1 \text{ day}} \times \frac{60 \text{ min}}{1 \text{ hr}} = 40,320 \text{ minutes}.$$

39. **Area and Volume Calculations.**

    a. The area of the pool's surface is 10 m × 5 m = 50 m^2. The pool's volume is 10 m × 5 m × 3 m = 150 m^3.

    b. The area of one of its two largest sides is 22 in × 15 in = 330 in^2. The package's volume is 22 in × 15 in × 12 in = 3960 in^3.

    c. The skyscraper's volume is 1000 ft × 25,000 ft^2 = 25,000,000 ft^3.

Conversions with Units Raised to Powers.

41. Since 1 foot equals 12 inches, 1 square foot equals 12^2 square inches. So 1 ft^2 = 144 in^2. This can also be written as

$$\frac{144 \text{ in}^2}{1 \text{ ft}^2} \text{ or } \frac{1 \text{ ft}^2}{144 \text{ in}^2}.$$

43. To convert 5 square feet to square inches, we use one of the conversion factors from Ex. 41:

$$5 \text{ ft}^2 \times \frac{144 \text{ in}^2}{1 \text{ ft}^2} = 720 \text{ in}^2.$$

45. Since 1 foot is 12 inches, 1 cubic foot is 12^3 cubic inches, i.e., 1 $\text{ft}^3 = 1728 \text{ in}^3$. This can also be written as

$$\frac{1728 \text{ in}^3}{1 \text{ ft}^3} \text{ or } \frac{1 \text{ ft}^3}{1728 \text{ in}^3}.$$

47. To convert 3 cubic yards to cubic inches, use one of the conversion factors from (a), and a corresponding one relating cubic yards to cubic feet. Since 1 yard equals 3 feet, 1 cubic yard equals $3^3 = 27$ cubic feet. Hence:

$$3 \text{ yd}^3 \times \frac{27 \text{ ft}^3}{1 \text{ yd}^3} \times \frac{1728 \text{ in}^3}{1 \text{ ft}^3} = 139,968 \text{ in}^3.$$

Currency Conversions.

49. 1 British pound is worth about 1.678 dollars, which is more than 1 dollar.

51. Converting 2500 pesos to dollars yields

$$2500 \text{ pesos} \times \frac{\$0.0943}{1 \text{ peso}} = \$235.75.$$

53. To convert \$100 to yen, note that

$$\$100 \times \frac{117.9 \text{ yen}}{\$1} = 11,790 \text{ yen}.$$

55. First we convert 5.50 euros to dollars:

$$5.50 \text{ euros} \times \frac{\$1.169}{1 \text{ euros}} = \$6.43.$$

Hence, gasoline in Germany sells for \$6.43 per gallon.

Working with Units.

57. If you travel 14 miles in 15 minutes, then your speed in miles per hour is:

$$\frac{14 \text{ miles}}{15 \text{ min}} \times \frac{60 \text{ min}}{1 \text{ hr}} = 56 \frac{\text{miles}}{\text{hr}}.$$

59. If you paid \$200,000 for 40 acres of land, then you paid $\frac{\$200,000}{40 \text{ acres}} = \$5000/\text{acre}$.

61. If you buy 4.7 pounds of apples priced at \$1.29 per pound, you will pay 4.7 lb $\times \frac{\$1.29}{1 \text{ lb}}$, which is about \$6.06.

63. The cost of 10 square yards of cloth, priced at \$2 per square yard, is 10 $\text{yd}^2 \times \frac{\$2}{1 \text{ yd}^2} = \$20$.

65. The floor area is 1520 square feet and there are 9 square feet in a square yard. Then the cost of covering the floor with carpet is:

$$1520 \text{ ft}^2 \times \frac{1 \text{ yd}^2}{9 \text{ ft}^2} \times \frac{\$18}{\text{yd}^2} = \$3040.$$

67. If you travel 1200 miles in 20 hours, then your average speed for the trip is $\frac{1200 \text{ miles}}{20 \text{ hr}} =$ 60 mph.

69. If you sleep (on average) 7.5 hours each night, then in a year you sleep

$$7.5 \frac{\text{hr}}{\text{night}} \times 365 = 2737.5 \text{ hours}.$$

What Went Wrong?

71. **Exam Question.** Sorry! You are wrong because your answer has units of lb/\$. The correct answer is 0.11 lb $\times \frac{\$7.70}{1 \text{ lb}} = \$0.85/\text{lb}$, i.e., 85 cents per pound.

73. **Exam Question.** Sorry! You are wrong because your large bag price answer has units of pounds per dollar. The comparable large bag price is $\frac{\$11}{50 \text{ lb}} = \frac{\$0.22}{\text{lb}}$, i.e., 22 cents per pound. Thus, the large bag is much cheaper *per pound* than the small bag, which costs 39 cents per pound.

Gas Mileage.

75. Multiplying $\frac{\text{gallons}}{\text{mile}} \times$ miles will cancel the miles and leave gallons:

$$\frac{1 \text{ gallon}}{28 \text{ miles}} \times 2500 \text{ miles} \approx 89.3 \text{ gallons}.$$

77. a. Time is distance divided by speed. Thus, at 55 mph, it will take $\frac{2000 \text{ miles}}{55 \text{ mph}} \approx 36.4$ hours and at 70 mph, it will take $\frac{2000 \text{ miles}}{70 \text{ mph}} \approx 28.6$ hours.
b. Multiplying miles $\times \frac{\text{gallons}}{\text{mile}} \times \frac{\text{dollars}}{\text{gallon}}$ will cancel the gallons and miles and leave dollars. At 55 mph, your gasoline cost is

$$2000 \text{ miles} \times \frac{1 \text{ gallon}}{38 \text{ miles}} \times \frac{\$1.65}{\text{gallon}} = \$86.84.$$

and at 70 mph your cost is

$$2000 \text{ miles} \times \frac{1 \text{ gallon}}{32 \text{ miles}} \times \frac{\$1.65}{\text{gallon}} = \$103.13.$$

79. **Filling a Pool.** Since 6 inches is 0.5 feet, the volume of water needed to fill the pool is

$$75 \text{ ft} \times 54 \text{ ft} \times 0.5 \text{ ft} = 2025 \text{ ft}^3.$$

Further Applications

81. **Full of Hot Air.** If an average human heart breaths 6 times per minute, exhaling half a liter of hot air each time, then since $6 \times 0.5 = 3$, we see that 3 liters of hot air are exhaled per minute. The amount of air exhaled in one day comes to

$$3\,\frac{\text{liters}}{\text{min}} \times 60\,\frac{\text{min}}{\text{hr}} \times 24\,\frac{\text{hr}}{\text{day}} = 4320\frac{\text{liters}}{\text{day}}.$$

83. **Dog Years.** a.

$$15 \text{ real years} \times \frac{7 \text{ dog years}}{1 \text{ real year}} = 105 \text{ dog years}.$$

b. The third year in the life of a human child starts when the child is two years old, and ends when the child is three years old. If dogs have a similar period, from their second to third (dog) birthdays, note that

$$2 \text{ dog years} \times \frac{1 \text{ real year}}{7 \text{ dog years}} \approx 0.2857 \text{ real years},$$

or about 0.2857 years $\times\ \frac{52 \text{ weeks}}{\text{year}} \approx 15$ weeks, and

$$3 \text{ dog years} \times \frac{1 \text{ real year}}{7 \text{ dog years}} \approx 0.4286 \text{ real years}$$

or about 0.4286 years $\times\ \frac{52 \text{ weeks}}{\text{year}} \approx 22$ weeks. Thus, "the terrible twos" for dogs is the period from about 15 to 22 (real) weeks in their lives.

85. **Home Project.** Solutions will vary.

Unit 2B

Does It Make Sense?

7. Makes sense. Two liters is about 8 glasses.
9. Makes sense. Many later model cars have kph as well as mph on the speedometer. If yours does, you can see that this is about 62 mph.
11. Does not make sense because it is so unlikely. Seven meters is about 23 feet and the world record is well below this.
13. Does not make sense. While milligrams do measure mass, a paperclip has a mass of about 1000 milligrams. (On the other hand, nanotechnology is likely to change drastically our sense of scale and possibility in this lifetime. Who knows?)
15. Makes sense. Ten million joules is about 2500 Calories, a fairly normal daily intake.
17. Does not make sense. This object has a density higher than that of water. It ought to sink, not to mention that it's pretty heavy.

Basic Skills and Concepts

Powers of 10.

19. $10^6 \times 10^5 = 10^{6+5} = 10^{11} = 100,000,000,000.$
21. $\frac{10^6}{10^5} = 10^{6-5} = 10^1 = 10.$
23. $10^{-2} \times 10^{-4} = 10^{-2-4} = 10^{-6} = 0.000001.$
25. $10^6 + 10^5 = 1,000,000 + 100,000 = 1,100,000.$
27. $10^{12} \times 10^9 = 10^{12+9} = 10^{21} = 1,000,000,000,000,000,000,000.$
29. $\frac{10^{15}}{10^{12}} = 10^{15-12} = 10^3 = 1000.$
31. $10^{-4} \times 10^{-6} = 10^{-4-6} = 10^{-10} = 0.0000000001.$
33. $10^8 + 10^5 = 100,000,000 + 100,000 = 100,100,000.$

USCS Units.

35. Solutions will vary of course, but for somebody who is 5 feet 6 inches, we get

$$(5 \text{ ft} \times \frac{12 \text{ in}}{\text{ft}}) + 6 \text{ in} = (60 + 6) \text{ in} = 66 \text{ in}.$$

37. A gallon of water weighs

$$128 \text{ oz} \times \frac{1 \text{ lb}}{16 \text{ oz}} = 8 \text{ lb}.$$

39. Since

$$\frac{1}{2} \text{ gal} \times \frac{8 \text{ pts}}{1 \text{ gal}} = 4 \text{ pt},$$

the jug holds 4 liquid pints. Equivalently, it holds

$$4 \text{ pt} \times \frac{28.88 \text{ in}^3}{1 \text{ pt}} \times \frac{1 \text{ dry pt}}{33.60 \text{ in}^3} \approx 3.44 \text{ dry pts}.$$

41. Converting bushels to cubic inches we have

$$150 \text{ bushels} \times \frac{4 \text{ pecks}}{\text{bushel}} \times \frac{8 \text{ dry qt}}{\text{peck}} \times \frac{67.2 \text{ in}^3}{\text{dry qt}} = 322,560 \text{ in}^3$$

Converting to cubic feet using $1 \text{ ft}^3 = (12 \text{ in})^3 = 1728 \text{ in}^3$, we have

$$322,560 \text{ in}^3 \times \frac{1 \text{ ft}^3}{1728 \text{ in}^3} \approx 187 \text{ ft}^3.$$

Metric Prefixes.

43. A millimeter is 1000 times smaller than a meter, since 1000 millimeters is 1 meter.
45. A gram is 1000 times smaller than a kilogram, since 1000 grams is 1 kilogram.
47. A square millimeter is 1,000,000,000,000 times smaller than a square kilometer. This is because 1000 millimeters is 1 meter and 1000 meters is 1 kilometer, so that there are $1000^2 = 1,000,000$ millimeters in a kilometer, and hence $1,000,000^2 = 1,000,000,000,000$ square millimeters in a square kilometer.

USCS-Metric Conversions.

49. Converting yields

$$10 \text{ m} \times \frac{3.28 \text{ ft}}{1 \text{ m}} = 32.8 \text{ ft}.$$

51. Converting, we get

$$880 \text{ yd} \times \frac{0.9144 \text{ m}}{1 \text{ yd}} \times \frac{1 \text{ km}}{1000 \text{ m}} \approx 0.8 \text{ km}.$$

53. Converting yields

$$20 \text{ gal} \times \frac{3.785 \text{ l}}{1 \text{ gal}} \approx 75.7 \text{ liters}.$$

55. Converting, we get

$$5 \text{ mL} \times \frac{0.03381 \text{ fl oz}}{1 \text{ mL}} \times \frac{1.805 \text{ in}^3}{1 \text{ fl oz}} \approx 0.3 \text{in}^3.$$

57. Since 1 foot is 0.3048 meters, $1 \text{ ft}^2 = (0.3048 \text{ m})^2 \approx 0.0929 \text{ m}^2$, and so

$$1200 \text{ ft}^2 \times \frac{0.0929 \text{ m}^2}{\text{ft}^2} \approx 111.5 \text{ m}^2.$$

Celsius-Fahrenheit Conversions.

Use the formulae:

$$F = 1.8C + 32 \text{ and } C = \frac{F - 32}{1.8}$$

59. a. $C = \frac{45-32}{1.8} \approx 7.2°\text{C}$.
    b. $F = 1.8(20) + 32 = 68°\text{F}$.
    c. $F = 1.8(-15) + 32 = 5°\text{F}$.
    d. $F = 1.8(-30) + 32 = -22°\text{F}$.
    e. $C = \frac{70-32}{1.8} \approx 21°\text{C}$.

Celsius-Kelvin Conversions.

Use the formulae:

$$K = C + 273.15 \text{ and } C = K - 273.15$$

61. a. $C = 50 - 273.15 = -223.15°\text{C}$.
    b. $C = 240 - 273.15 = -33.15°\text{C}$.
    c. $K = 10 + 273.15 = 283.15°\text{K}$.
63. **Basketball Power.** Burning 800 calories per hour can be converted to joules per second as follow:

$$\frac{800 \text{ Cal}}{1 \text{ hr}} \times \frac{4184 \text{ j}}{1 \text{ Cal}} \times \frac{1 \text{ hr}}{60 \text{ min}} \times \frac{1 \text{ min}}{60 \text{ s}} \approx 930 \frac{\text{j}}{\text{s}},$$

or 930 watts. This is enough to keep nine 100-watt bulbs shining.

Electric Bills.

65. a. 1250 kilowatt-hours is 1250 × 3.6 million joules, which is 4500 million, or 4.5 billion, joules.

    b. The average power used in watts is the total number of joules used per second. Since there are

$$60 \frac{\text{s}}{\text{min}} \times 60 \frac{\text{min}}{\text{hr}} \times 24 \frac{\text{hr}}{\text{day}} \times 30 \frac{\text{days}}{\text{month}},$$

i.e., 2,592,000 seconds in June, the average power used is:

$$\frac{4,500,000,000 \frac{\text{j}}{\text{month}}}{2,592,000 \frac{\text{s}}{\text{month}}} \approx 1736 \frac{\text{j}}{\text{s}} = 1736 \text{ watts}.$$

    c. If each liter of burned oil releases 12 million joules of energy, then to produce 4500 million joules we'll need to burn

$$4500 \text{ million j} \times \frac{1 \text{ L}}{12 \text{ million j}} = 375 \text{ L}.$$

This can be checked to be about 99 gallons.

Densities.

67. Density here is mass per unit volume measured in grams per cubic centimeter: $\frac{40 \text{ grams}}{10 \text{ cm}^3} = 4 \frac{\text{g}}{\text{cm}^3}$. This is greater than the density of water so the pebble will sink.
69. The average population density of the United States is

$$\frac{280,000,000 \text{ people}}{3,500,000 \text{ mi}^2} = 80 \frac{\text{people}}{\text{mi}^2}.$$

71. The population density of New Jersey is
$$\frac{8,400,000 \text{ people}}{7419 \text{ mi}^2} \approx 1132 \frac{\text{people}}{\text{mi}^2},$$
and that of Wyoming is
$$\frac{490,000 \text{ people}}{970,000 \text{ mi}^2} \approx 0.5052 \frac{\text{people}}{\text{mi}^2}.$$
New Jersey's population density is over 2000 times that of Wyoming!

73. **Blood-Alcohol Content: Wine.**

a. There are $20 \times 2 = 40$ grams of alcohol in her 4000 milliliters blood or
$$\frac{40 \text{ g}}{4000 \text{ mL}} \times \frac{100}{100} = 1 \frac{\text{g}}{100 \text{ mL}.}$$
(Notice that her weight is not part of the calculations.) If all the alcohol were absorbed immediately, the woman would be in a coma.

b. After 3 hours, 30 grams of alcohol have left her body leaving 10 grams. This is one fourth of what it was before so her BAL is now $\frac{1}{4} \times 1 \frac{\text{g}}{\text{mL}} = 0.25 \frac{\text{g}}{100 \text{ mL}}$.

Since the AMA states that brain function is impaired at $0.04 \frac{\text{g}}{100 \text{ mL}}$, she ought to have someone escort her home.

Further Applications

75. **Metric Mile.**

a. In order to compare the metric mile to the USCS mile we must find a common set of units. Note that 1 mile is 1.6093 kilometers, or 1609.3 meters, and $1500 - 1609.3 = -109.3$ meters. So, a metric mile is 109.3 meters shorter than a USCS mile, and since $-\frac{109.3}{1609.3} = -0.0679$, the metric mile is about 6.8% shorter than a USCS mile.

b. Solutions will vary.

77. **Tallest Mountain?** The total height of Mauna Kea from its ocean floor base to its peak is $13,796 + 18,200 = 31,996$ feet. Converting to miles and kilometers, in turn, we get
$$31,996 \text{ ft} \times \frac{1 \text{ mi}}{5280 \text{ ft}} \times \frac{1.6093 \text{ km}}{\text{mi}} = 9.75 \text{ km}.$$
The total height of Mauna Kea is thus greater than the above sea level height of Mount Everest (29,023 feet), but to assert that the Hawaiian mountain is taller is to ignore the fact that there is more to Mount Everest than meets the eye; a fair comparison should take into account its own rise from the ocean floor.

Gems and Gold.

79. A nugget that is 25% gold is 6-karat gold, since 100% is 24-karat gold.

81. A 2.5-carat diamond weighs $2.5 \times 0.2 = 0.5$ grams.

83. **Refrigerator Cost.** A 350-watt refrigerator consumes energy at the rate of 350 joules per second. Since there are
$$\frac{60 \text{ s}}{1 \text{ min}} \times \frac{60 \text{ min}}{1 \text{ hr}} \times \frac{24 \text{ hr}}{1 \text{ day}} \times 365 \text{ days},$$
i.e., 31,536,000 seconds in a year, the unit uses $31,536,000 \times 350 = 11,038$ million joules per year. Dividing by 3.6 million joules per kilowatt-hour yields 3066 kilowatt-hours. Each kilowatt-hour costs \$0.08, so the total cost is $\$0.08 \times 3066 = \$245.28$.

85. **Compact Fluorescent Light Bulbs.** Using the 25-watt bulb in place of the 100-watt one saves 75 watts, and since there are
$$\frac{60 \text{ s}}{1 \text{ min}} \times \frac{60 \text{ min}}{1 \text{ hr}} \times 10,000 \text{ hr}$$
i.e., 36 million seconds in 10,000 hours, the bulb substitution saves 75×36 million, or 2700 million joules. Dividing by 3.6 million joules we get 750 kilowatt-hours. Since each kilowatt-hour costs \$0.08, the total saving over the lifespan of the fluorescent bulb is $\$0.08 \times 750 = \$60$.

87. **Coal Power Plant.** Since there are
$$\frac{60 \text{ s}}{1 \text{ min}} \times \frac{60 \text{ min}}{1 \text{ hr}} \times \frac{24 \text{ hr}}{1 \text{ day}} \times 30 \text{ days}$$
i.e., 2.592 million seconds in a month, the plant can generate 1 billion watts of power, i.e., 1 billion joules per second. In a month it will generate 1 billion j $\times$ 2.592 million, or 2592 million million (i.e., trillion), joules. Dividing by 3.6 million joules we get 720 million kilowatt-hours. If each kilogram of coal yields about 450 kilowatt-hours (kwh) of energy when burned,

then the coal required to fuel this power plant each month is

$$720 \text{ million kwh} \times \frac{1 \text{ kg}}{450 \text{ kwh}} = 1.6 \text{ million kg}$$

If a typical home used 1000 kilowatt-hours of energy per month, then this power plant can supply:

$$720 \text{ million kwh} \times \frac{1 \text{ home}}{1000 \text{ kwh}} = 720,000 \text{ homes.}$$

Solar Energy.

89. A 1-square-meter panel with 20% efficiency generates 20% of 1000, i.e., 200 watts of power. This 200 watts of power is 200 joules per second, and since there are $6 \times 60 \times 60 = 21,600$ seconds in 6 hours, we see that each day (which yields 6 hours of direct sunlight) leads to the production of $200 \times 21,600 = 4,320,000$ joules of energy.
The 200 watts of power which the panels can generate only applies to the 6 hours out of 24 which they are actually receiving direct sunlight. So, on average, their power is $\frac{6}{24} \times 200$ watts, namely 50 watts.

91. **Wind Power: One Turbine.** The rate at which energy is produced, or power, is 200 kilowatts. Energy is power × time. The time is one year so we will need to multiply 200 by the number of hours in a year

$$200 \text{ kw} \times 24\frac{\text{hrs}}{\text{day}} \times 365\frac{\text{days}}{\text{year}} = 1,752,000\frac{\text{kwh}}{\text{year}}$$

If each household uses 10,000 kwh each year, then

$$\frac{1,752,000 \text{ kwh}}{10,000\frac{\text{kwh}}{\text{household}}} \approx 175 \text{ households}$$

Currency Conversions. In problems 93-98, the current conversion factor and the answer have been left blank, (...). Answers will depend on current information.

93.

$$\frac{0.60 \text{ euros}}{\text{kg}} \times \frac{\$(...)}{\text{euro}} \times \frac{2.205 \text{ kg}}{\text{lb}} = \frac{\$(...)}{\text{lb}}$$

95.

$$\frac{15 \text{ km}}{\text{liter}} \times \frac{1 \text{ miles}}{1.6093 \text{ km}} \times \frac{1 \text{ liters}}{0.2642 \text{ gal}} \approx 35\ \frac{\text{mi}}{\text{gal}}$$

97.

$$\frac{3.5\pounds}{\text{liter}} \times \frac{\$(...)}{\pounds} \times \frac{1 \text{ liter}}{33.81 \text{ oz}} = \frac{\$(...)}{\text{oz}}$$

99. **Personal Energy Audit.** Solutions will vary.

Unit 2C

Does It Make Sense?

3. Does not make sense. That's not the way problem solving works. There's no single recipe that always succeeds, only general guidelines (such as the four-step process in the book) that can help.
5. Makes sense (if you didn't let the double negatives fool you!). The answer to a problem MUST make sense or something has gone wrong somewhere.

Basic Skills and Concepts

7. **Box Office.** One way to solve this is to make a list of all possible adult ticket sales (zero up to 5), calculate those sales, and see if the leftover amount can be accounted for by children's tickets:

Adult tickets sold	Adult ticket sales	Revenue left for child tickets	Child tickets sold
0	0	150	10
1	30	120	8
2	60	90	6
3	90	60	4
4	120	30	2
5	150	0	0

(One could also have made a list of the possible number of children's tickets sold, noticing that since 150 is even, there must be an even number of children's tickets sold.) Algebraic formulas such as those typically associated with mixture problems will probably not be very successful here because there is not enough information for a unique solution.

More on Jack and Jill.

9. If Jill's time in the first race was 10 seconds, then her pace was 100 m $\div$ 10 s = 10 m/s, or 10 meters per second. Jack's pace would therefore be 95 $\div$ 10 s = 9.5 meters per second. For the second race, Jill's time would be 105 m $\div 10\frac{\text{m}}{\text{s}}$ = 10.5000 seconds, and Jack's would be 100 m $\div 9.5\frac{\text{m}}{\text{s}}$ = 10.5263 seconds, so Jill would win by 0.0263 seconds. Note how the assumptions here amount to a doubling of the paces, and hence a halving of the times taken to run the race, and a halving of the winning margin.

11. **Cars and Canary.** The distance between the cars is shrinking at a rate of 180 kilometers per hour (the combined speed of the two cars), and hence the cars will meet after 150 km $\div$ $180\frac{\text{km}}{\text{hr}} = \frac{5}{6}$ hours. Meanwhile, the canary, flying at 120 kilometers per hour, will have flown $\frac{5}{6}$ hrs $\times$ 120 $\frac{\text{km}}{\text{hr}}$ = 100 kilometers.

13. **Mixing Marbles.** Pile 1 originally starts as (15B,0W), Pile 2 as (0B,15W), and three marbles are transferred from the first to the second pile. Thus, Pile 1 becomes (12B,0W) and Pile 2 (3B,15W). Next, three marbles are transferred back from Pile 2 to Pile 1. Four possibilities result, depending on how many of these three are black, as tabulated below.

Transfers from 2 to 1	New Pile 1	New Pile 2
3B	(15B,0W)	(0B,15W)
2B	(14B,1W)	(1B,14W)
1B	(13B,2W)	(2B,13W)
0B	(12B,3W)	(3B,12W)

Note how in each case the number of black marbles in Pile 2 equals the number of white marbles in Pile 1.

15. **Wedding Decorations.** Lay out a rectangle as in Figure 2.11. The dimensions here will be 3 ft by 12 ft. The height (or base, depending on how you look at it) of each triangle is $\frac{12}{10}$ = 1.2 ft. By the Pythagorean theorem, each hypotenuse is $\sqrt{3^2 + 1.2^2} \approx 3.23$ ft. Since there are 10 turns, each column requires about $10 \times 3.23 = 32.3$ ft of ribbon. Since there are 20 columns, you will need $20 \times 32.3 = 646$ ft.

Bowed Rail.

17. The bow and the ground make approximately an isosceles triangle with very small angles in the bottom corners. (By the way, surveyors often use this and other methods for such estimates.) The bow is part of a circle whose circumference is much greater than 1/2 mile. Such a circle could not be used "nicely" to estimate the height of the bow.

19. **China's One-Child Policy.** If 10,000 families have children according to the one-son policy, then 5000 families have a son as their first, and therefore only child. Of the other 5000 families who had a daughter as their first child, 2500 have a son as their second child, and no more children. Of the other 2500 families, who had a daughter as their second (as well as first) child, 1250 have a son as their third child, and no more children. Of the other 1250 families, who had a daughter as their third (as well as first and second) child, 625 have a son as their fourth child, and no more children. Of the other 625 families, who had a daughter as their fourth child, about 312 have a son as their fifth child, and no more children. Of the other 312 families, who had a daughter as their fifth child, about 156 have a son as their sixth child, and no more children. Of the other 156 families, who had a daughter as their sixth child, about 78 have a son as their seventh child, and 78 had a daughter, and so on. In this scenario, keeping track up to the seventh child, we see that the total number of sons is $5000+2500+1250+625+312+156+78 = 9921$. The total number of girls is also $5000 + 2500 + 1250 + 625 + 312 + 156 + 78 = 9921$! So boy and girls are being born in equal numbers, and since there are $9921 + 9921 = 19,842$ total for 10,000 families, this yields an average of 1.9842 children per family. If we do the bookkeeping past the seventh child, assuming that families continue having children until a boy is born, the average gets closer and closer to 2.

Further Applications

21. **Gardening Supplies.** A table works nicely:

top soil	fertilizer
0	25
3	22
6	19
9	16
12	13
15	10
18	7
21	4
24	1

23. **Stereo Wire 1.** The drawing below utilizes the hint given in the problem. From Pythagoras' Theorem: $d = \sqrt{16^2 + 12^2} = 20$ feet.

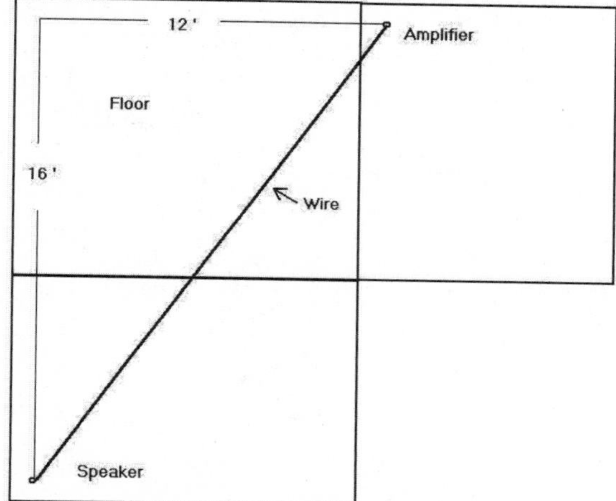

25. **Bridge Height.** To use the triangle method of example 6, we will need two sides. The horizontal side is $100/2 = 50$ meters and the hypotenuse is $102/2 = 51$ meters. So the height is $\sqrt{51^2 - 50^2} \approx 10$ meters.

Puzzle Problems.

27. If it takes 30 seconds to walk between the first and third floors of a building, then it takes 15 seconds to walk up one floor. Hence, to walk from the first to the sixth floor takes five times 15, i.e., 75 seconds.

29. If you draw one, two or three apples from the basket, they could all be of different types. However, once you draw a fourth you must have (at least) two of one kind, since there are only three kinds available.

31. If I am somebody's brother, yet have no brothers myself, then that somebody (the blind fiddler in this case) must be a woman.

33. By selecting a fruit from the box labeled *Apples and Oranges*—which being incorrectly labeled must contain *only* apples or oranges—you immediately learn how that box should be labeled. Let's suppose you selected an apple, then the box labeled *Oranges* must contain both apples and oranges, and the box labeled *Apples* must contain only oranges. On the other hand, if you selected an orange, then the box labeled *Oranges* must contain only apples and the box labeled *Apples* must contain both apples and oranges. Thus, with just one selection, you can determine the correct labeling for all three boxes. Note, however, that if you start by selecting from one of the other boxes you learn less and must make a second selection, so our solution is the best possible.

35. Clearly the woman must ferry the animals across with her one at a time, being careful to never leave unattended any creatures which can harm each other. Her first crossing must therefore take the goose to the other side. She returns alone, and picks up either of the other animals for a second crossing to the other side. However, she needs to return *with* the goose, which she exchanges for the one remaining creature for the third crossing to the other side. It is safe to leave the mouse and wolf together on the other side, and she goes back one last time to pick up the goose again. After her fourth crossing to the other side she has made seven crossings in total, counting the three return trips.

37. Since half of the rope length is 75 feet, and the midpoint of the rope is 25 feet from the ground and the poles are 100 feet high, the ropes must be vertical and the flagpoles right next to each other (no distance between them).

39. If you draw one or two socks from the drawer, they could be different colors. However, once you draw a third sock you must have (at least)

two of one color, since there are only two colors available.

41. Prisoner 1 cannot see red hats on both Prisoners 2 and 3; if he did, he would know he had a white hat (and would be freed). Therefore the hats on Prisoners 2 and 3 must be either both white, or one of each color, and Prisoner 2 knows this! Therefore if Prisoner 2 sees a red hat on Prisoner 3, Prisoner 2 knows he has a white hat (and would be freed). Since each of Prisoners 1 and 2 claim to be unable to determine the color of his own hat, Prisoner 3 can deduce that he has a white hat, and he is freed.

42-51. Solutions will vary.

Unit 3A

Does It Make Sense?

7. Makes sense. The statement just means that population has been declining in these countries.
9. Makes sense. It would be true, for example, if the younger child weighed 100 pounds and the older child weighed 125 pounds.
11. Does not make sense. For example, $120 is 20% more than $100, but $100 is not 20% less than $120. (It is about 17% less than $120.)
13. Makes sense. In this case, the 700% more common means 8 times as many cancers in the group than in the general population.
15. Makes sense. This would be the case if the old rate of return was 10%, so a 50% increase would raise the return to 15%.

Basic Skills and Concepts

Review of Fractions.

17. $1/4 = 0.25 = 25\%$.
19. $0.45 = 45\% = 9/20$.
21. $0.33333\ldots = 33.333\ldots\% = 1/3$.
23. $23\% = 0.23 = 23/100$.
25. $1/8 = 0.125 = 12.5\%$.
27. $1.34 = 134\% = 67/50$.
29. $0.65 = 65\% = 13/20$.
31. $99\% = 0.99 = 99/100$.

Review of Ratios.

33. The ratio of A to B is $\frac{A}{B} = \frac{10}{2} = 5$, the ratio of B to A is $\frac{B}{A} = \frac{2}{10} = 0.2$, and A is 500% of B.
35. The ratio of A to B is $\frac{A}{B} = \frac{11}{1} = 11$, the ratio of B to A is $\frac{B}{A} = \frac{1}{11} \approx 0.091$, and A is 1100% of B.
37. The ratio of A to B is $\frac{A}{B} = \frac{75}{480} = 0.15625$, the ratio of B to A is $\frac{B}{A} = \frac{480}{75} = 6.4$, and A is 15.625% of B.
39. The ratio of A to B is $\frac{A}{B} = \frac{7{,}500{,}000}{16{,}500{,}000} \approx 0.4545$, the ratio of B to A is $\frac{B}{A} = \frac{16{,}500{,}000}{7{,}500{,}000} = 2.2$, and A is about 45.45% of B.
41. The ratio of A to B is $\frac{A}{B} = \frac{359{,}000}{290{,}000} \approx 1.2379$, the ratio of B to A is $\frac{B}{A} = \frac{290{,}000}{359{,}000} \approx 0.8078$, and A is about 123.79% of B.
43. The ratio of A to B is $\frac{A}{B} = \frac{1500}{2200} \approx 0.6818$, the ratio of B to A is $\frac{B}{A} = \frac{2200}{1500} \approx 1.4667$, and A is about 68.18% of B.

Percentages as Fractions.

45. 25 is about 22.12% of 113, because $\frac{25}{113} \approx 0.2212$.
47. 1234 is about 41.01% of 3009, because $\frac{1234}{3009} \approx 0.4101$.
49. 23 is about 18.70% of 123, because $\frac{23}{123} \approx 0.1870$.
51. **Salary Comparison.** In absolute terms, John's salary increased $8000 whereas Mary's increased $10000; thus Mary's increase was greater than John's increase. However, in relative terms the salary increases were the same, since John's was $\frac{\$8000}{\$20{,}000} = 0.40 = 40\%$ and Mary's was $\frac{\$10{,}000}{\$25{,}000} = 0.40 = 40\%$.

Percentage Change.

53. The absolute change in the US population was (281 - 76) = 205 million. The relative change was $\frac{205}{76} \approx 2.70$ or 270%.
55. The absolute change is $1483 - 2226 = -743$ newspapers, and the percentage change is $-\frac{743}{2226} \times 100\% \approx -33.4\%$.

Percentage Difference.

57. Taking the daily circulation figure for the NYT as the reference value, the absolute difference is $1.77 - 1.07 = 0.7$ million newspapers, and the percentage difference is $\frac{0.7}{1.07} \times 100\% \approx 65.42\%$.
59. Taking the U.S. tourist figure as the reference value, the absolute difference is $66 - 48 = 18$ million international arrivals, and the percentage difference is $\frac{18}{48} \times 100\% = 37.50\%$.
61. Taking the female open-heart surgery figure as the reference value, the absolute difference is $504{,}000 - 209{,}000 = 295{,}000$ operations, and the percentage difference is $\frac{295{,}000}{209{,}000} \times 100\% \approx 141.15\%$.

***Of* vs. *More Than*.**

63. Jack's weight is $\frac{100+40}{100} = 1.4$ times Jill's, so his weight is 140% of hers.
65. The population of Montana is $\frac{100-20}{100} = 0.80$ times the population of New Hampshire, so

Montana's population is 80% of New Hampshire's.

Price and Sales.

67. The wholesale cost is (100-50)% = 50% of the retail cost, i.e., 0.5 times the retail cost. So the retail cost is $\frac{1}{0.50} = 2$ times the wholesale cost.
69. The retail cost is (100+40)% = 140% of the wholesale cost, i.e., 1.4 times the wholesale cost.

Percentages of Percentages.

71. The absolute difference in percentages of high school seniors using alcohol is $52.7\% - 68.2\% = -15.5\%$, this is a 15.5 percentage point drop. In relative terms, the difference is $-\frac{15.5\%}{68.2\%} \approx -0.2273$, which reflects a drop of about 22.73%.
73. The absolute difference in the five-year survival rate for Caucasians for all forms of cancer is 60% - 39% = 21%, so there was a 21 percentage point rise. In relative terms, the difference is $\frac{21\%}{39\%} \approx 0.5385$, which reflects a rise of about 53.85%.
75. **Care in Wording.** Assume 30% of city employees in Carson City ride the bus to work. If "the percentage of city employees in Freetown who ride the bus to work is *10% higher* than in Carson City," then the percentage of city employees in Freetown who ride the bus to work is $\frac{100+10}{100} \times 30\% = 33\%$. On the other hand, if "the percentage of city employees in Freetown who ride the bus to work is *10 percentage points higher* than in Carson City," then the percentage of city employees in Freetown who ride the bus to work is 10% + 30% = 40%. In the first case, we are told how much higher the Freetown rate is as a percentage *of* the Carson City rate, so we add 10% *of* the lower rate to get the higher rate. In the second case, we are told how much higher than the Carson City rate the Freetown rate in absolute percentage points, which means that we add 10 percentage points *to* the lower rate to get the higher rate.

Solving Percentage Problems.

77. A bicycle with a $699 price tag will cost $\frac{100+7.6}{100} \times \$699 = \$752.12$ when subjected to a local sale tax rate of 7.6%.
79. A car with a $17,600 price tag will cost $\frac{100+6.5}{100} \times \$17,600 = \$18,744$ when subjected to a local sale tax rate of 6.5%.
81. Leaving $22 for an $18.75 dinner bill means that your tip was $22 - $18.75 = $3.25 in absolute terms. In relative terms, you tipped at a rate of $\frac{\$3.25}{\$18.75} \approx 0.1733$ or 17.33%.
83. If the original smoking rate R jumped 45 percent, to 18.3 percent, then R satisfies $1.45 \times R = 18.3\%$. So, $R = \frac{18.3\%}{1.45} \approx 12.62\%$.

Shifting Reference Value.

85. False. Her weight after losing 10% was 0.90 times her original weight, and following the subsequent 10% weight gain it went up to (1.10)(0.90) = 0.99 times—i.e., 99% *of*—her original weight, which is 1% less than her original weight.
87. False. Your final taxes are (1.06)(1.05) = 1.1130 times—or 111.30% *of*—your original salary, which is 11.3% more than your original taxes.

Is It Possible?

89. Not possible. One price cannot be more than 100% less than another price.
91. Possible; e.g., if the average house price increased from $100,000 to $550,000.
93. Possible; this means that your computer speed is three and a half times mine.
95. **Average Percentages.** No, you cannot simply average the averages for classes of different sizes.

Further Applications

Analyzing Percentage Statements.

97. True; blond haired women comprise (0.10)(0.60) = 0.06 = 6% of the class.
99. False; some of the hotels with restaurants may also have pools. (If all of them do, only 70% of the hotels in town have a restaurant and a pool.)

Solving News Percentages.

101. Since 75% of $100 billion is $75 billion, the value of U.S. trade with Mexico that is delivered by

truck is almost \$75 billion.

103. A 20% growth in a sales value of \$3 billion will lead to $\frac{100+20}{100} \times \$3$ billion $= \$3.6$ billion being spent on bagels next year.
105. Last winter, $\frac{80}{100+16} \approx 68.97\%$ of people were not worried about losing their jobs.
107. Sixty percent of the prisoners will be re-arrested: $0.60 \times 625,000 = 375,000$
109. This week's stock price at close was 103% of last week's, so last week's stock price at close was $\frac{\$13.48}{1.03} \approx \$13.09$

Unit 3B

Does It Make Sense?

9. Makes sense. If a book has 250 words per page (fairly typical), then $10^5 = 100,000$ words means only 400 pages.
11. Makes sense. That is roughly a 20-story building.
13. Does not make sense. A typical stadium holds 50,000 or more people–no one could sign that many autographs in a reasonable amount of time. (For example, at 10 seconds per autograph, it would take 500,000 seconds–which is almost 140 hours–to sign that many autographs.)

Basic Skills and Concepts

Review of Scientific Notation.

15. a. $5 \times 10^6 = 5,000,000 = 5$ million.
    b. $7 \times 10^9 = 7,000,000,000 = 7$ billion.
    c. $2 \times 10^{-2} = 0.02 = 2$ hundredths.
    d. $8 \times 10^{11} = 800,000,000,000 = 800$ billion.
    e. $1 \times 10^{-7} = 0.0000001 = 1$ ten millionth.
    f. $9 \times 10^{-4} = 0.0009 = 9$ ten thousandths.
17. a. $600 = 6.0 \times 10^2$.
    b. $0.9 = 9 \times 10^{-1}$.
    c. $50,000 = 5 \times 10^4$.
    d. $0.003 = 3 \times 10^{-3}$.
    e. $0.0005 = 5 \times 10^{-4}$.
    f. $70,000,000,000 = 7.0 \times 10^{10}$.
19. a. $(3\times 10^4)\times(8\times 10^5) = (3\times 8)\times(10^4\times 10^5) = 24 \times 10^9 = 2.4 \times 10^{10}$.
    b. $(6.3\times 10^2)+(1.5\times 10^1) = 630+15 = 645 = 6.5 \times 10^2$.
    c. $(9\times 10^3)\times(5\times 10^{-7}) = (9\times 5)\times(10^3\times 10^{-7}) = 45 \times 10^{-4} = 4.5 \times 10^{-3}$.
    d. $(4.4 \times 10^{99})/(2 \times 10^{11}) = (4.4/2) \times (10^{99}/10^{11}) = 2.2 \times 10^{88}$.

They Don't Look That Different!

21. a. 10^{35} is 10^9, or 1 billion, times larger than 10^{26}.
    b. 10^{27} is 10^{10}, or 10 billion, times larger than 10^{17}.
    c. 1 billion $= 1 \times 10^9$ is 10^3, or 1000, times larger than 1 million $= 10^6$.
    d. 7 trillion $= 7\times 10^{12}$ is 10^9, or 1 billion, times larger than 7 thousand $= 7 \times 10^3$.
    e. 2×10^{-6} is 10^3, or 1 thousand, times larger than 2×10^{-9}.
    f. 6.1×10^{29} is 10^2, or 100, times larger than 6.1×10^{27}.

Using Scientific Notation.

23. Total annual energy consumption in the US is about 10^{20} joules.
25. The hard drive on my computer has a capacity of 1.2×10^{10} bytes.
27. The diameter of a typical bacterium is about 10^{-6} meters.

Approximation with Scientific Notation.

29. a. No rounding or estimating (or calculator!) is needed in this problem. Since $20,000 = 2 \times 10^4$ and $100 = 10^2$, we have $2 \times 10^4 \times 10^2 = 2 \times 10^6$ or 2,000,000.
    b. We could approximate this quotient by

$$\frac{9 \times 10^3}{3 \times 10^1} = 3 \times 10^2 = 300.$$

A calculator yields 311; so our estimate was reasonably close.

c. Note that the answer here will be negative. We can approximate this product by

$$-12 \times 12 \times 10^3 = -144 \times 10^3 = -1.44 \times 10^5.$$

The actual value is about -1.49×10^5; our estimate was reasonably close.

d. Again, no rounding or estimating is needed. Since 250 million = 2.5×10^8, we have

$$(2.5 \times 10^8)(4 \times 10^1) = 10 \times 10^9 = 10^{10}$$

or 10 billion.

e. We could approximate this product by $7 \times 300 = 2100$, which is not too far from the actual value of about 2169.

f. We could approximate this quotient by

$$\frac{6.6 \times 10^6}{3.3 \times 10^1} = 2 \times 10^5 = 200,000.$$

A calculator yields about 200,948, so our estimate was not too far off.

Perspective Through Estimation.

31. A 10-story building is between 100 and 120 feet high. A football field is 100 yards—or 300 feet—long, which is almost three times longer than the building is high.

33. It is not unusual for Americans to put 15,000 to 20,000 miles on a single car in a year. Assume an average American (excluding traveling business people) takes two airplane trips per year of 5000 miles. This amounts to 10,000 miles of flying. To the extent that these assumptions are accurate, we can conclude that Americans drive more than they fly each year.

Order of Magnitude Estimates.

35. We will find the amount spent on movies by estimating the number of people who go to the movies, how often they go, and the amount spent on admission tickets. Let's assume that 100 million of the U.S. population of 280 million go to the movies. If these people go 10 times per year, on average, and pay $7 for admission, on average, then the total spent per year will be

$$10^8 \text{ persons} \times \frac{10 \text{ movies}}{\text{person} \times \text{year}} \times \frac{\$7}{\text{movie}}$$

which works out at $7 billion per year. Our ticket price estimate reflects big city prices, and is probably too high as a national average, especially if we take lower children's prices into account. With a $5 ticket price average, and assuming that 150 million people attend movies an average of 20 times a year, our estimate would jump to $15 billion per year. It is difficult to give a precise estimate with more accurate information concerning movie going habits and ticket prices.

37. If we assume that you drink about 2 pints of water per day, then in a year you drink 2 times 365 pints of water. Converting to gallons we get:

$$\frac{2 \text{ pints}}{\text{day}} \times \frac{365 \text{ day}}{\text{year}} \times \frac{1 \text{ gallon}}{8 \text{ pint}} = 90 \frac{\text{gallons}}{\text{year}}.$$

39. One way to approach this problem is to estimate the number of gallons a person uses per week and then convert that to an annual figure. If a person fills the tank with 20 gallons once a week for 52 weeks of the year, then the total gasoline used per year is

$$\frac{20 \text{ gallons}}{\text{week}} \times \frac{52 \text{ weeks}}{\text{year}} = 1040 \frac{\text{gallons}}{\text{year}}.$$

An alternative approach is to estimate using the number of miles driven in a year and the gas mileage of the car. Let's assume that annual driving amounts to 20,000 miles and that, on average, the car gets 20 miles per gallon of gas. Then we get the following estimate of gasoline used per year:

$$\frac{20,000 \text{ miles}}{\text{year}} \times \frac{1 \text{ gallon}}{20 \text{ miles}} = 1000 \frac{\text{gallons}}{\text{year}}.$$

The two estimates are rather close which increases the confidence that can be placed in them.

Energy Comparisons.

41. Each hour of running requires 4×10^6 joules (j) of energy, and the metabolism of each bar of candy releases 10^6 joules of energy, so a four hour run would require the energy of

$$4 \text{ hrs} \times \frac{4 \times 10^6 \text{ j/hr}}{10^6 \text{ j/candy bar}} = 16 \text{ candy bars}.$$

43. Each kilogram of coal, when burned, releases 1.6×10^9 joules of energy, and the fission of

one kilogram of uranium-235 releases 5.6×10^{13} joules of energy. Since

$$\frac{5.6 \times 10^{13} \text{ joules}}{1.6 \times 10^{9} \text{ joules}} = 3.5 \times 10^{4},$$

the fission of uranium-235 releases 35,000 times more energy than burning coal, kilogram by kilogram.

45. Since the fusion of hydrogen in 1 liter of water releases 7×10^{13} joules (j) of energy, and an average home uses 5×10^{7} joules of electrical energy per day, the amount of water required to generate (via fusion) the needs of such a home for one day would be

$$\frac{5 \times 10^{7} \text{ j}}{7 \times 10^{13} \text{ j/liter}} \approx 0.7 \text{ microliters.}$$

47. The fission of one kilogram of uranium-235 releases 5.6×10^{13} joules (j) of energy, and the U.S. annual energy consumption is 1×10^{20} joules, so the annual energy needs of the U.S. would be met by

$$\frac{1 \times 10^{20} \text{ j}}{5.6 \times 10^{13} \text{ j/kg}} \approx 1.8 \text{ million } \frac{\text{kg}}{\text{year}}.$$

Scale Ratio.

49. If 1 cm on the map represents 1 km $= 10^3$ m $= 10^5$ cm on the ground, the scale ratio for this map is 1 to 100,000.

51. If 2 inches on the map represents 0.5 mile on the ground, then as 1 mile is 5280 ft $= 5280 \times 12$ in $= 63,360$ in, we see that 2 inches on the map represents 31,680 inches on the ground. Hence, 1 inch on the map represents 15,840 inches on the ground, and the scale ratio for this map is 1 to 15,840.

53. If 5 cm on the map represents 100 km $= 100 \times 10^5$ cm $= 10^7$ cm on the ground, the scale ratio for this map is 5 to 10,000,000, which is 1 to 2,000,000.

55. If 1 ft on the map represents 100 meters $= 100 \times 3.28$ ft $= 328$ feet on the ground, the scale ratio for this map is 1 to 328.

57. **Scale Model Solar System.** We are given that the scale ratio for our model should be 1 to 10 billion ($= 10^{10}$). Thus, to find scaled sizes or distance, we divide the real sizes or distances by 10^{10}. Because the data table gives so many sizes and distances to put on this scale, it's easiest to look for general rules.

Note that many of the planet diameters are on the order of 10,000 km (10^4 km). On the 1 to 10 billion scale, a real diameter of 10^4 km becomes a scaled diameter of $\frac{10^4 \text{ km}}{10^{10}} = 10^{-6}$ km, which is easier to visualize in millimeters. Since 1 km equals 10^6 mm, we see that 10^{-6} km equals exactly one millimeter; thus the scale of 1 to 10 billion is equivalent to a scale where 1 mm corresponds to 10,000 km.

Now it is easy to convert the real diameters to scaled diameters. The earth's real diameter of about 12,760 km becomes a scaled diameter of about 1.3 mm, and Jupiter's real diameter of about 143,000 km becomes a scaled diameter of about 14.3 mm (which equals 1.43 cm). The second column in the table here shows the Model (scaled) diameters for the nine planets.

Object	Model Diameter	Model Distance
Mercury	0.5 mm	6 m
Venus	1.2 mm	11 m
Earth	1.3 mm	15 m
Mars	0.7 mm	23 m
Jupiter	14.3 mm	78 m
Saturn	12.0 mm	143 m
Uranus	5.2 mm	287 m
Neptune	4.8 mm	450 m
Pluto	0.2 mm	590 m

We can apply a similar argument to the distances. A real distance of 100 million km (10^8 km) becomes a scaled distance of $\frac{10^8 \text{ km}}{10^{10}} = 10^{-2}$ km, i.e., 10 meters (since there are $1000 = 10^3$ meters in one kilometer). Thus the 1 to 10 billion scale means that 10 m corresponds to 100 million km. Now, the Earth's real distance of about 150 million km from the Sun becomes a scaled distance of 15 meters, and Pluto's real distance of about 5,900 million km from the Sun becomes a scaled distance of 590 meters. This explains the third column above.

Putting things in context, it should be clear that "space" is pretty empty. For example, if Neptune were the size of the tip of a ballpoint pen, it would be over four football field lengths away from the sun!

59. **Universal Timeline.** If 14 billion years is represented by a timeline which is 100 meters long, then 1 billion years is represented by a distance of $\frac{100}{14} \approx 7.14$ meters along the timeline. Similarly, 10,000 years is represented by a distance of $10^4 \times \frac{100}{14 \times 10^9}$ meters, or about 0.071 of one millimeter.

Further Applications

Making Numbers Understandable.

61. A marriage rate of approximately 2.2 million per year in the U.S. translates to
$$\frac{2.2 \times 10^6 \text{ marriages}}{\text{year}} \times \frac{1 \text{ year}}{365 \text{ days}} \approx 6027 \frac{\text{marriages}}{\text{day}}.$$

63. A suicide rate of approximately 30,000 per year in the U.S. translates to
$$\frac{30,000 \text{ suicides}}{\text{year}} \times \frac{1 \text{ year}}{365 \text{ days}} \approx 82 \frac{\text{suicides}}{\text{day}}.$$

65. Let's assume that a stack of thirty \$1 bills is about 0.3 cm high. Then a national debt of about \$6.9 trillion translates to a stack of dollar bills which is
$$6.9 \times 10^{12} \text{ bills} \times \frac{0.5 \text{ cm}}{50 \text{ bills}} \times \frac{1 \text{ km}}{10^5 \text{ cm}},$$
or, approximately 680,000 kilometers high. This too is not feasible, as it exceeds the distance from the earth to the moon!

67. Assuming that each stadium can hold 70,000 people, then 1.7 million college students with new bachelor's degrees could fill up
$$1.7 \times 10^6 \text{ students} \times \frac{1 \text{ stadium}}{70,000 \text{ students}},$$
or, approximately 24 stadiums.

69. **Amazing Amazon.** If the daily discharge of 4.5 trillion gallons can supply all U.S. households for five months, then $4.5/5 = 0.9$ trillion gallons can supply all U.S. households for one month. Assuming roughly 100 million U.S. households, this translates to $\frac{0.9 \times 10^{12}}{100 \times 10^6} =$ 9000 gallons per household per month, or about 300 gallons per day. This is reasonable since the actual per household usage for water is about 375 gallons per day.

71. **Stellar Corpses: White Dwarfs and Neutron Stars.**
a. We are told that the sun in its white dwarf incarnation will resemble a sphere of radius 6400 kilometers $= 6.4 \times 10^8$ centimeters, and have a mass of 2×10^{30} kilograms. Recall that a sphere of radius r has volume $\frac{4}{3}\pi r^3$. Since density is mass per unit volume, we compute:
$$\frac{2 \times 10^{30} \text{ kg}}{\frac{4}{3}\pi \times (6.4 \times 10^8 \text{ cm})^3} \approx 1.8214 \times 10^3 \frac{\text{kg}}{\text{cm}^3},$$
getting about 1800 kg/cm^3.
b. If a teaspoon measures about 4 cubic centimeters, then the mass of a teaspoon of the white dwarf would be roughly:
$$4 \text{ cm}^3 \times 1800 \frac{\text{kg}}{\text{cm}^3} = 7200 \text{ kg},$$
which is roughly the mass of a large car.
c. We are dealing with a neutron star of radius 10 kilometers having a mass of $1.4 \times 2 \times 10^{30}$ kilograms, i.e., 2.8×10^{30} kilograms. Since 10 kilometers $= 10 \times 10^5 = 10^6$ centimeters, to find the density of the neutron star we compute:
$$\frac{2.8 \times 10^{30} \text{ kg}}{\frac{4}{3}\pi \times (10^6 \text{ cm})^3} \approx 6.68 \times 10^{11} \frac{\text{kg}}{\text{cm}^3}.$$
One cubic centimeter of this weighs about 668 billion kilograms, which is over ten times the total mass of Mount Everest (5×10^{10} kg, or, 50 billion kilograms).

Sampling Problems.

73. A stack of 10 pennies is roughly 1.5 cm high, so the thickness of one penny is approximately $1.5/10 = 0.15$ cm $= 1.5$ mm.
A stack of 10 nickels is roughly 1.8 cm high, so the thickness of one nickel is approximately $1.8/10 = 0.18$ cm $= 1.8$ mm.
A stack of 10 dimes is roughly 1.3 cm high, so the thickness of one dime is approximately $1.3/10 = 0.13$ cm $= 1.3$ mm.

A stack of 10 quarters is roughly 1.5 cm high, so the thickness of one quarter is approximately $1.7/10 = 0.17$ cm $= 1.7$ mm. (Similar calculations may be done using inches, but the metric answers are easier to work with and understand.) The thickness of these coins are of the same order of magnitude, so clearly it is to your advantage to take your height stacked in quarters, since the quarter is at least two and a half times as valuable as any of the other coins.

75. Solutions may vary.

Unit 3C

Does It Make Sense?

7. Does not make sense. There's no chance that anyone could know to such precision what next year's deficit will be.
9. Does not make sense. It would be nearly impossible to find a scale that could measure your weight to 0.0001 pound in the first place, and even if you did, your weight would have changed by more than 0.0001 pound within minutes after making the measurement (due to water loss from sweat, shedding of skin, etc.).
11. Makes sense. Since registration requires doing something specific (in this case, filling out a form and paying a fee), it should be possible to get an exact count of the number of people who do it - as long as great care is taken to make sure that no recording errors occur.
13. Makes sense. For a company with revenue of \$1 billion, a \$1 million error would be only 0.1%, which is a fairly small relative error.

Basic Skills and Concepts

Review of Rounding.

15.

a. 2.	b. 15.	c. 779.
d. 4.	e. 14.	f. 235.
g. 2000.	h. 89.	i. -14.

Counting Significant Digits.

17. The number 96.2 has three significant digits, because all digits are non-zero. It is precise to the nearest tenth (0.1) of a km/hr.
19. The number 100.020 has six significant digits, because the right-most zero is usually unnecessary, so the fact that it is included makes it significant. It is precise to the nearest thousandth (0.001) of a second.
21. The number 0.00098 has two significant digits, because it can be written 9.8×10^4. It is precise to the nearest 0.00001 mm.
23. The number 0.0002020 has four significant digits, because it can be written 2.020×10^{-4} and the right-most zero is usually unnecessary, so the fact that it is included makes it significant. It is precise to the nearest 0.0000001 meters.
25. The number 300,000 has only one significant digit, because it can be written 3×10^5. It is precise to the nearest 100,000.
27. The number 3×10^5 has five significant digits. Since it equals 300,000, it is precise to the nearest whole number.

Rounding with Significant Digits.

29. $1452 \times 9076.7 = 13,179,368.4$. For two significant digits, round the million's place giving 13,000,000.
31. $46371 \div 0.00728 \approx 6,369,642.857$. For three significant digits, round in the 10,000's place: 6,370,000.
33. $(3.4 \times 10^9) \div (4.1 \times 10^{-6}) \approx 8.29268 \times 10^{14}$. For two significant digits, round just right of the decimal point: 8.3×10^{14}.

Sources of Errors.

35. There is likely to be random error due to miscounting because the intersection is busy, as well as systematic error (a particular person counting may well have their own bias) due to interpretation of what counts as a sports utility vehicle.
37. There is likely to be random error due to miscalculation of the average, and systematic error due to underreporting of incomes on tax returns.
39. There is likely to be random error due to errors in reading the scale, but no systematic error

since the scale is well calibrated.

41. There is likely to be random error due to miscounting.

43. **Tax Audit.** The errors referred to in (1) are likely to be random error; those in (2) are more likely to be systematic (probably due to under-reporting).

45. **Safe Air Travel.** An altimeter set to 2500 feet in a city that is actually at 5280 feet will read $5280 - 2500 = 2780$ feet too low at takeoff and throughout the subsequent flight. This is a systematic error.

Absolute and Relative Errors.

47. The absolute error is $\$(19.00 - 18.50) = \$0.50$; the relative error $\frac{\$0.50}{\$18.50} \approx 0.027 = 2.7\%$.

49. The absolute error is $\$(48 - 65) = -\$17$; the relative error $-\frac{\$17}{\$65} \approx -0.2615 = -26.15\%$.

51. The absolute error is $(5.25 - 5)$ cups $= -0.25$ cups; the relative error is $-\frac{0.25 \text{ in}}{5.5 \text{ in}} \approx -0.04545 = -4.545\%$.

53. The absolute error is $(11.7 - 12)$ mi $= -0.3$ mi; the relative error $-\frac{0.3 \text{ mi}}{12 \text{ mi}} = -0.025 = -2.5\%$.

Accuracy and Precision.

55. The tape measure is more accurate because it got closer to your true height than the laser did; but the laser is more precise, as it claimed to gauge your height to a greater degree of precision than the tape did.

57. The digital scale is more precise and more accurate than the clinical scale: it measures to a greater precision and got closer to your true weight than the clinical scale did.

Combining Measured Numbers.

For problems 59-66, recall the Rounding Rule for Addition and Subtraction: an answer obtained by adding or subtracting two approximate numbers should be rounded to the same precision as the least precise of the two numbers. Also recall the Rounding Rule for Multiplication and Division: in multiplication and division, the answer should be given to the same number of significant digits as the number in the problem with the fewest significant digits.

59. Note that 140 liters $-$ 1.09 liters $=$ 138.91 liters, but since the volume of 140 liters is the least precise (to the nearest ten), we should round this difference to the nearest ten also, yielding 140 liters (again!).

61. The weight 9.7 kg has two significant digits, whereas 165 kg has three. The product of the given numbers is easily checked to be 1600.5 kg^2, but this should be rounded to two significant digits, namely 1600 kg^2.

63. Note that 36 miles $+$ 2.2 miles $=$ 38.2 miles, but since the first given distance was the least precise (to the nearest mile only), we should round the sum to the nearest mile also, yielding 38 miles.

65. The figure \$112.4 million has four significant digits, whereas 480,000 residents has only two. The appropriate quotient of these numbers is \$234.17 per resident, but rounded to two significant digits the answer should be listed as \$230 per resident.

Further Applications

Believable Facts?

67. Random and systematic errors could be present. The claim is not believable with the given precision, even if it is an official census count.

69. Random and systematic errors could be present. The claim is believable with the given precision; it could be a reasonable projection.

71. Random and systematic errors could be present. The claim is believable with the given precision; presumably it's based on actual averaged measurements, rounded to the nearest degree.

73. Random and systematic errors could be present; the claim is not believable with the given precision, no matter what data it is based on.

Unit 3D

Does It Make Sense?

5. Does not make sense. The statement does not take into account inflation. In fact, as shown

in Figure 3.4, the real cost of gasoline today is much lower than it was in 1918.

7. Makes sense. Franklin lived more than 200 years ago, and the value of a penny back then is more like that the value of a dollar today than it is of a penny today.

9. Does not make sense. The year that you choose as the reference for prices does not affect the real trends.

Basic Skills and Concepts

Gasoline Price Index.

11. Since index number $= \frac{\text{value}}{\text{reference value}} \times 100$, we see that the current price index number for gasoline is $\frac{180\text{ c}}{56.7\text{ c}} \times 100 = 317.46$.

13. Since the price indices are based on the 1975 value, and 1995 has a price index of 212.5, a tank of gasoline that cost \$10 in 1975 cost $2.125 \times \$10 = \$21.25$, in 1995.

15. Of course, the 1965 price index entry is 100. In order to recast the gasoline price indices listed in Table 3.2 with the 1965 price as the reference value, we must calculate the ratio of $\frac{\text{year price}}{\text{1965 price}}$. For example, to get the 1955 index number, we have

$$\frac{\text{1955 price}}{\text{1965 price}} = \frac{29.1}{31.2} \approx 0.9327$$

so the 1955 price is about 93.3% of the 1965 price, and thus corresponds to a price index of 93.3 in the new table below. The other entries of the new table are calculated in a similar way.

Year	Price	Price as % of 1965 price	Price Index (1965 = 100)
1955	29.1c	93.3%	93.3
1965	31.2c	100.0%	100.0
1975	56.7c	181.7%	181.7
1985	119.6c	383.3%	383.3
1995	120.5c	386.2%	386.2
2000	155.0c	496.8%	496.8

Understanding the CPI.

17. Since

$$\frac{\text{CPI}_{2002}}{\text{CPI}_{1975}} = \frac{179.9}{53.8} \approx 3.34$$

a standard of living that cost \$20,000 to maintain in 1975 would cost about $3.34 \times \$20,000 = \$66,800$, or about \$67,000, to maintain in 2002.

19. The inflation rate from 1977 to 1978 was

$$\frac{\text{CPI}_{1978} - \text{CPI}_{1977}}{\text{CPI}_{1977}} = \frac{65.2 - 60.6}{60.6} \approx 0.0759$$

or about 7.6%.

21. Since

$$\frac{\text{CPI}_{2000}}{\text{CPI}_{1979}} = \frac{172.2}{72.6} \approx 2.3719,$$

a loaf of bread that cost \$0.75 in 1979 would cost $2.3719 \times \$0.75 = \$1.78$ in 2000.

23. Since

$$\frac{\text{CPI}_{1975}}{\text{CPI}_{2000}} = \frac{53.8}{172.2} \approx 0.3124,$$

admission to a movie cost that cost \$7.00 in 2000, would have cost $0.3124 \times \$7 = \$2.19$ in 1975.

25. Since

$$\frac{\text{CPI}_{2002}}{\text{CPI}_{1973}} = \frac{179.9}{44.5} \approx 4.04,$$

every dollar in 1973 had the same purchasing power that \$3.88 did in 2000. To put it another way, a dollar in 1973 had 3.88 times the purchasing power that a dollar did in 2000.

Housing Price Index. In problems 27-30, we note that to get the value of a house in City A which is comparable to a house in City B, the calculation goes thus

$$\text{Value in City A} = \text{Value in City B} \times \frac{\text{City A index}}{\text{City B index}}$$

27. If a house is valued at \$250,000 in Denver, then a comparable house in Palo Alto should have a value of

$$\$250,000 \times \frac{\text{Palo Alto Index}}{\text{Denver Index}} = \$250,000 \times \frac{365}{87} = \$1,048,850$$

or about \$1 million. A comparable house in Sioux City should cost

$$\$250,000 \times \frac{\text{Sioux City Index}}{\text{Denver Index}} = \$250,000 \times \frac{47}{87} \approx \$135,057$$

or about \$135,000. A comparable house in Boston should cost

$$\$250,000 \times \frac{\text{Boston Index}}{\text{Denver Index}}$$

$$= \$250,000 \times \frac{182}{87} \approx \$522,988$$

or about \$523,000.

29. If a house is valued at \$250,000 in Cheyenne, then a comparable house in Spokane should have a value of

$$\$250,000 \times \frac{\text{Spokane Index}}{\text{Cheyenne Index}}$$

$$= \$250,000 \times \frac{78}{75} = \$260,000.$$

A comparable house in Denver should cost

$$\$250,000 \times \frac{\text{Denver Index}}{\text{Cheyenne Index}}$$

$$= \$250,000 \times \frac{87}{75} = \$290,000.$$

A comparable house in Juneau should cost

$$\$250,000 \times \frac{\text{Juneau Index}}{\text{Cheyenne Index}}$$

$$= \$250,000 \times \frac{100}{75} \approx \$333,333$$

or about \$333,000.

Further Applications

31. **Health Care Spending.** Since $\frac{1500 \text{ billion}}{73 \text{ billion}} \approx$ 20.55, total spending on health care increased by a factor of 20.55 between 1973 and 2002. This is about five times the corresponding increase in the CPI over the same period:

$$\frac{\text{CPI}_{2002}}{\text{CPI}_{1971}} = \frac{179.9}{44.4} \approx 4.05.$$

For another perspective on the same figures, note that the \$73 billion spent on health care in the U.S. in 1973 was equivalent to $\$73 \times 10^9 \times 4.05 \approx \$2.96 \times 10^{11}$, or \$296 billion in 2002 dollars, which is less than a quarter of the \$1.5 trillion actually spent on health care in 2002.

33. **Private College Costs.** The relative change (between 1980 and 2002) in the average cost of attending a private college was $\frac{\$25100-\$5900}{\$5900} \approx$ 3.2542, or around 325%—so that costs went up by over a factor of 4—and the CPI went up by a factor of a little over 2:

$$\frac{\text{CPI}_{2002}}{\text{CPI}_{1980}} = \frac{179.9}{82.4} \approx 2.18.$$

Thus the private college costs went up about twice as fast as the overall rate of inflation.

35. **Home Prices—South.** The relative change (between 1990 and 2000) in the price of a typical single-family home in the South was $\frac{\$123,600-\$75,300}{\$75,300} \approx 0.6414$, or around 64%—so that costs went up by a factor of 1.64—and the CPI went up by a factor of around 1.3:

$$\frac{\text{CPI}_{2000}}{\text{CPI}_{1990}} = \frac{172.2}{130.7} \approx 1.3175.$$

Thus the house price change in the South was somewhat higher than the overall rate of inflation.

Federal Minimum Wage.

37. This can be read directly from the table: \$2.78.
39. In 1996, actual dollars are the same as 1996 dollars.
41. The 1979 minimum hourly wage of \$2.90 was equivalent to

$$\$2.90 \times \frac{\text{CPI}_{1996}}{\text{CPI}_{1979}} = \$2.90 \times \frac{156.9}{72.6} = \$6.27$$

in 1996 dollars. This is consistent with the minimum wage table entry for 1979.

43. The purchasing power of the minimum wage was highest in 1968, since that is the year in the table with the highest entry in the 1996 dollars column.
45. **Project: Convenience Store Index.** Solutions will vary.

Unit 3E

Does It Make Sense?

5. Makes sense. This is an example of Simpson's paradox, which can occur just as shown in the acne drug example in the text.
7. Does not make sense. Only a small percentage of bags will contain banned materials, so this

is much like the polygraph example in the text, in which many or most of the positives will be false.

9. Does not make sense. It's quite possible for both sides to be telling the truth, if they are looking at the issue in different ways.

Basic Skills and Concepts

11. **Batting Percentages.** In the first half of the season, Josh's batting average was $\frac{50}{150} \approx 0.333$, and Jude's batting average was $\frac{10}{50} = 0.200$, so Josh had the higher batting average. In the second half of the season, Josh's batting average was $\frac{35}{70} = 0.500$, and Jude's batting average was $\frac{70}{150} \approx 0.467$, so Josh had the higher batting average here too. However, combining the figures for both halves of the season, Josh's overall batting average was $\frac{50+35}{150+70} = 0.386$, and Jude's overall batting average was $\frac{10+70}{50+150} = 0.400$. Thus, Jude had the higher batting average overall. These results illustrate Simpson's paradox because Jude had the higher batting average overall despite the fact that Josh had the higher average in each half of the season considered separately.

13. **Test Scores.**

a. New Jersey had higher scores (283, 252 respectively) than Nebraska in both the white and non-white categories, yet Nebraska had the higher overall average (277) across both racial categories.

b. The percentage of non-whites in Nebraska is much less than in New Jersey.

c. If 87% of Nebraska students were white, with an average of 281, and the remaining 13% were non-white, with an average of 250, then assuming that N Nebraska students took the test, $0.87 \times N$ of them were white with scores (on average) of 281, whereas $0.13 \times N$ of them were non-white with scores (on average) of 250. Thus, their overall average score was

$$\frac{(0.87 \times N \times 281) + (0.13 \times N \times 250)}{N}$$
$$= (0.87 \times 281) + (0.13 \times 250) = 276.97.$$

d. If 66% of New Jersey students were white, with an average of 283, and the remaining 34% were non-white, with an average of 252, then assuming that M New Jersey students took the test, $0.66 \times M$ of them were white with scores (on average) of 283, whereas $0.34 \times M$ of them were non-white with scores (on average) of 252. Thus, their overall average score was

$$\frac{(0.66 \times M \times 283) + (0.34 \times M \times 252)}{M}$$
$$= (0.66 \times 283) + (0.34 \times 252) = 272.46.$$

e. Although Nebraska had lower scores in both categories, it came out ahead overall.

15. **Tuberculosis Deaths.** a. In NYC, the death rate for whites was $\frac{8400}{4{,}675{,}000}$ or about 0.18%, and for non-whites it was $\frac{500}{92{,}000}$ or about 0.54%. The overall death rate was $\frac{8400+500}{4{,}675{,}000+92{,}000}$ or about 0.19%,

b. In Richmond, the death rate for whites was $\frac{130}{81{,}000}$ or about 0.16%, and for non-whites it was $\frac{160}{47{,}000}$ or about 0.34%. The overall death rate was $\frac{130+160}{81{,}000+47{,}000}$ or about 0.23%,

c. The death rate for both whites and non-whites in New York was higher than in Richmond; yet the overall death rate was higher in Richmond than in New York. This occurred here because the percentage of non-whites in New York was significantly less than that in Richmond.

More Accurate Mammograms.

17. Of all the women who test positive, only $\frac{95}{590} \approx$ 16% actually have a malignancy.

19. **Polygraph Test.** a. If the drug use rate is 1%, then $(0.01)(2000) = 20$ people actually use drugs, and $2000 - 20 = 1980$ do not. Next, 90% of users test positive, i.e., are deemed by the polygraph to have lied, so $(0.90)(20) = 18$ of the 20 users test positive, and $20 - 18 = 2$ do not. Similarly, 90% of the non-users test negative, i.e., are deemed to have told the truth, this accounts for $(0.90)(1980) = 1782$ people. The remaining $1980 - 1782 = 198$ non-users test positive. Overall, $18 + 198 = 216$ people are

deemed to have lied, and $2+1782 = 1784$ people are deemed to have told the truth.

b. All 216 people who test positive are accused of lying, but only 18 of these were actually lying. The other 198 were telling the truth: $\frac{198}{216}$, or about 91.67%, were falsely accused.

c. The polygraph claims that 1784 people were telling the truth, of whom 1782 really were; the other 2 were lying; thus, $\frac{1782}{1784}$ or about 99.89% of those found telling the truth were actually telling the truth.

21. **Political Math.** The housing program will see an increase of 1%, since it will grow from \$1 billion to \$1.01 billion. This represents an increase in actual dollars. However, the increase is less than the 3% projected increase in the CPI, which effectively amounts to a cut: the program increase is not sufficient to keep up with inflation.

Further Applications

23. **Better Drug.** a. Drug B's cure rate for men was $\frac{196}{200}$, or 98%, and for women was $\frac{101}{900}$, or about 11.22%. Meanwhile, drug A's cure rate for men was $\frac{400}{800}$, or 50%, and for women was $\frac{5}{100}$, or 5%. So drug B comes out ahead both for men and for women.

b. Overall, drug A had a better cure rate ($\frac{5+400}{100+800}$ or 45%) than drug B ($\frac{101+196}{900+200}$ or 27%).

c. Since the drugs had different effects on men and women, the individual cure rates should be cited and used for evaluation.

25. **Hiring Statistics.** Consider the men who applied: their acceptance rate for white-collar positions was 15%, their acceptance rate for blue-collar positions was 75%, and their overall acceptance rate was

$$\frac{(0.15)(200) + (0.75)(400)}{200 + 400} = 55\%.$$

Next, consider the women who applied: their acceptance rate for white-collar positions was 20%, and their acceptance rate for blue-collar positions was 85% – both higher than the corresponding rates for men. Yet the women's overall acceptance rate was

$$\frac{(0.20)(200) + (0.85)(100)}{200 + 100} \approx 41.67\%.$$

Within each category—white-collar and blue-collar positions—the percentage of women hired was greater than the percentage of men hired, but overall, the hiring rate for men was higher than for women. This paradox can be resolved by noting that the number of blue-color jobs $(455 - 70 = 385)$ was over five times greater than the number of white-collar jobs (70).

27. Possible argument: These 400 people constitute $\frac{400}{280,000,000} \approx 0.00014\%$ of the total population (about 280 million), yet they paid 1.6% of all taxes collected in 2000. Clearly, they are paying a disproportionate share.

29. Possible argument: In 1993, when tax share declined for the wealthiest Americans, their share of income also declined. This suggests that the wealth is redistributed to other sectors of the economy, boosting revenues from other sources.

31. **2003 Tax Cut.**

a. In relative terms, a \$211 tax cut for a single person making \$41,000 is $\frac{211}{41,000} \approx 0.005$ or about one half of one percent. A \$12,838 tax cut for a single person making \$530,000 is $\frac{12,838}{530,000} \approx 0.024$ or about 2.4%. In other words, the tax cut for the latter was nearly five times greater in relative terms.

b. In relative terms, a \$1208 tax cut for a family of four making \$41,000 is $\frac{1208}{41,000} \approx 0.029$ or about 2.9%. A cut of \$13,442 for a family of four making \$530,000 is $\frac{13,442}{530,000} \approx 0.025$ or about 2.5%. In other words the tax cuts for families of four is more nearly the same in relative terms.

c. Answers will vary.

Unit 4A

Does It Make Sense?

9. Does not make sense. The simple interest will be higher during the first year, but compounding will rapidly catch up and pass it within a few years.
11. Does not make sense. The compounding period certainly matters, as might fees, requirements for minimum balance or minimum length of time you hold the account, etc.
13. Make sense. The 5.1% by which your account grew is the annual percentage yield, which will be a little higher than the interest rate as long as interest is compounded more than once a year.

Basic Skills and Concepts

Algebra Review.

15. Given $x - 4 = 6$, we add 4 to both sides to get $x = 6 + 4 = 10$.
17. Given $y + 5 = 10$, we subtract 5 from both sides to get $y = 10 - 5 = 5$.
19. Given $2z = 12$, we divide both sides by 2 to get $z = 12/2 = 6$.
21. Given $3x = 15$, we divide both sides by 3 to get $x = 15/3 = 5$.
23. Given $2x - 5 = 13$, we first add 5 to both sides to get $2x = 13 + 5 = 18$, then divide by 2 to get $x = 18/2 = 9$.
25. Given $3n + 4 = 13$, we first subtract 4 from both sides to get $3n = 13 - 4 = 9$, then divide by 3 to get $n = 9/3 = 3$.
27. Given $4x + 8 = 24$, we first subtract 8 from both sides to get $4x = 24 - 8 = 16$, then divide by 4 to get $n = 16/4 = 4$.
29. Given $5 - 2w = 9$, we first subtract 5 from both sides to get $5 - 2w - 5 = 9 - 5 = 4$, i.e., $-2w = 4$, then divide by -2 to get $w = 4/(-2) = -2$.

Simple Interest.

31. The annual interest is $500(0.05) = \$25$. Over 5 years the interest comes to $\$25(5) = \$125$. The investment is then worth $\$500 + 125 = \$625$.
33. The annual interest is $2000(0.03) = \$60$. Over 20 years the interest comes to $\$60(20) = \$1200$. The investment is then worth $\$2000 + 1200 = \$3200$.

Simple vs. Compound Interest.

35. Since Yancy is earning simple interest at an annual rate of 5%, her initial investment of \$500 grows by \$25 at the end of each year. After 5 years, her balance is up to \$625, which is a \$125 increase in absolute terms. In relative terms, her balance has increased by $\frac{\$125}{\$500} = 0.25$, i.e., 25%.

Samantha, on the other hand, invests the same amount of money at 5% compound interest. After the first year she too gets \$25 in interest and has a balance of \$525. However after the second year, she gets $0.05 \times \$525 = \$26.25$ in interest, resulting in a new balance of \$551.25. After the third year, she gets $0.05 \times \$551.25 = \$27.56$ in interest, resulting in a new balance of \$578.81. Similarly, after the fourth and fifth years she gets more "interest on her interest," as tabulated below, ending up with a balance of \$638.14.

	Yancy		Samantha	
Year	Interest	Balance	Interest	Balance
0	-	\$500	-	\$500
1	\$25	\$525	\$25	\$525
2	\$25	\$550	\$26.25	\$551.25
3	\$25	\$575	\$27.56	\$578.81
4	\$25	\$600	\$28.94	\$607.75
5	\$25	\$625	\$30.39	\$638.14

After 5 years, Samantha's balance is up by \$138.14, which in relative terms is $\frac{\$138.14}{\$500} = 0.276$, i.e., a 27.6% increase.

Compound Interest.

37. If we invest \$2000 at an APR of 3% for 10 years, we accumulate a balance of

$$\$2000 \times (1 + 0.03)^{10} = \$2687.83.$$

39. If we invest \$30,000 at an APR of 7% for 25 years, we accumulate a balance of

$$\$30,000 \times (1 + 0.07)^{25} = \$162,822.98.$$

41. If we invest \$10,000 at an APR of 6% for 25 years, we accumulate a balance of

$$\$10,000 \times (1 + 0.06)^{25} = \$42,918.71.$$

Compounding More Than Once a Year.

For these problems, we use the formula

$$A = P(1 + \frac{APR}{n})^{nY}$$

43. Investing \$1000 at an APR of 3.5% compounded monthly for 10 years yields:

$$A = \$1000(1 + \frac{0.035}{12})^{120} = \$1418.34.$$

45. Investing \$5000 at an APR of 5.6% compounded quarterly for 20 years yields:

$$A = \$5000(1 + \frac{0.056}{4})^{80} = \$15,205.70.$$

47. Investing \$1000 at an APR of 7% compounded monthly for 10 years yields:

$$A = \$1000(1 + \frac{0.07}{12})^{180} = \$2848.95.$$

49. Investing \$5000 at an APR of 6.2% compounded quarterly for 30 years yields:

$$A = \$5000(1 + \frac{0.062}{4})^{120} = \$31,663.68$$

Annual Percentage Yield (APY).

51. Investing \$1000 for 1 year at an APR of 2.5% compounded daily yields $A = \$1000(1 + \frac{0.025}{365})^{365} = \$1025.30$, which results in an APY of $\frac{\$25.30}{\$1000} = 0.0253 = 2.53\%$.
53. Investing \$1000 for 1 year at an APR of 3.25% compounded monthly yields $A = \$1000(1 + \frac{0.0325}{12})^{12} = \$1032.99$, which results in an APY of $\frac{\$32.99}{\$1000} = 0.03299 \approx 3.30\%$.

Continuous Compounding.

In these problems, use the formula

$$A = Pe^{APR \times Y}.$$

55. If we invest \$1000 for 1 year at 4% compounded continuously, we end up with $A = \$1000e^{0.04\times 1} = \$1040.81$, and an APY of $\frac{\$40.81}{\$1000} = 0.04081 = 4.08\%$. Investing for 5 years we get $A = \$1000e^{0.04\times 5} = \$1221.40$, and investing for 20 years we get $A = \$1000e^{0.04\times 20} = \$2225.54$.

57. If we invest \$10,000 for 1 year at 6% compounded continuously, we end up with $A = \$10000e^{0.06\times 1} = \$10,618.37$, and an APY of $\frac{\$618.37}{\$10000} = 0.06184 \approx 6.18\%$. Investing for 5 years we get $A = \$10000e^{0.06\times 5} = \$13,498.59$, and investing for 20 years we get $A = \$10000e^{0.06\times 20} = \$33,201.17$.
59. If we invest \$5000 for 1 year at 6.5% compounded continuously, we end up with $A = \$5000e^{0.065\times 1} = \$5335.80$, and an APY of $\frac{\$335.80}{\$5000} = 0.06716 \approx 6.72\%$. Investing for 5 years we get $A = \$5000e^{0.065\times 5} = \$6920.15$, and investing for 20 years we get $A = \$5000e^{0.065\times 20} = \$18,346.48$.

Planning Ahead with Compounding.

In these problems, we use the formulae

$$P = \frac{A}{(1 + \frac{APR}{n})^{nY}} \quad \text{and} \quad P = \frac{A}{e^{APR\times Y}},$$

for interest compounded n times a year and continuously, respectively.

61. To end up with \$10,000 after 10 years at an APR of 5% compounded annually, you must start with

$$P = \frac{\$10000}{(1 + 0.05)^{10}} = \$6139.13 \approx \$6140.$$

63. To end up with \$10,000 after 10 years at an APR of 6% compounded monthly, you must start with

$$P = \frac{\$10000}{(1 + \frac{0.06}{12})^{120}} = \$5496.33 \approx \$5497$$

College Fund.

65. To get \$100,000 after 18 years at an APR of 4% compounded daily, you must start with

$$P = \frac{\$100000}{(1 + \frac{0.04}{365})^{6570}} = \$48,677.15 \approx \$48,678.$$

67. To get \$100,000 after 18 years at an APR of 9% compounded monthly, you must start with

$$P = \frac{\$100000}{(1 + \frac{0.09}{12})^{216}} = \$19,909.86 \approx \$19,910.$$

Further Applications

Small Rate Differences.

69. After 10 years Chang has $\$500 \times (1+0.035)^{10} = \$705.30$; after 30 years he has $\$500 \times (1 + 0.035)^{30} = \$1403.40$. After 10 years Kio has $\$500 \times (1 + 0.0375)^{10} = \$722.52$; after 30 years she has $\$500 \times (1+0.0375)^{30} = \$1508.74$. Hence, Kio has \$17.22 more than Chang after 10 years, and since $\frac{\$17.22}{\$705.30} = 0.024$, Kio's balance is 2.4% higher than Chang's.
After 30 years the change is more dramatic: Kio has \$105.34 more than Chang, and since $\frac{\$105.34}{\$1403.40} = 0.075$, Kio's balance is 7.5% higher than Chang's. Consequently, a small interest rate difference gets magnified over time.

71. **Comparing Annual Yields.** If we invest \$1000 for 1 year at an APR of 6.6% compounded quarterly, we end up with $A = \$1000(1 + \frac{0.066}{4})^4 = \$1067.65$, which results in an APY of $\frac{\$67.65}{\$1000} = 0.06765$, i.e., 6.77%. If the interest is compounded monthly, we get $A = \$1000(1 + \frac{0.066}{12})^{12} = \$1068.03$, and an APY of 6.80%. Daily compounding leads to $A = \$1000(1 + \frac{0.066}{365})^{365} = \$1068.22$, and an APY of 6.82%.
Compounding monthly as opposed to quarterly increases the APY noticeably, but increasing the frequency of compounding from monthly to daily has a smaller effect.

73. **Rates of Compounding.** For Account 1, after Y years the balance is given by $\$1000(1 + 0.055)^Y$, and the interest is that amount less the initial \$1000. Letting $Y = 1, 2, \ldots, 10$ yields half of the table below (in which we rounded to the nearest dollar).

	Account 1		Account 2	
Year	Interest	Balance	Interest	Balance
0	-	\$1000	-	\$1000
1	\$55	\$1055	\$57	\$1057
2	\$58	\$1113	\$59	\$1116
3	\$61	\$1174	\$63	\$1179
4	\$65	\$1239	\$67	\$1246
5	\$68	\$1307	\$70	\$1317
6	\$72	\$1379	\$74	\$1391
7	\$76	\$1455	\$79	\$1470
8	\$80	\$1535	\$83	\$1553
9	\$84	\$1619	\$87	\$1640
10	\$89	\$1708	\$93	\$1733

For Account 2, after Y years the balance is $\$1000(1 + \frac{0.055}{365})^{365Y}$, and the interest is that amount less the initial \$1000. By varying Y, we obtain the other half of the table.
After 10 years, Account 1 has increased in value by \$708, which in relative terms is 70.8%. Account 2 has increased in value by \$733, which in relative terms is 73.3%.

75. **Comparing Investment Plans.** Bernard invests \$1600 at 4% compounded annually, so after Y years he has $A = \$1600(1 + 0.04)^Y$. For $Y = 5$ we get \$1946.64, and for $Y = 20$ we get \$3505.80.
Carla invests \$1400 at an APR of 5% compounded daily; after Y years she has $A = \$1400(1+\frac{0.05}{365})^{365Y}$. For $Y = 5$ we get \$1797.60, and for $Y = 20$ we get \$3805.33.
Hence, Bernard has the higher accumulated balance after 5 years, but Carla comes out ahead after 20 years: Carla's higher APR and more frequent compounding allows her to more than make up for her smaller investment given sufficient time.

77. **Retirement Fund.** You wish to have \$75,000 after 35 years. Under Plan A, you get an APR of 5% compounded annually, so you must start by investing $P = \frac{\$75{,}000}{(1+0.05)^{35}} \approx \$13{,}597$. Under Plan B, you get an APR of 4.5% compounded continuously, so you must start by investing $P = \$75{,}000 \div e^{0.045 \times 35} \approx \$15{,}525.57$.

Finding Time Periods.

79. Investing \$1000 at an APR of 8% for Y years yields $A = 1000(1.08)^Y$. For $Y = 10$ we get

$A = \$2158.92$, which falls quite a bit short short of tripling our \$1000. Trying $Y = 15$ we get $A = \$3172.17$, which more than triples our money. Trying $Y = 14$ we get $A = \$2937.19$, which is a bit short of our goal. However, since the interest is being compounded only once a year, we must settle for 15 years and an overshoot of our goal.

81. As above we seek the smallest whole number Y so that $A = 1000(1.07)^Y$ comes out to be \$100,000 or larger. For $Y = 25$ we get $A = \$5427.43$, which is far short of our desired goal. $Y = 50$ yields $A = \$29,457.03$, which is still short. $Y = 75$ yields $A = \$159,876.02$, which is a considerable overshoot! Trying $Y = 65, 70, 68,$ and 69 in succession we find that 68 years is not enough, and 69 gives us \$106,532.14. Since the interest is being compounded only once a year, we must settle for 69 years.

Unit 4B

Does It Make Sense?

9. Makes sense. That's exactly what savings plans are all about.
11. Does not make sense. It's true that stocks have out-performed other investments over the historical long-term, but there have been many historical periods when stocks did not perform well as investments. Moreover, there's no guarantee that past trends will continue in the future.
13. Does not make sense. No one can make a promise like that, so such a claim would clearly mark the fund as a scam. Don't be fooled by such advertisements, no matter how common they may be!

Basic Skills and Concepts

Review of Powers and Roots.

15. $4^3 = 4 \times 4 \times 4 = 64$.
17. $2^3 \times 2^5 = 2^{3+5} = 2^8 = 256$.
19. $3^6 \div 3^2 = 3^{6-2} = 3^4 = 81$.
21. $4^{-2} = \frac{1}{4^2} = \frac{1}{4\times4} = \frac{1}{16}$.
23. $4^5 \times 4^{-2} = 4^{5-2} = 4^3 = 64$.
25. $5^3 \div 5^{-4} = 5^{3-(-4)} = 5^7 = 78,125$.

Solving with Powers and Roots.

27. Given $x^2 = 100$, we get $x = \pm 10$.
29. Given $x^3 = 27$, we get $x = 3$.
31. Given $x^{\frac{1}{3}} = 2$, we get $x = 2^3 = 8$.
33. Given $x^{\frac{1}{5}} = 2$, we get $x = 2^5 = 32$.

Savings Plan Formula.

35. Use the savings plan formula. Investing \$100 (P=100) each month at 12% (APR =0.12) for 9 months (Y=0.75 and nY=9) gives
$$100 \times \frac{(1+\frac{0.12}{12})^9 - 1}{\frac{0.12}{12}} = \$936.85.$$
37. Investing \$200 (P=200) each month at 6% (APR =0.06) for 18 months (Y=1.5 and nY=18) gives
$$100 \times \frac{(1+\frac{0.06}{12})^{18} - 1}{\frac{0.06}{12}} = \$3757.16.$$

Investment Plans.

Recall the formula:
$$A = PMT \times \frac{(1+\frac{APR}{n})^{nY} - 1}{\frac{APR}{n}}.$$

39. Depositing \$50 monthly for 40 years at 5% yields
$$A = \$50 \times \frac{(1+\frac{0.05}{12})^{12\times40} - 1}{\frac{0.05}{12}} = \$76,301.01.$$
This is about 3 times the total deposits $\$50 \times 12 \times 40 = \$24,000$ made.
41. Depositing \$200 monthly for 18 years at 7% yields
$$A = \$200 \times \frac{(1+\frac{0.07}{12})^{12\times18} - 1}{\frac{0.07}{12}} = \$86,144.21.$$
This is about twice the total amount of deposits made over the 18 years, which is $\$200\times12\times18 = \$43,200$.

Investment Planning.

Use the inverted savings plan formula, which gives the PMT in terms of the amount A saved:
$$PMT = \frac{A \times \frac{APR}{n}}{(1+\frac{APR}{n})^{nY} - 1}.$$

43. To create a college fund worth \$150,000 by making monthly deposits for 18 years, assuming an APR of 7.5%, you must deposit

$$\frac{\$150,000 \times \frac{0.075}{12}}{(1+\frac{0.075}{12})^{12\times 18}-1} = \$329.96$$

each month.

45. To save up \$10,000 to buy a car, by making monthly deposits for 3 years at an APR of 5.5%, you must deposit

$$\frac{\$10,000 \times \frac{0.055}{12}}{(1+\frac{0.055}{12})^{12\times 3}-1} = \$256.13$$

each month.

47. **Comfortable Retirement.** First, we need to figure out how much you must save by the time you reach 60. In order to draw an annual income of \$50,000 from then on, without end, if we assume an APR of 6%, then the amount saved must satisfy $A \times 0.06 = \$50,000$. Hence, $A = \frac{\$50,000}{0.06} = \$833,333$. Next, in order to save \$833,333 after 30 years of monthly deposits at 6%, you must deposit

$$\frac{\$833,333 \times \frac{0.06}{12}}{(1+\frac{0.06}{12})^{12\times 30}-1} = \$829.59$$

each month.

Total and Annual Returns.

Recall:

$$\text{total return} = \frac{A-P}{P},$$

$$\text{annual return} = \left(\frac{A}{P}\right)^{\frac{1}{Y}} - 1.$$

49. Since 100 shares of the stock in question cost you \$5500, and you sold the stock after five years for \$10,300, the total return was $\frac{10300-5500}{5500} \approx 87.3\%$, and the annual return was about

$$\left(\frac{10300}{5500}\right)^{\frac{1}{5}} - 1 \approx 13.4\%.$$

51. Since the shares cost you \$5500, and you receive \$11,300 for them after 10 years, the total return was $\frac{11300-5500}{5500} = 1.0545 = 105.45\%$, and the annual return was

$$\left(\frac{11300}{5500}\right)^{\frac{1}{10}} - 1 \approx 7.5\%.$$

53. Since the shares cost you \$4500, and you only receive \$2500 for them after 3 years, the total return was $\frac{2500-4500}{4500} \approx -44.44\%$ (a loss), and the annual return was about

$$\left(\frac{2500}{4500}\right)^{\frac{1}{3}} - 1 \approx -17.8\%.$$

55. Since the shares cost you \$7500, and you sold the stock after 8 years for \$12,600, the total return was $\frac{12600-7500}{7500} = 0.6800 = 68.00\%$, and the annual return was

$$\left(\frac{12600}{7500}\right)^{\frac{1}{8}} - 1 \approx 6.7\%.$$

57. **Historical Returns.** Investing \$500 for 70 years (starting in 1930) in small-company stocks, whose average annual return over the period in question was 12.4%, yields $\$500 \times (1+0.124)^{70}$, which is roughly \$1,789,006. Investing in large-company stocks, whose average annual return over the period in question was 11.1%, yields $\$500 \times (1+0.111)^{70}$, which is roughly \$792,418. Investing in long-term corporate bonds, whose average annual return over the period in question was only 5.6%, yields $\$500 \times (1+0.056)^{70}$, which is roughly \$22,670. Investing in U.S. Treasury bills, whose average annual return over the period in question was a mere 3.8%, yields $\$500 \times (1+0.038)^{70}$, which is roughly \$6804.

Reading Stock Tables.

59. Closing at \$24.42, Maytag (MTG) had the largest gain, \$0.31. The closing price two days ago was $\$24.42 - 0.31 = \$24.11$.

61. Of the four stocks, Monsanto had the smallest gap between 52-week high and trading prices yesterday. They had a 52-week high of \$22.60 and traded as high as \$21.86 yesterday. (Note:

It is incidental that the high yesterday was closest to the 52-week high; it might just as well have been the low that came closest.)

63. The dividend for Monsanto is paying \$0.52 per share annually, so if you own 1000 shares, your dividend is $1000 \times 0.52 = \$520$.

65. Maytag has the highest yield. That is, that stock has the highest rate of return in dividends of the four.

Price-to-Earning Ratio.

67. a. Yes, Maytag earned a profit last year because its PE ratio is 12. This means that the stock is currently selling at 12 times the profit per share.
b. $\frac{\text{share price}}{\text{PE ratio}} = \frac{24.42}{12} = \$2.04$.
c. A PE ratio of 12 - 14 is typical performance for reasonably priced stocks, so this stock is neither expensive nor cheap.

69. a. No, the dd in the PE ratio column means that Motorola is operating at a loss.
b. No information available to determine losses.
c. Not applicable.

71. a. Yes Mueller Industries earned a profit last year because its PE ratio is 16. This means that the stock is currently selling at 16 times the profit per share.
b. $\frac{\text{share price}}{\text{PE ratio}} = \frac{27.11}{16} = \$1.69$.
c. A PE ratio of 16 is over the 12 - 14 range, but not by much. So this stock is neither expensive nor cheap.

Bond Yields. Recall that

$$\text{current yield} = \frac{\text{annual interest}}{\text{current price}}.$$

73. The current yield of a \$1000 Treasury Bond with a coupon rate of 2% and a market value of \$950 is $\frac{0.02 \times \$1000}{\$950} \approx 2.11\%$.

75. The current yield of a \$1000 Treasury Bond with a coupon rate of 5.5% and a market value of \$1100 is $\frac{0.055 \times \$1000}{\$1100} = 5\%$.

Bond Interest. Recall that

$$\text{annual interest} = \text{current yield} \times \text{current price}.$$

77. The annual interest on a \$1000 Treasury Bond with a current yield of 3.9% that is quoted at 105 points is $3.9\% \times (105\% \times \$1000) = \$40.95$.

79. The annual interest on a \$1000 Treasury Bond with a current yield of 6.2% that is quoted at 114.3 points is $6.2\% \times (114.3\% \times \$1000) = \$70.87$.

81. **Mutual Fund Growth.** If you invested \$500 in SocInvBdA 3 years ago, and reinvested all dividends and gains, then since the annual return was 10% according to Figure 4.6 (see the 3-Year column in the SocInvBdA entry), your investment would now be worth $\$500 \times (1 + 0.10)^3 = \$665.50$.

Further Applications

Who Comes Out Ahead?

83. Yolanda deposits \$100 monthly for 10 years at 5%, yielding

$$A = \$100 \times \frac{(1 + \frac{0.05}{12})^{12 \times 10} - 1}{\frac{0.05}{12}} = \$15,528.23.$$

Overall, she deposits $\$100 \times 12 \times 10 = \$12,000$. Zach deposits \$1200 once a year for 10 years at 5%, yielding

$$A = \$1200 \times \frac{(1 + \frac{0.05}{1})^{1 \times 10} - 1}{\frac{0.05}{1}} = \$15,093.47.$$

Overall, he deposits $\$1200 \times 10 = \$12,000$. Thus we see that although both people deposit the same amount of money overall, and have the same APR, Yolanda comes out ahead. This is because her interest is compounded more frequently.

85. Juan deposits \$200 monthly for 10 years at 6%, yielding

$$A = \$200 \times \frac{(1 + \frac{0.06}{12})^{12 \times 10} - 1}{\frac{0.06}{12}} = \$32,775.87.$$

Overall, he deposits $\$200 \times 12 \times 10 = \$24,000$. Maria deposits \$2500 once a year for 10 years at 6.5%, yielding

$$A = \$2500 \times \frac{(1 + \frac{0.065}{1})^{1 \times 10} - 1}{\frac{0.065}{1}} = \$33,736.06.$$

Overall, she deposits $\$2500 \times 10 = \$25,000$. Maria comes out just ahead of Juan, despite her less frequent compounding. This is because her APR is higher than his, and overall she deposits a bit more than he does.

Comparing Investment Plans.

87. If you deposit \$50 monthly for 15 years at 7%, you will end up with

$$A = \$50 \times \frac{(1 + \frac{0.07}{12})^{12\times 15} - 1}{\frac{0.07}{12}} = \$15,848.11,$$

which is considerably short of your desired goal of \$50,000. This investment plan is far from adequate.

89. If you deposit \$100 monthly for 15 years at 6%, you will end up with

$$A = \$100 \times \frac{(1 + \frac{0.06}{12})^{12\times 15} - 1}{\frac{0.06}{12}} = \$29,081.87,$$

which is still short of your desired goal of \$50,000. This investment plan is far from adequate.

91. **Total Return on Stock.** If you bought Mossimo stock 1 year ago for \$5.80 per share and sell it at the closing price of \$8.25 per share, then since no dividends were paid on this stock, your absolute gain per share equals your capital gain per share less your commission. This comes out to be $\$8.25 - \$5.80 - \$0.25 = \$2.20$. The total return is the relative gain per share: $\frac{\$2.20}{\$5.80} \approx = 37.9\%$.

93. **Death and the Maven (A True Story).** Since a \$5000 nest egg turned into a \$22 million fortune over a period of 50 years, the total return was $\frac{22,000,000-5000}{5000} = 4399 = 439,900\%$— in other words her nest egg grew *by a factor of over 400!* The annual return was

$$\left(\frac{22,000,000}{5000}\right)^{\frac{1}{50}} - 1 \approx 18.3\%.$$

Unit 4C

Does It Make Sense?

7. Makes sense. This is often the case in the early years of a long-term loan.

9. Does not make sense. If you only make the minimum payments, your credit card debt will grow with time, which means your financial situation will worsen. If it worsens enough, you won't have ANY of your own money to keep.

11. Makes sense. By the third year, the adjustable rate will at most have risen to 6% - the same as your fixed rate option. Thus, if you are planning to move, you are clearly better off with the ARM that gives you a lower rate during the first two years (and possibly longer, if the adjustable rate stays low).

Basic Skills and Concepts

Loan Terminology.

13. a. For this loan, the starting principal is \$40,000, the APR is 7%, the number of payments per year is 12, the loan term is 20 years, and the payment amount is \$310.

b. Overall, you will make $12 \times 20 = 240$ payments, and the total payments will be $\$310 \times 240 = \$74,400$.

c. \$40,000 of the payments pays off the principal, and the remaining $\$74,400 - \$40,000 = \$34,400$ is all interest.

Loan Payments.

Recall the formula:

$$PMT = \frac{P \times \frac{APR}{n}}{1 - (1 + \frac{APR}{n})^{-nY}}.$$

15. a. A 20-year loan of \$25,000 at an APR of 10% requires monthly payments of

$$\frac{\$25,000 \times \frac{0.10}{12}}{1 - (1 + \frac{0.10}{12})^{(-12\times 20)}} = \$241.26.$$

b. The total payments over the term of the loan will be $\$241.26 \times 12 \times 20 = \$57,902.40$.

c. \$25,000 of the payments pays off the principal, and the remaining $\$57,902.40 - \$25,000 = \$32,902.40$ is all interest.

17. a. A 30 year mortgage of \$150,000 at an APR

of 7.5% requires monthly payments of

$$\frac{\$150,000 \times \frac{0.075}{12}}{1-(1+\frac{0.075}{12})^{(-12\times 30)}} = \$1048.82.$$

b. The total payments over the term of the mortgage will be $\$1048.82 \times 12 \times 30 = \$377,575.20$.

c. $150,000 of the payments pays off the principal, and the remaining $\$377,575.20 - \$150,000 = \$227,575.20$ is all interest.

19. a. A 15 year mortgage of $100,000 at an APR of 9% requires monthly payments of

$$\frac{\$100,000 \times \frac{0.09}{12}}{1-(1+(\frac{0.09}{12})^{(-12\times 15)}} = \$1014.27.$$

b. The total payments over the term of the mortgage will be $\$1014.27 \times 12 \times 15 = \$182,568.60$.

c. $100,000 of the payments pays off the principal, and the remaining $\$182,568.60 - \$100,000 = \$82,568.60$ is all interest.

21. a. A 3-year loan of $5000 at an APR of 12% requires monthly payments of

$$\frac{\$5000 \times \frac{0.12}{12}}{1-(1+\frac{0.12}{12})^{(-12\times 3)}} = \$166.07.$$

b. The total payments over the term of the loan will be $\$166.07 \times 12 \times 3 = \$5978.52$.

c. $5000 of the payments pays off the principal, and the remaining $\$5978.52 - \$5000 = \$978.52$ is all interest.

23. a. A 15-year loan of $50,000 at an APR of 8% requires monthly payments of

$$\frac{\$50,000 \times \frac{0.08}{12}}{1-(1+\frac{0.08}{12})^{(-12\times 15)}} = \$477.83.$$

b. The total payments over the term of the loan will be $\$477.83 \times 12 \times 15 = \$86,009.40$.

c. $50,000 of the payments pays off the principal, and the remaining $\$86,009.40 - \$50,000 = \$36,009.40$ is all interest.

Principal and Interest Payments.

25. A 30 year mortgage of $100,000 at an APR of 8.5% requires monthly payments of

$$\frac{\$100,000 \times \frac{0.085}{12}}{1-(1+\frac{0.085}{12})^{(-12\times 30)}} = \$768.91.$$

Note that the monthly interest rate here is $\frac{0.085}{12} \approx 0.0070833$. For a $100,000 starting loan principal, the interest due at the end of the first month is $0.0070833 \times \$100,000 = \$708.33$. So of the $768.91 first monthly payment, $\$768.91 - \$708.33 = \$60.58$ goes towards the principal. This effectively reduces the loan to $\$100,000.00 - \$60.58 = \$99,939.42$.
The interest due at the end of the second month is $0.0070833 \times \$99,939.42 = \$707.90$. So of the $768.91 second monthly payment, $\$768.91 - \$707.90 = \$61.01$ goes towards the principal. This effectively reduces the loan to $\$99,939.42 - \$61.01 = \$99,878.41$.

End of Month	Interest paid	Toward principal	New principal
1	$708.33	$60.58	$99,939.42
2	$707.90	$61.01	$99,878.41
3	$707.47	$61.44	$99,816.97

A similar argument shows that an additional $61.44 is paid towards the principal at the end of the third month, and the loan is thereby reduced to $99,816.97.

27. **Choosing an Auto Loan.** A 3-year loan of $10,000 at an APR of 7% requires monthly payments of

$$\frac{\$10,000 \times \frac{0.07}{12}}{1-(1+\frac{0.07}{12})^{(-12\times 3)}} = \$308.77,$$

which is much more than you can afford. Borrowing the same amount of money for 4 years at 7.5% requires monthly payments of

$$\frac{\$10,000 \times \frac{0.075}{12}}{1-(1+\frac{0.075}{12})^{(-12\times 4)}} = \$241.79,$$

which is still beyond the reach of your budget. A 5-year loan of $10,000 at 8% requires monthly payments of

$$\frac{\$10,000 \times \frac{0.08}{12}}{1-(1+\frac{0.08}{12})^{(-12\times 5)}} = \$202.76,$$

which is affordable. This is the only loan which meets your needs.

Credit Card Debt.

29. If you pay off a credit card debt of \$2500 in 1 year at an APR of 18%, your monthly payments will be

$$\frac{\$2500 \times \frac{0.18}{12}}{1-(1+\frac{0.18}{12})^{(-12\times 1)}} = \$229.20,$$

and the total payments will be 12 × \$229.20 = \$2750.40.

31. If you pay off a credit card debt of \$2500 in 3 years at an APR of 21%, your monthly payments will be

$$\frac{\$2500 \times \frac{0.21}{12}}{1-(1+\frac{0.21}{12})^{(-12\times 3)}} = \$94.19,$$

and the total payments will be 36 × \$94.19 = \$3390.84.

33. **Credit Card Debt.** Suppose we make monthly payments of \$200 towards a balance of \$1200 at an APR of 18%, which is equivalent to a monthly interest rate of 1.5%. At the end of each month, you reduce your balance by \$200 but also increase it by \$75, plus the interest on the previous month's balance.

At the end of the first month your balance becomes: \$1200.00 − \$200 + \$75 + (1.5% × \$1200.00) = \$1093.00. At the end of the second month it's: \$1093.00 − \$200 + \$75 + (1.5% × \$1093.00) = \$984.49. At the end of the third month the balance is: \$984.40 − \$200 + \$75 + (1.5% × \$984.40) = \$874.17.

Continuing in this way, we get the entries in the last column of the following table.

M	Payment	Expenses	Interest	Balance
0	-	-	-	\$1200.00
1	\$200	\$75	\$18.00	\$1093.00
2	\$200	\$75	\$16.40	\$984.40
3	\$200	\$75	\$14.77	\$874.17
4	\$200	\$75	\$13.11	\$762.28
5	\$200	\$75	\$11.43	\$648.71
6	\$200	\$75	\$9.73	\$533.44
7	\$200	\$75	\$8.00	\$416.44
8	\$200	\$75	\$6.25	\$297.69
9	\$200	\$75	\$4.47	\$177.16
10	\$200	\$75	\$2.66	\$54.82

At the end of the tenth month the balance becomes: \$177.16−\$200+\$75+(1.5%×\$177.16) = \$54.82. The eleventh payment of \$200 is more than we need to pay this off; a partial payment suffices.

35. **Credit Card Woes.** Suppose we make irregular payments ranging from zero to \$500 per month towards paying off a credit card debt of \$300, all the while incurring additional monthly expenses, as documented in the second and third columns of the table below. The APR is 18%, so that the monthly interest rate is 1.5%.

M	Payment	Expenses	Interest	Balance
0	-	-	-	\$300
1	\$300	\$175	\$4.50	\$179.50
2	\$150	\$150	\$2.69	\$182.19
3	\$400	\$350	\$2.73	\$134.92
4	\$500	\$450	\$2.02	\$86.94
5	0	\$100	\$1.30	\$188.24
6	\$100	\$100	\$2.82	\$191.06
7	\$200	\$150	\$2.87	\$143.93
8	\$100	\$80	\$2.16	\$126.09

At the end of the first month your balance becomes: \$300.00 − \$300 + \$175 + (1.5% × \$300.00) = \$179.50. At the end of the second month it's: \$179.50 − \$150 + \$150 + (1.5% × \$179.50) = \$182.19, and so on. At the end of the eighth month the balance becomes: \$143.93−\$100+\$80+(1.5%×\$143.93) = \$126.09.

In spite of the fact that for 7 of the 8 months, expenses did not exceed payments, the initial balance has only been reduced by a bit more than half: the accumulating interest and continued spending counteracts much of our well-intentioned payments.

Fixed Rate Options.

37. With the first option, the monthly payments will be

$$\frac{\$100,000 \times \frac{0.08}{12}}{1-\left(1+\frac{0.08}{12}\right)^{(-12\times 30)}} = \$733.76,$$

and the total payments will be $12 \times 30 \times \$733.76 = \$264,153.60$.
With the second option, the monthly payments will be

$$\frac{\$100,000 \times \frac{0.075}{12}}{1-\left(1+\frac{0.075}{12}\right)^{(-12\times 15)}} = \$927.01,$$

and the total payments will be $12 \times 15 \times \$927.01 = \$166,861.80$.
Payments for the 15-year loan will be larger than for the 30-year loan; so you do need more money each month to make the payments. However, with the 15-year mortgage, you will pay the loan off sooner and also pay less overall: in the end, the 30-year mortgage costs over 50% more than the 15-year mortgage. If the higher payment is affordable, the first option is probably a better one. (Not considered here are the tax consequences of mortgage interest payments—a subject which is addressed in Unit 4D.)

39. With the first option, the monthly payments will be

$$\frac{\$120,000 \times \frac{0.0715}{12}}{1-\left(1+\frac{0.0715}{12}\right)^{(-12\times 30)}} = \$810.49,$$

and the total payments will be $12 \times 30 \times \$810.49 = \$291,776.40$.
With the second option, the monthly payments will be

$$\frac{\$120,000 \times \frac{0.0675}{12}}{1-\left(1+\frac{0.0675}{12}\right)^{(-12\times 15)}} = \$1061.89,$$

and the total payments will be $12 \times 15 \times \$1061.89 = \$191,140.20$.
Payments for the 15-year loan will be larger than for the 30-year loan; so you do need more money each month to make the payments. However, with the 15-year mortgage, you will pay the loan off sooner and also pay less overall: in the end, the 30-year mortgage costs over 50% more than the 15-year mortgage. If the higher payment is affordable, the first option is a better one.

Closing Costs.

41. With the first option, the monthly payments will be

$$\frac{\$80,000 \times \frac{0.08}{12}}{1-\left(1+\frac{0.08}{12}\right)^{(-12\times 30)}} = \$587.01,$$

and the closing costs of \$1200.
With the second option, the monthly payments will be

$$\frac{\$80,000 \times \frac{0.075}{12}}{1-\left(1+\frac{0.075}{12}\right)^{(-12\times 30)}} = \$559.37,$$

the closing costs are \$1200, and we must also pay 2% of the principal (the points). Thus the total extra costs for the second option come to $\$1200 + (0.02 \times \$80,000) = \$1200 + \$1600 = \$2800$.
The total payout for the first option—which includes 30 years of 12 monthly payments as above—is $\$211,323.60 + \$1200 = \$212,523.60$. The total payout for the second option is $\$201,373.20 + \$2800 = \$204,173.20$. The second loan, with its lower interest rate, is the better option, despite the points.

43. With the first option, the monthly payments will be

$$\frac{\$80,000 \times \frac{0.0725}{12}}{1-\left(1+\frac{0.0725}{12}\right)^{(-12\times 30)}} = \$545.74,$$

and closing costs of \$1200, and we must also pay 1% of the principal (the points). Thus the total extra costs for the first option come to $\$1200 + (0.01 \times \$80,000) = \$1200 + \$800 = \$2000$.
With the second option, the monthly payments will be

$$\frac{\$80,000 \times \frac{0.0675}{12}}{1-\left(1+\frac{0.0675}{12}\right)^{(-12\times 30)}} = \$518.88,$$

the closing costs are = \$1200, and we must also pay 3% of the principal (the points). Thus the total extra costs for the second option come to $\$1200 + (0.03 \times \$80,000) = \$1200 + \$2400 = \$3600$.

The total payout for the first option—which includes 30 years of 12 monthly payments as above—is $\$196,466.40 + \$2000 = \$198,466.40$. The total payout for the second option is $\$186,796.80 + \$3600 = \$190,396.80$. The second loan, with its lower interest rate, is the better option, despite the additional points.

45. **Accelerated Loan Payment.**

a. A 20-year loan of \$25,000 at an APR of 9% requires monthly payments of

$$\frac{\$25,000 \times \frac{0.09}{12}}{1 - \left(1 + \frac{0.09}{12}\right)^{(-12 \times 20)}} = \$224.93.$$

b. If we pay off the loan in 10 years instead of 20 years, the payments increase to:

$$\frac{\$25,000 \times \frac{0.09}{12}}{1 - \left(1 + \frac{0.09}{12}\right)^{(-12 \times 10)}} = \$316.69.$$

c. For the 20-year loan, the total payments are $12 \times 20 \times \$224.93 = \$53,983.20$, and for the 10-year loan they are $12 \times 10 \times \$316.69 = \$38,002.80$.

47. **ARM Rate Approximations.** For the 7% fixed rate \$150,000 loan, the interest payments in the first year will be approximately $7\% \times \$150,000 = \$10,500$. For the 5% ARM loan, the interest payments in the first year will be approximately $5\% \times \$150,000 = \$7500$. Thus the ARM loan will save you about \$3000 in the first year, which comes out to \$250 per month. If the ARM later rises to 8.5%, the annual interest will increase to roughly $8.5\% \times \$150,000 = \$12,750$. This is \$2250 *more* than the interest on the fixed rate loan, which is about \$188 more per month.

Further Applications

49. **How Much House Can You Afford?** The loan payment formula

$$PMT = \frac{P \times \frac{APR}{n}}{1 - \left(1 + \frac{APR}{n}\right)^{-nY}}$$

can be turned around to yield:

$$P = PMT \times \frac{1 - \left(1 + \frac{APR}{n}\right)^{-nY}}{\frac{APR}{n}}.$$

In our case, since we can make monthly payments of \$500 on a 30-year loan at 9%, we can afford a loan principal of:

$$P = \$500 \times \frac{1 - \left(1 + \frac{0.09}{12}\right)^{-12 \times 30}}{\frac{0.09}{12}} \approx \$62,141.$$

Now suppose we have the cash on hand to make a 20% down payment, this means that we must borrow the remaining 80%. Since we can afford to borrow \$62,141, we can afford to buy a house for which \$62,141 represents 80% of the cost. As can easily be checked, such a house costs \$77,676.

51. **Student Loan Consolidation.**

a. The 15-year loan of \$10,000 at an APR of 8% requires monthly payments of

$$\frac{\$10,000 \times \frac{0.08}{12}}{1 - \left(1 + \frac{0.08}{12}\right)^{(-12 \times 15)}} = \$95.57,$$

the 20-year loan of \$15,000 at an APR of 8.5% requires monthly payments of

$$\frac{\$15,000 \times \frac{0.085}{12}}{1 - \left(1 + \frac{0.085}{12}\right)^{(-12 \times 20)}} = \$130.17,$$

and the 10-year loan of \$12,500 at an APR of 9% requires monthly payments of

$$\frac{\$12,500 \times \frac{0.09}{12}}{1 - \left(1 + \frac{0.09}{12}\right)^{(-12 \times 10)}} = \$158.34.$$

b. The total payments for the 15-year loan are $\$95.57 \times 12 \times 15 = \$17,202.60$, the total payments for the 20-year loan are $\$130.17 \times 12 \times 20 = \$31,240.80$, and the total payments for the 10-year loan are $\$158.34 \times 12 \times 10 = \$19,000,80$. Adding these up we get \$67,444.20.

c. A 20-year loan of $\$10,000 + \$15,000 + \$12,500 = \$37,500$ at an APR of 8.5% requires monthly payments of

$$\frac{\$37,500 \times \frac{0.085}{12}}{1 - \left(1 + \frac{0.085}{12}\right)^{(-12 \times 20)}} = \$325.43,$$

which amounts to $325.43 × 12 × 20 = $78,103.20 over the term of the loan.

There is something to be said for this consolidated loan: you make one simple payment each month to one bank, and overall you pay not too much more than if you stick with the three separate loans. On the other hand, while the three loans require you to pay $384.08 (the sum of the three individual payments) monthly at first, this drops to $225.74 (the sum of the payments for the 15- and 20-year loans) after 10 years, and again 5 years later, as two of the loans are paid off.

53. **Project: Choosing a Mortgage.** Solutions will vary.

Unit 4D

Does It Make Sense?

11. Does not make sense. Taxes are affected by many factors besides gross income, such as deductions and the type of income (wages versus dividends or capital gains)
13. Makes sense. This can be the case because of the benefit of the mortgage interest deduction.
15. Makes sense. This could be the case if their incomes put them in the category where they are subject to a marriage penalty.
17. Makes sense. At an income of $7,000, you won't owe any ordinary income tax (because of the personal exemption and standard deduction), but you'll still owe FICA tax of 15.3% on the entire income.

Basic Skills and Concepts

Income on Tax Forms.

The 2003 tax code states that you may deduct a maximum of $3000 of your IRA contributions unless you are 50 years or older. In that case, the maximum is $3500. In Problems 19-22, it is assumed that all of the individuals are less than 50 years old.

19. Antonio's gross income is $47,200 + 2400 = $49,600. He may deduct $3000 for his IRA contribution giving an adjusted gross income of $46,600. Finally, his taxable income is $46,600 − 3050 − 7400 = $36,150.
21. Isabella's gross income is $88,750 + 4900 = $93,650. He may deduct only $3000 for her IRA contribution giving an adjusted gross income of $90,650. Finally, her taxable income is $90,650 − 3050 − 9050 = $78,550.

Should You Itemize?

23. Your deductions come to $8600 + 2700 + 645 = $11,945. Since this is more than the standard deduction, you should itemize.

Income Calculations.

25. Suzanne's gross income is her wages plus her interest: $33,200 + $350 = $33,550. Her contribution to a tax-deferred plan is an adjustment to her gross income. So her AGI (adjusted gross income) is $33,550 − $500 = $33,050. She can take a personal exemption of $3050 and the standard deduction of $4750 (because her itemized deductions do not exceed the standard deduction). This gives her a taxable income of $33,050 − $3050 − $4750 = $25,250.
27. Wanda's gross income consists of salary and interest, which total $35,400 + $500 = $35,900. With no adjustments, her AGI (adjusted gross income) is also $35,900. Her total exemptions are 3 × $3050 = $9150 and she should take the standard deduction of $4750. So her taxable income is $35,900 − $9150 − $4750 = $22,000.

Marginal Tax Calculations.

29. Gene is single and in the 25% marginal tax bracket, so his first $7000 is taxed at 10%, the next (28400-7000) is taxed at 15%, and the remainder (35400-28400) is taxed at 25%. His tax bill is 0.10(7000) + 0.15(28,400 − 7000) + 0.25(35,400 − 28,400) = $5660.
31. Bobbi is in the 28% marginal tax bracket for married people filing separately. Her first $7000 is taxed at 10%, the next (28,400-7000) is taxed at 15%, the next (57,325-28,400) is taxed at 25%, and the remaining income (77,300-57,325) is taxed at 28%. Her tax bill is 0.10(7000) +

$0.15(28,400 - 7000) + 0.25(57,325 - 28,400) + 0.28(77,300 - 57,325) = \$16,734.25$.

33. Paul is in the 25% marginal tax bracket for head of household. His first \$10,000 is taxed at 10%, the next (38,050-10,000) is taxed at 15%, and his remaining income (89,300-38,050) is taxed at 25%. His tax bill initially computes to $0.10(10,000)+0.15(38,050-10,000)+0.25(89,300 - 38,050) = \$18,020$, and with his \$1000 tax credit his tax bill is reduced to \$17,020.

35. This couple is in the 25% marginal tax bracket for married people filing jointly. Their first \$14,000 is taxed at 10%, the next (56,800-14,000) is taxed at 15%, and the remaining income (105,500-56,800) is taxed at 25%. Their tax bill initially computes to $0.10(14,000) + 0.15(56,800 - 14,000) + 0.25(105,500 - 56,800) = \$19,995$, and with a \$2000 tax credit their tax bill is reduced to \$17,995.

Tax Credits and Tax Deductions.

37. Midori and Tremaine will save a full \$500 in taxes because of their tax credit.

39. Rosa will have no tax savings because she claims the standard deduction, so her \$1000 charitable contribution is not used as a deduction.

41. Sebastian's \$1000 charitable contribution reduces his taxable income by \$1000, so he will save 28% of \$1000, or \$280.

Rent or Own?

43. The apartment rent is \$1600 per month. The house mortgage payments cost \$2000 per month, of which the interest of \$1800 is tax deductible. This will save you $33\% \times \$1800 = \$594$, so that the true monthly cost of the mortgage is $\$2000 - \$594 = \$1406$. Thus, buying the house is actually cheaper!

45. **Varying Value of Deductions.** The \$10,000 each Maria and Steve pay in mortgage interest is tax deductible. This will save Maria $33\% \times \$10,000 = \$3300$, so that the true cost to her is $\$10,000 - \$3300 = \$6700$. Steve, meanwhile, saves $15\% \times \$10,000 = \$1500$, so that the true cost to him is $\$10,000 - \$1500 = \$8500$. The true cost of the mortgage interest is lower for Maria because of her higher tax bracket.

FICA Taxes.

47. Luis's entire income of \$28,000 is subject to the 7.65% FICA tax: $7.65\% \times \$28,000 = \$2142$. To find his federal income tax, first note that his adjusted gross income is $\$28,000 - \$2500 = \$25,500$, due to the tax-deferred contribution. We then subtract the \$3050 personal exemption and \$4750 standard deduction to get his taxable income: $\$25,500 - \$3050 - \$4750 = \$17,700$. This income is taxed at the 15% marginal rate: 10% on the first \$7000 and 15% on the rest: $0.10(7000)+0.15(17,700-7000) = \$2305$. Thus Luis's FICA tax and income tax total is $\$2142 + \$2305 = \$4447$. Then his overall tax rate is $\frac{\$4447}{\$28,000} \approx 15.9\%$

49. Jack's salary of \$44,800 is subject to the 7.65% FICA tax of $7.65\% \times \$44,800 = \$3427$. To find his income tax, note that his gross income is salary plus interest: $\$44,800 + \$1250 = \$46,050$. Therefore his adjusted gross income is $\$46,050 - \$2000 = \$44,050$, due to his tax-deferred contribution. We then subtract the \$3050 personal exemption and \$4750 standard deduction to get his taxable income: $\$44,050 - \$3050 - \$4750 = \$36,250$. The first \$7000 of this income is taxed at the 10% marginal rate, the next (28,400-7000) is taxed at 15%, and the rest (36,250-28,400) at the 25% rate: $0.10(7000)+0.15(28,400-7000)+0.25(36,250-28,400) \approx \$5873$. Thus Jack's FICA tax and income tax total is $\$3427 + \$5873 = \$9300$. His overall tax rate is $\frac{\$9300}{\$46,050} \approx 2\%$.

51. Brittany's salary of \$48,200 is subject to the 7.65% FICA tax: $7.65\% \times \$48,200 = \$3687$. To find her taxable income we subtract the \$3050 personal exemption and \$4750 standard deduction from her salary: $\$48,200 - \$3050 - \$4750 = \$40,400$. This puts Brittany in the 25% marginal tax bracket as a single person. Her fed-

eral tax is $0.10(7000) + 0.15(28,400 - 7000) + 0.25(40400 - 28,400) = \$6910$. Thus her FICA tax and income tax total is $\$3687 + \$6910 = \$10,597$. Her overall tax rate is $\frac{\$10,597}{\$48,200} \approx 22\%$.

Dividends and Capital Gains.

53. Pierre has only ordinary income and no capital gains; his gross income and adjusted gross income are $120,000, all of which is subject to FICA tax and income tax. For the FICA tax, the first $87,000 is taxed at a rate of 7.65%, the rest is taxed at 1.45%. Thus his FICA tax is $0.0765(87,000) + 0.0145(120,000 - 87,000) = \$7134$. To find Pierre's income tax, we subtract the $4750 standard deduction and $3050 personal exemption to get his taxable income: $\$120,000 - \$4750 - \$3050 = \$112,200$. This puts Pierre in the 28% marginal tax bracket as a single person. His income tax is $0.10(7000)+0.15(28,400-7000)+0.25(68,800-28,400) + 0.28(112,200 - 68,800) = \$26,162$. Thus Pierre's FICA tax and income tax total is $\$7134 + \$26,162 = \$33,296$. His overall tax rate is $\frac{\$33,296}{\$120,000} \approx 27.7\%$.
By contrast, all of Katarina's income is capital gains. She owes no FICA taxes. Her gross income can be reduced by the $4750 standard deduction and $3050 personal exemption to give her a taxable income of $\$120,000 - \$4750 - \$3050 = \$112,200$. As capital gains for a single person, this income is taxed at 5% for the first $28,400 and 15% for the remainder. So Katarina's income tax is $0.05(28,400) + 0.15(112,200 - 28,400) = \$13,990$. Her overall tax rate is $\frac{\$13,990}{\$120,000} \approx 11.7\%$.
Although Pierre and Katarina have the same gross income, Katharine pays considerably less in taxes because her income consists of capital gains.

Tax-Deferred Savings Plans.

55. With a taxable income of $18,000, your marginal tax rate is 15%. Thus each $400 contribution to a tax-deferred savings plan will reduce your tax bill by $15\% \times \$400 = \$60$. In other words, $400 will go into your tax-deferred savings account each month, but your monthly paychecks will decrease by only $\$400 - \$60 = \$340$. Annually, you will take home $12 \times \$60 = \$720$ more pay.

57. With a taxable income of $90,000, your marginal tax rate is 25%. Thus each $800 contribution to a tax-deferred savings plan will reduce your tax bill by $0.25 \times \$800 = \$200$. In other words, $800 will go into your tax-deferred savings account each month, but your monthly paychecks will decrease by only $\$800 - \$200 = \$600$. Annually, you will take home $12 \times \$200 = \$2400$ more pay.

Further Applications

Marriage Penalty.

59. If Gabriella and Roberto file as a married couple, their combined adjusted gross income is $\$44,500 + \$33,400 = \$77,900$. They can claim two exemptions for a reduction of $2 \times \$3050 = \$6100$. They would take the standard deduction for married couples of $9500. So their taxable income is $\$77,900 - \$6100 - \$9500 = \$62,300$. This places them in the 25% marginal tax bracket. Their tax bill is $0.10(14,000) + 0.15(56,800-14,000)+0.25(62,300-56,800) = \$9195$.
Let's see what happens if Gabriella and Roberto file separately using the single tax rates. Her taxable income is $\$44,500 - \$3050 - \$4750 = \$36,700$ (subtracting one exemption and a standard deduction). This puts her in the 25% marginal tax bracket with a tax bill of $0.10(7000) + 0.15(28,400 - 7000) + 0.25(36,700 - 28,400) = \$5985$. Similarly, Roberto's taxable income is $\$33,400 - \$3050 - \$4750 = \$25,600$, putting him in the 15% marginal tax bracket with a tax bill of $0.10(7000)+0.15(25,600-7000) = \$3490$. Their combined tax bill filing as two individuals is $\$5985 + \$3490 = \$9475$, which is more than their tax bill would be as a married couple. They are not penalized for being married.

61. Together, Mia and Steve have $2 \times 185,000 =$

$370,000 in gross income. Their deductions amount to $2(3050) + 9500 = \$15,600$. Their taxable income then is $370,000 - 15,600 = \$354,400$. This puts them in the 35% tax bracket and their tax bill is: $0.10(14,000) + 0.15(56,800-14,000)+0.25(114,650-56,800)+ 0.28(174,700 - 114,650) + 0.33(311,950 - 174,700) + 0.35(354,400 - 311,950) == \$99,246.50$.
If Mia filed separately, her taxable income would be $185,000 - 3050 - 4750 = \$177,200$, putting her in the 33% tax bracket. Her tax bill would then be: $0.10(7000) + 0.15(28,400 - 7000) + 0.25(68,800 - 28,400) + 0.28(143,500 - 68,800) + 0.33(177,200 - 143,500) = \$46,047$. The tax for Steve would be the same, so their total tax would be $92,094. This is $7152.50 less than if they filed jointly, so, there is a marriage penalty.

63. **Estimating Your Taxes.** Solutions will vary.

Unit 4E

Does It Make Sense?

9. Makes sense. It's true for many people, though certainly not all.
11. Does not make sense. The government spends Social Security's "off-budget" surplus each year, so if that money were reduced it would cause the rest of the government's deficit to rise.
13. Does not make sense. If you believe 10-year projections, you haven't learned the lessons of history.

Basic Skills and Concepts

15. **Personal Budget Basics.**
 a. The total of your outlays is $\$10,000+\$5500+ \$1200 + \$8200 = \$24,900$, which is well under your net income of $34,000, so you have a very comfortable surplus.
 b. Your projected outlays for next year total $\$10,000 + \$5500 + \$1200 + \$8200 + \$8500 =$ $33,400, while your income is expected to be $103\% \times \$34,000 =$ $35,020. You should have a (modest) surplus.
 c. In this scenario, your projected outlays for next year total $101\% \times (\$10,000 + \$5500 + \$1200 + \$8200) + \$7500 =$ $32,649. Again, you can afford the additional $7500 in tuition and fees without going into debt.
17. **Per Worker Debt.** If each one of the 150 million workers in the U.S. assumed an equal share of the $7 trillion federal debt, this would amount to
$$\frac{\$7 \times 10^{12}}{150 \times 10^6 \text{ workers}} = \frac{\$7 \times 10^{12}}{1.5 \times 10^8 \text{ workers}},$$
or about $47,000 per worker.
19. **The Wonderful Widget Company Future.**
 a. Assuming an interest rate of 8.2%, the 2005 interest payment will be $8.2\% \times \$773,000$ (see Example 3), which to the nearest thousand is $63,000.
 b. The total outlays for 2005 come to $\$600,000+\$200,000+\$250,000$ plus the $63,000 interest payment (see above) on the debt as it stood at the end of 2004; these all add up to $1,113,000.
The year-end surplus or deficit is the $1,050,000 in total receipts for 2005 less the $1,113,000 total outlays for that year. This is a deficit of $63,000.
At the end of 2005, the accumulated debt now stands at $\$773,000 + \$63,000 = \$836,000$.
 c. Assuming an interest rate of 8.2% for the next year, the 2006 interest payment will be $8.2\% \times \$836,000$, which to the nearest thousand is $69,000.
 d. The total outlays for 2006 will come to $\$600,000 + \$200,000$ plus the $69,000 interest payment (see above) on the debt as it stood at the end of 2005; these all add up to $869,000.
The year-end surplus or deficit will be the $1,100,000 in total receipts for 2006 less the $869,000 total outlays for that year This is a surplus of $231,000.
At the end of 2006, the accumulated debt will stand at $\$836,000 - 231,000 = \$605,000$.

e. Solutions will vary.

21. **Budget Projections.** The total receipts for 2002 were \$1853 billion. A 1% decrease in total receipts would have lead to a 1% × \$1853, or, roughly \$18.5 billion, increase in the deficit, so that the deficit would have been about \$158 + \$18.5 = \$176.5 billion.
The total outlays for 2002 were \$2011 billion. A 0.05% increase in total outlays would have lead to a 0.5% × \$2011, or, roughly \$10 billion, increase in the deficit, so that the deficit would have been about \$158 + \$10 = \$168 billion.

Budget Analysis.

23. Individual income taxes accounted for 0.46 × \$1853 ≈ \$852 billion of the total receipts.
25. Excise taxes accounted for 0.03 × \$1853 ≈ \$56 billion of the total receipts.
27. Medicare accounted for *o*.12 × \$2011 ≈ \$221 billion of the total outlays.
29. **On and Off Budget.** The \$160 billion which was supposed to be deposited in the Social Security trust fund was the off-budget surplus, and when this is subtracted from the \$50 billion unified surplus, we obtain an on-budget deficit of \$110 billion.
31. **Social Security Finances.** Cut government spending, borrow money, raise taxes.

Further Applications

33. **Counting the Federal Debt.** It will take 7 trillion seconds to count \$7 trillion, at a rate of one dollar per second. Since there are 60 × 60 × 24 × 365 = 31,536,000 seconds in a year, the count will take

$$\frac{7 \times 10^{12} \text{ secs}}{31,536,000 \ \frac{\text{secs}}{\text{year}}},$$

which comes out to about 222,000 years.

35. **Rising Debt.** Assuming a growth rate of 1%, after 10 years the federal debt would be $\$7 \times 10^{12} \times (1+0.01)^{10}$, which is about \$7.7 trillion. After 50 years it would be $\$7 \times 10^{12} \times (1+0.01)^{50}$, which is about \$11.5 trillion.

37. **Budget 2005.** Since surplus (if positive) or deficit (if negative) equals total receipts less outlays, then outlays equal total receipts less surplus or plus deficit, depending. Thus the projected outlays for 2005 are about \$2135+\$208 = \$2343 billion, or \$2.343 trillion.
A 5% increase in total outlays would lead to a 5% × \$2343, or, about \$117 billion, increase in the deficit. A 5% decrease in total receipts would lead to an additional 5%×\$2135, or, \$107 billion, increase in the deficit, So the projected deficit would be about \$208 + 117 + 107 = \$432 billion.

39. **Retiring the Public Debt.** To pay off a debt on \$4 trillion in 10 years at an APR of 4% requires annual payments of

$$\frac{\$4 \text{ trillion} \times 0.04}{1-(1.04)^{-10}},$$

which is about \$493 billion.

41. **National Debt Lottery.** A simple division shows that

$$\frac{\$7 \times 10^{12}}{\$150 \times 10^{6} \text{ /week}} \approx 46,667 \text{ weeks},$$

or roughly 897 years are required to pay off the debt at this rate.

Unit 5A

Does It Make Sense?

9. Does not make sense. The sample must be a subset of the population, so it cannot be larger than the population.
11. Does not make sense. The control group should get an inactive treatment, not different active treatment.
13. Make sense. We can never be certain that the poll is going to prove correct.

Basic Skills and Concepts

Population and Sample.

15. Population: registered voters in California; sample: 1026 people selected for interviews; population parameters: approval ratings of candidates for all voters; sample statistics: approval ratings of candidates for those in sample.
17. Population: all new model computers; sample: one computer selected for measurements; population parameter: speed of all new model computers on specific tasks; sample statistic: speed of the selected computer on specific tasks.
19. Population: all adult Americans; sample: 1010 selected adults; population parameters: rankings of professions by all adult Americans; sample statistics: rankings of professions by those in sample.

Steps in a Study.

21. Step 1: population is all students at the school; goal is to determine annual pizza consumption. Step 2: Choose a representative sample. Step 3: Determine annual pizza consumption for those in sample. Step 4: Infer annual pizza consumption for all students. Step 5: Assess results; formulate conclusion.
23. Step 1: population is all adult American women; goal is to determine mean height of these women. Step 2: Choose a representative sample. Step 3: Determine mean height for those in sample. Step 4: Infer mean height for all adult American women. Step 5: Assess results; formulate conclusion.
25. Step 1: population is all alkaline batteries; goal is to determine mean lifetime of these batteries. Step 2: Choose a representative sample. Step 3: Determine mean lifetime of batteries in sample. Step 4: Infer mean lifetime of all alkaline batteries. Step 5: Assess results; formulate conclusion.
27. **Representative Sample?** The entire track team would of course be a representative—but unnecessarily large—sample! The seniors would not be a representative sample, as age could be an important factor. The putters and throwers, or sprinters, would not be representative either, as their high energy activities may result in additional caloric intake.

Identifying the Sampling Method.

29. This is an example of stratified sampling. Perhaps the IRS auditor wishes to ensure that people above and below a certain income threshold were audited.
31. This is an example of stratified sampling. People in different age groups were selected so that the survey would not just sample the young or old.
33. This is an example of simple random sampling. It's easy to automate and carry out.

Type of Study.

35. Observational, not case-control.
37. Observational, not case-control.
39. Experiment; treatment group consists of plants treated with fertilizer; control group consists of plants treated with no fertilizer; neither placebo nor blinding are needed.

Which Type of Study?

41. An observational study would be best: this will preclude any deliberate under- or over-estimating which might arise.
43. An case-control observational study would be best: since the artificial flavoring is potentially harmful, it would not be ethical to require any study participants to take it.
45. An experimental study would be best: have some people take an aspirin a day, and a control

group who take a placebo a day.

Margin of Error.

47. The confidence interval for the percentage of voters in favor of the Republican candidate is obtained by subtracting and adding the margin of error, namely 2.5%, from the sample statistic, which is 53%. This yields: 50.5% to 55.5%. Since this is (just) above the 50% mark, it is probably safe for the Republican party to plan a victory party.

49. The confidence interval for the January unemployment rate is obtained by subtracting and adding the margin of error of 0.2% from 4.2%, which yields 4.0% to 4.4%. The confidence interval for the February unemployment rate is obtained by subtracting and adding the margin of error of 0.2% from 4.3%, which yields 4.1% to 4.5%. Since these confidence intervals overlap so much, we cannot conclude that unemployment rates increased as claimed.

Further Applications

51. The proportion of people showing improvement in the treatment group was three times as high as in the control group: there is evidence the treatment is effective.

53. The proportion of people showing improvement in the treatment group was almost twice as high as in the control group: there is evidence that the treatment is effective.

Interpreting Real Studies.

55. a. The goal was to determine what percentage of adults thought their children would have a higher standard of living than they had. Population is all parents; population parameter is percentage of all parents who think their children will have a higher standard of living than they had.

    b. Sample is 748 parents surveyed; sample statistic is percentage of parents in sample who respond yes to the question.

    c. The confidence interval is 63% plus or minus 3.6%, namely 59.4% to 66.6%.

57. a. The goal of the study was to determine the unemployment rate for June 2003. Population is presumably all Americans of working age; population parameter is percentage of working-age people who are unemployed.

    b. Sample is working-aged people in the 60,000 households surveyed; sample statistic is percentage of those people who are unemployed.

    c. The confidence interval is 6.4% plus or minus 0.2%, namely 6.20% to 6.6%.

59. a. The goal of the study was to determine the percentage of adult Americans who believe that humans would be cloned within the next 50 years. Population is all adult Americans; population parameter is percentage of all adult Americans who believe that humans will be cloned within 50 years.

    b. Sample is the 1546 adults Americans surveyed; sample statistic is percentage of those people who responded yes to the question.

    c. The confidence interval is 51% plus or minus 3%, namely 48% to 54%.

Unit 5B

Does It Make Sense?

5. Does not make sense. The TV survey may have suffered from bias, such as selection or participation bias. The professional survey was more likely conducted well, and could give valid results even with a fairly small sample.

7. Does not make sense. It's essentially impossible to be sure you've identified all the potential confounding variables, let alone to control for all of them properly.

Basic Skills and Concepts

Would You Believe This Study?

9. You should doubt the results of this study. A survey of visitors to a natural foods store is inherently biased, and a survey is not a good way to evaluate the effectiveness of a treatment. It should be evaluated through a carefully controlled experiment.

11. You should doubt the results of this study. The Democrats have a built-in bias in this case, though it's still possible they will conduct the study fairly.
13. You should doubt the results of this study. The return postcard makes the survey suffer from participation bias, because people choose whether to return the postcard.
15. You should doubt the results of this study. It's very difficult to define happiness, so it's almost impossible to prove that one group is more likely to be happy than another.
17. You should doubt the results of this study. Since accident rates depend on both driver ages and on intoxication, these are both potential confounding variables in a study of accident rates that does not control for them.
19. You should doubt the results of this study. A sensitive issue like this will get honest answers only if people are confident that their answers will be confidential. Despite the letter's promise, many people will not trust that they'll remain anonymous when they provide their names and addresses.

Would You Believe This Claim?

21. You should doubt this claim. It's hard to believe that an unemployment study could overturn all of economic theory. The economists are more likely either exaggerating the importance of their work, or misinterpreting their results altogether.
23. You should doubt this claim. Nobody lives that long, so anyone who claims they can make it happen is probably either delusional or a fraud.

Further Applications

Bias.

25. There is possible conflict of interest. It's debatable if an unfavorable review would be aired on a network owned by Disney.
27. There is probably selection bias. People who vote during this period are unlikely to represent a good cross-section of all voters.
29. There is probably selection bias. Marines are unlikely to represent a good cross-section of all 18- to 24-year olds.
31. There is possible conflict of interest. It is in the interest of the company to find that their product poses no threat.
33. **It's All in the Wording.** Solutions will vary.

Stat-Bytes.

35. What was the sample and sample size? How was "great deal of confidence" measured? Which military leaders were considered?
37. What was the sample and sample size? Is self-reporting accurate?
39. What was the sample for the first estimate? The sample size? Similar questions could be asked concerning the second estimate. Furthermore, since a ten-year period is implied, the revenue growth figure is hard to access without relevant inflation and cost of living increase information.

Accurate Headlines?

41. Apart from the fact that "98% of (all) movies" is not the same as "98% of top rental movies," the summary merely claimed that 98% of the top rental movies contained drug use, or drinking or smoking.
43. The headline could be true, but it cannot be justified by the cited evidence: the sample is extremely small and there could be conflict of interest bias in the study.

Unit 5C

Does It Make Sense?

7. Does not make sense. Both State and State Capitol are names (qualitative data), so neither column actually has a frequency (number) to record. Without a frequency column, it's not a frequency table.
9. Does not make sense. The width of the bars on a qualitative bar graph is arbitrary, so just because they are different in width does not make them wrong.

11. Does not make sense. The locations of the wedges are arbitrary, so having a particular wedge in a different place doesn't matter.
13. Does not make sense. It is possible to make a bar chart with qualitative data.

Basic Skills and Concepts

Frequency Tables.

15.

Grade	Freq.	Rel. freq.	Cum. freq.
A	4	0.17	0.17
B	7	0.29	0.46
C	8	0.33	0.79
D	3	0.13	0.92
F	2	0.08	1.00
Total	24	1.00	

Qualitative vs. Quantitative.

17. This variable is qualitative. Blood types are associated with names, e.g., Type O+, not numbers.
19. This variable is qualitative. Like grades, the responses are measuring quality.
21. This variable is qualitative. The responses are not numerical.
23. This variable is qualitative. The choices are not numerical.

Binned Frequency Tables.

25.

Bin	Freq.	Rel. freq.	Cum. freq.
95–99	2	0.08	0.08
90–94	2	0.08	0.16
85–89	6	0.24	0.40
80–84	3	0.12	0.52
75–79	4	0.16	0.68
70–74	1	0.04	0.72
65–69	4	0.16	0.88
60–64	0	0.00	0.88
55–59	1	0.04	0.92
50–54	1	0.04	0.96
<50	1	0.04	1.00
Total	25	1.00	

27. **Largest Cities.**

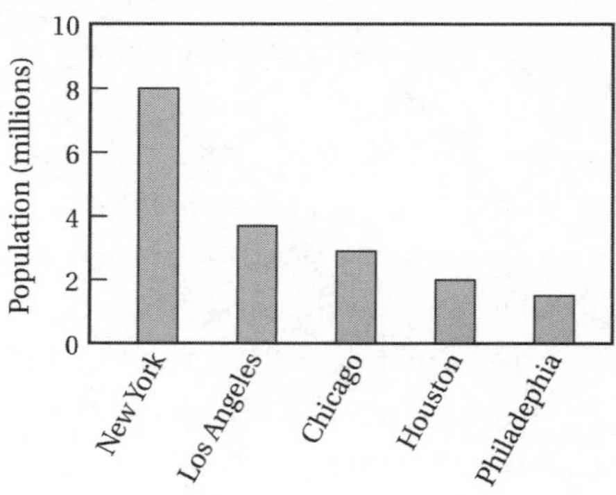

29.

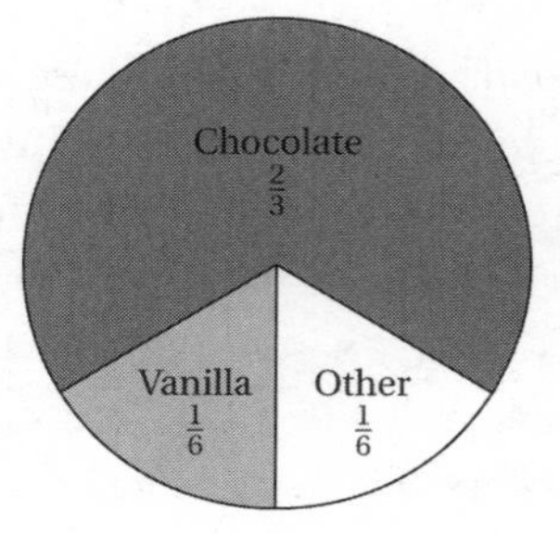

31. **Government Income.**

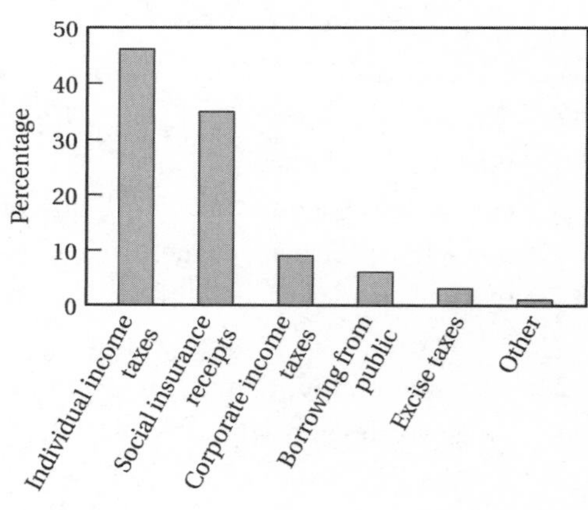

33. **Oscar-Winning Actors.**

Bin	Freq.	Rel. freq.
20–29	0	0.00
30–39	12	0.35
40–49	13	0.38
50–59	5	0.15
60–69	3	0.09
70–79	1	0.03
Total	34	1.00

Here is a histogram for the data:

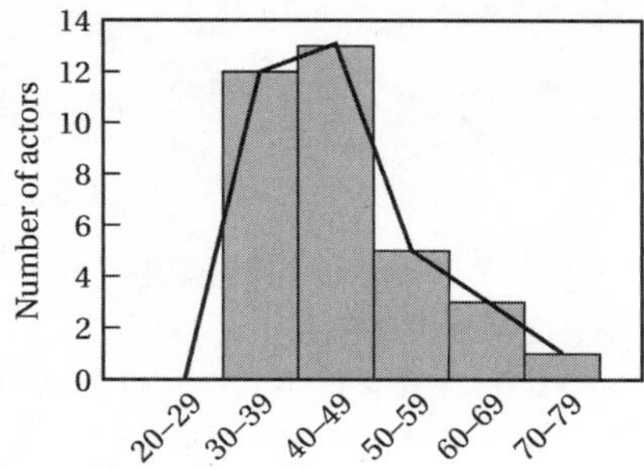

Clearly most actors win their Oscars in their 30s or 40s. None won any in their 20s.

35. **Homicide Rates.** Answers may vary.

Further Applications

Statistical Graphs.

37. a. The teams are qualitative categories.

b. Here is a bar graph for this data:

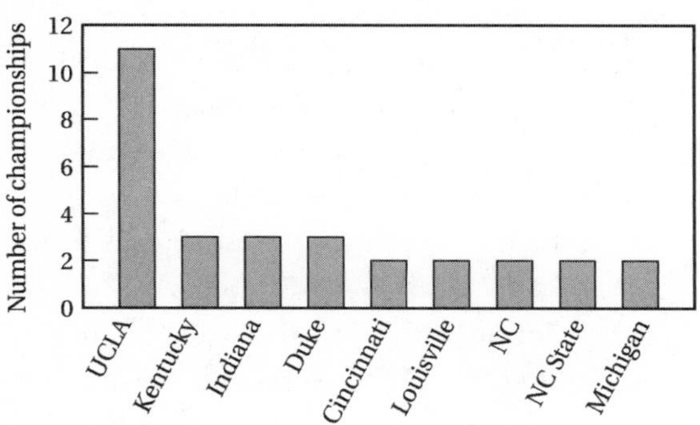

c. UCLA won about four times as many championships as any other team, and the other teams performances are all on a par with each other.

39. a. The ethnic groups are qualitative categories.

b. Here is a bar graph for this data:

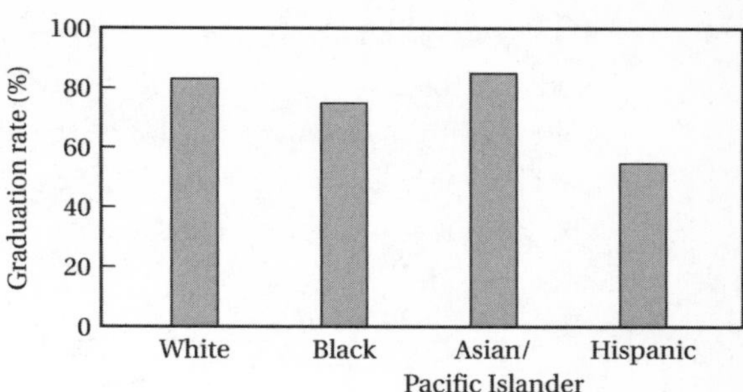

c. The first three graduation rates do not differ that much from each other; all are significantly higher than the rate for Hispanics.

41. a. The land masses are qualitative categories.

b. Here is a bar graph for this data:

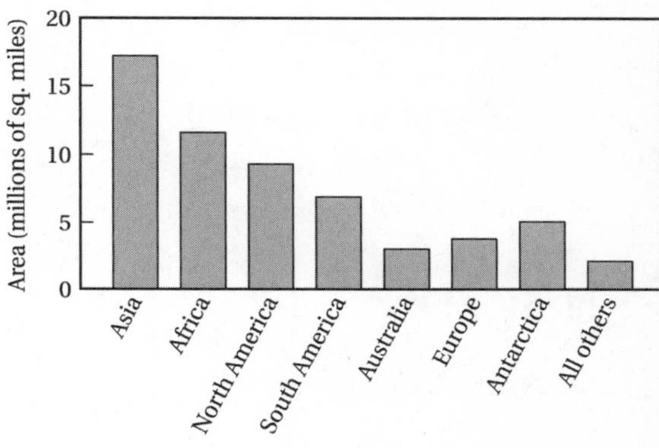

c. The land masses come in a great variety of areas, with no one size dominating.

43. a. The religions are qualitative categories.

b. Here is a bar graph for this data:

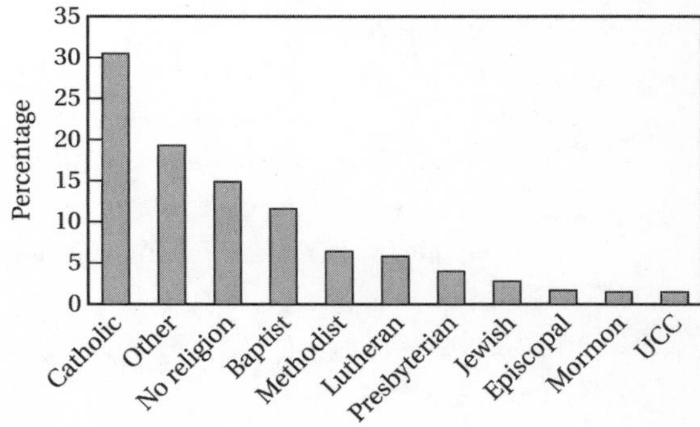

c. Only two religions, namely Catholics and

Baptists, dominate, accounting for about 31% and 12% of the students respectively. No other religion even accounts for 10% of the students.

45. a. The years are quantitative categories.

b. Here is a line graph for the data:

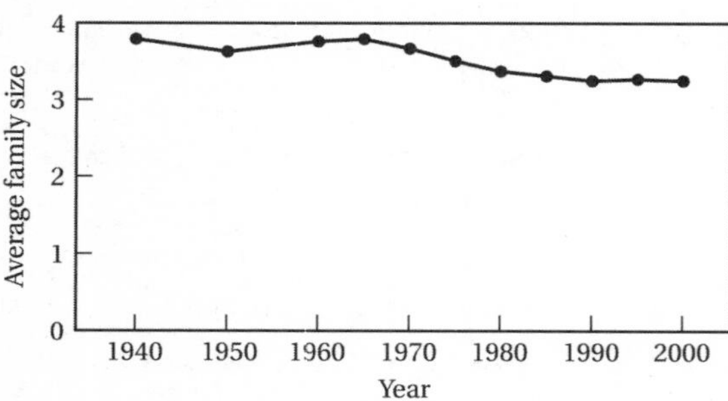

c. The average family size dropped from 1940 to 1950, almost regained its former level by 1965, and then declined steadily until 1990. There was a slight increase in the first half of the 1990s.

Unit 5D

Does It Make Sense?

9. Does not make sense. A 3-dimensional appearance does not add any information. It is purely decorative.

11. Makes sense. If you want it to look dramatic, this is one way to do it.

Basic Skills and Concepts

13. **Net Grain Production.**

a. China, India, and Russia all had to import grain in 1990.

b. China, India, and Russia are all expected to need to import grain in 2030.

c. It suggests that considerably more grain will need to be grown around the world over the next 30 years.

15. **Stack Plot.**

a. Look at the gap between the line for the disease and the one above it. The death rate for cancer increased; for tuberculosis it decreased; for cardiovascular disease it increased then decreased with overall decrease; and for pneumonia it decreased.

b. The death rate for cardiovascular disease reached a maximum of about 500 (deaths per 100,000) in 1950.

c. The death rate for cancer in 2000 was about 210 (deaths per 100,000).

d. If the lines of the graph are extended, it appears that cancer may overtake cardiovascular disease as the leading cause of death.

17. **Federal Spending.**

a. The percentage of the budget that went to net interest was: about 78% − 70% = 8% in 1980; about 85% − 70% = 15% in 1990. The width of the net interest band was about the same in 1995 and 2000 as in 1990, or about 15%.

b. The percentage of the budget that went to defense was: about 78% − 26% = 52% in 1960; about 70% − 47% = 23% in 1980; and about 74% − 57% = 17% in 2000.

c. The percentage of the budget that went to payment for individuals was: about 27% in 1960; about 47% in 1980; and about 57% in 2000.

19. **School Segregation.** There are regional differences. E.g., the probability that a black student would have white classmates is, in general, much higher in the northern states, and lower in many parts of the south and southwest, as well as in some specific cities (Chicago, Detroit, New York). Other southern cities stand out, such as Atlanta, which has a cluster of historically black colleges.

U.S. Age Distribution.

21. a. Each bar represents a percentage of the population for a particular age group in a particular year.

b. There has been a general decrease in the percentage of people in the youngest age category.

c. The data displayed here are truly three-dimensional.

23. **Extending the Olympic Graph.** You need to know the number of women and what percentage of participants are women. If you knew total number of participants and number of women, you could get the percentage in the little pie shown, but you would have the same information if you knew how many men and how many women. So there's more than one possible answer here.

25. **Volume Distortion.** While the height of the 2000 TV in the figure is about 4 times the height of the 1980 TV, the visual perception is based on the area or volume discrepancy, depending on whether one pays attention to the depth of the TVs as depicted. The area of the 2000 TV is about $4 \times 4 = 16$ times the area of the 1980 TV. The volume of the 2000 TV is about $4 \times 4 \times 4 = 64$ times the area of the 1980 TV. Either way one interprets the picture, one gets the impression of a growth factor far in excess of 4.

27. **Comparing Earnings.** Note that the zero point for weekly earnings is not on the graph. As a result, the graph is deceptive and a casual reader might come away with the mistaken impression that men earn about ten times as much as women. In reality, the men's weekly earnings appears to be about 44% greater than women's, since $\frac{750-520}{520} = 44\%$. Here is a fairer picture:

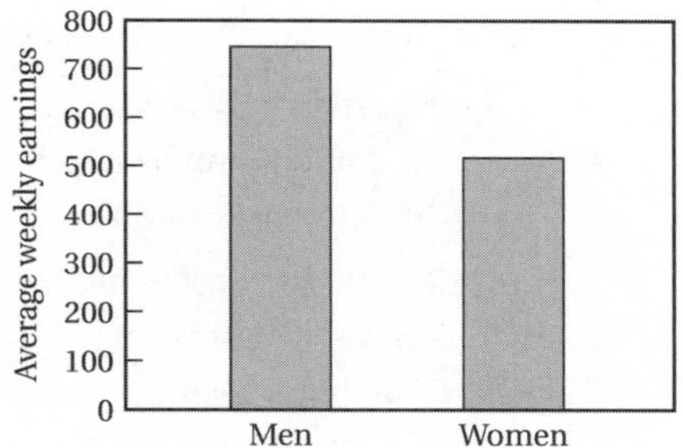

29. **Computer Sales.** The first graph has an ordinary, while the second has an exponential scale:

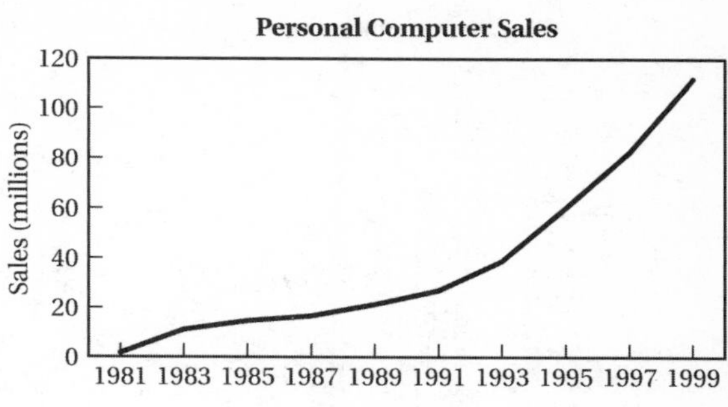

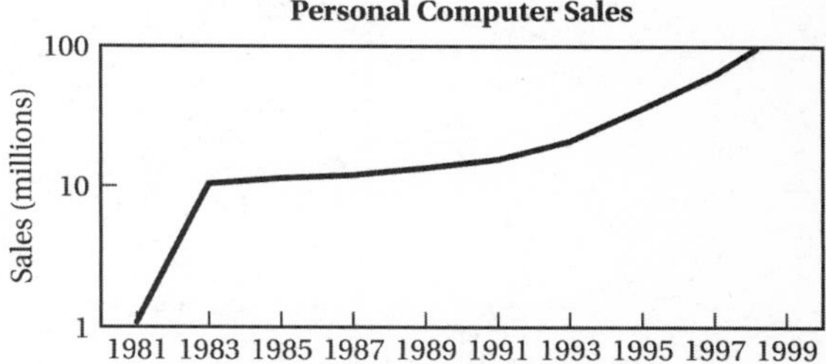

31. **World Population.**

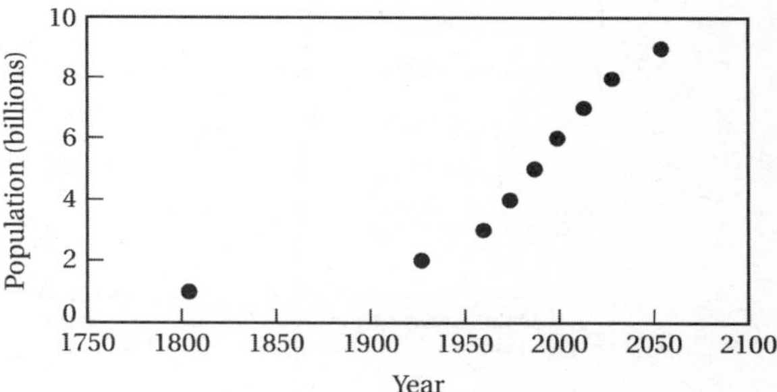

What this graph makes clear is that there has been a steady upward trend in world population in the past 50 years quite unlike anything experienced before.

Further Applications

33. **Alcohol on the Road.** A single graph can display this data:

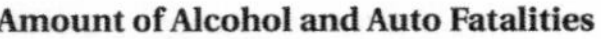

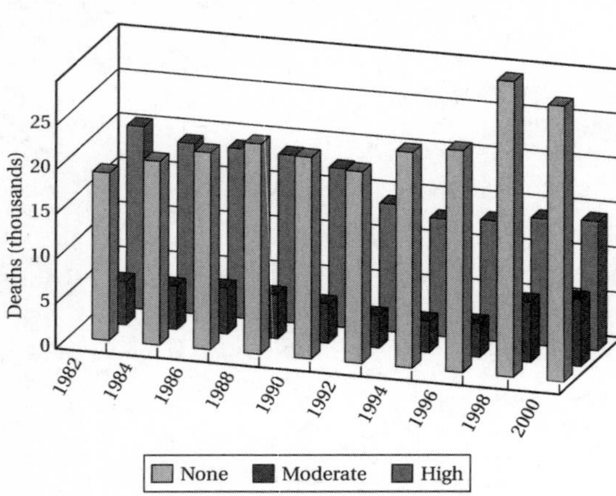

We see that over the period in question there was a steady increase in the number of fatalities not involving alcohol, and a corresponding drop in the numbers of fatalities in each the other two categories (accidents involving moderate or high alcohol).

35. **Firearm Fatalities.** A single graph cannot meaningfully display this data because the U.S. figure so overwhelms the rest. Here is a bar graph excluding the U.S.:

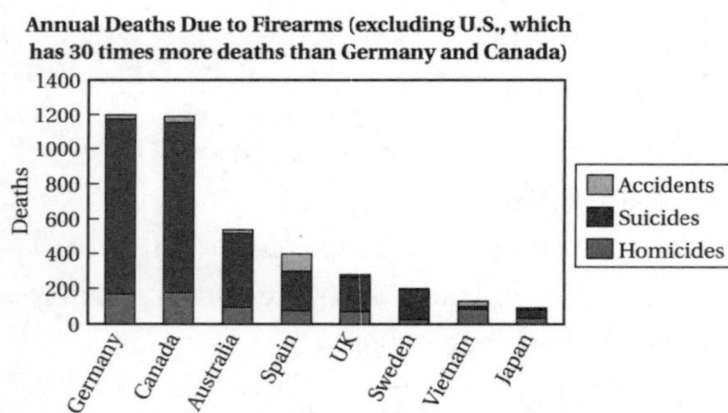

We see that Germany and Canada have much higher numbers of deaths due to firearms than the other countries listed. However, even Germany's figure is dwarfed by the U.S.'s, by a factor of 30.

Unit 5E

Does It Make Sense?

7. Makes sense. A negative correlation in this case means higher ticket prices correlate with lower ticket sales. Thus, lowering the price tends to go with higher ticket sales.
9. Does not make sense. Correlation alone never proves causality. The correlation could be a coincidence, or both variables could be responding to a common underlying cause.
11. Makes sense. In the absence of a correlation, there's no reason to suspect causality.

Basic Skills and Concepts

Interpreting Scatter Diagrams.

13. a. The variables are city mpg and car weight.

    b. The correlation is negative because the overall trend is"down". It may appear that a curve may fit quite well and the correlation is somewhat strong, though not perhaps linear.

    c. The heavier the car, the more gas it will consume for city driving.

15. a. The variables are % of income to charity and salary level.

    b. Just because the data do not seem to lie along a curve does not mean that they are not correlated. The best line through the data would appear to slope down, especially if the outliers were removed. The data appears to be negatively correlated, but not strongly.

    c. The higher the salary earned, the smaller the percentage of income is given to charity, with notable exceptions.

Types of Correlation.

17. Body weight could be measured in pounds; calorie intake in calories. We'd expect a weak positive correlation: increased calorie intake should result in increased body weight in some people.
19. The rate of pedaling would be measured in revolutions per minute; the bicycle speed in miles per hour. We'd expect a strong positive correlation: the faster you pedal the faster the bike would go in general.
21. The blood-alcohol content could be measured in percentage alcohol in the bloodstream; the reaction time in seconds. We'd expect a strong

positive correlation: for most people, the higher the blood-alcohol content, the greater the reaction time.

23. The weight of a car could be measured in pounds; the price in dollars. We'd expect a weak positive correlation: the heavier the car, the more expensive it might be.

Further Applications

Making Scatter Diagrams.

25. a.

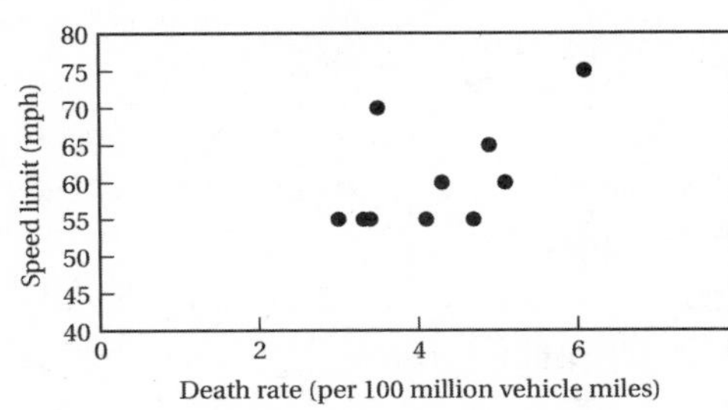

b. There is a weak positive correlation.

c. The correlation could be explained by asserting that in countries with higher speed limits, people tend to drive faster, and are more likely to have more frequent and more serious accidents.

27. a.

Percent of population below poverty level

20
15
10
5
0

20,000 25,000 30,000 35,000

Per capita personal income (dollars)

b. There is a weak negative correlation.

c. The correlation could be explained by asserting that in states that have lower per capita income, income is more uniformly distributed meaning that relatively fewer persons are very poor or very rich.

29. a.

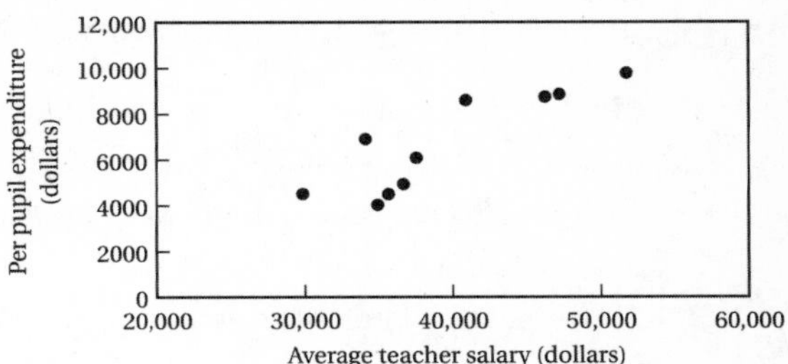

b. There is a strong positive correlation.

c. The correlation could be explained by asserting that the money spent on students includes the amount spent on teachers; ergo, the more that is spent on students, the more likely it is that teachers' salaries will be higher.

Correlation and Causality.

31. There is a positive correlation between the crime rate and the number of people in prison. This may be due to a common underlying cause: increased criminal activity.

33. There is a positive correlation between gasoline prices and the number of airline passengers. This may be a case of direct cause: people opting to fly long distances rather than drive them.

35. The cost of deer hunting permits is positively correlated with deer sightings. This is probably a case of direct cause: the more expensive the hunting permit, the fewer people take one out and hunt, so that more live deer will be sighted.

37. **Identifying Causes: Headaches.**

a. Guideline 1.

b. Guideline 2.

c. Guideline 3.

d. The above observations suggest that perhaps your headaches are caused by bad air in the building in which you work (there is a "disease" called sick building syndrome).

39. **Longevity of Orchestra Conductors.** People do not decide to become conductors until relatively later in life, say over 30 years of age. Having already survived this many years, a person's life expectancy is longer than average.

Unit 6A

Does It Make Sense?

7. Makes sense. The mean is the balance point of the data set, so it can fall almost anywhere within the data range, depending on the precise data values.
9. Makes sense. The outlier will pull up the mean, but won't significantly affect the median.
11. Does not make sense. The mean, median, and mode will not be the same in a skewed distribution.

Basic Skills and Concepts

Mean, Median, and Mode.

13. The mean is 671.37, obtained by dividing the sum of the six numbers by 6. The median is 672.2, obtained by averaging the middle two numbers when arranged in ascending order. The mode is 672.2 because it occurs most frequently.
15. The mean is 0.188, obtained by dividing the sum of the twelve numbers by 12. The median is 0.165, obtained by averaging the middle two numbers when arranged in ascending order. The mode is 0.16 because it occurs most frequently.
17. The mean is 9.5, obtained by dividing the sum of the fifteen numbers by 15. The median is 10, which is the middle number when arranged in ascending order. The modes are 5,10,15 because they occur most frequently.
19. **Outlier Coke.** The mean weight is 0.8124 pounds, obtained by dividing the sum of the weights by 7. The median is 0.8161 pounds, which is the middle weight when the numbers are arranged in ascending order. The weight 0.7901 pounds is an outlier. Excluding this value, the mean of the remaining 6 numbers is 0.8161 pounds and the median is 0.8163 pounds.

Appropriate Average.

21. The median would give a better description of the average income of all adults in a large city then mean or mode. Using the mean would allow a small number of outliers at the high end to pull the average up so that it would be not representative of the data as a whole. The mode has no significance here.
23. The median would give a better description of the average number of times that people change jobs in their careers than mean or mode. Using the mean would allow a small number of outliers at the high end (frequent change) or low end (little or no change) to increase or decrease the average so that it is not representative of the data as a whole. The mode would be significant if the majority of numbers assumed the mode value.
25. The mean or median would give a better description of the average daily high temperature for a month than the mode. If there are many outliers, then the median would be preferred.

Describing Distributions.

27. Here we assume that A scores correspond to higher numerical scores, and so appear to the right of the B and C scores in the frequency distribution histogram.

    a. We expect one peak, on the right, corresponding to the A scores.

    b. The distribution would be left-skewed, since the mean scores would be less than the median score of an A score.

    c. The variation would be small, since two thirds of the scores were A's.
29. a. We expect two peaks corresponding to two different classes of vehicles.

    b. The distribution would be roughly symmetric, since about half of the vehicles are compact cars.

    c. The variation would be quite large, since SUV's weigh much more than compact cars.
31. a. We expect no peaks in sales in San Diego.

    b. The distribution would be roughly symmetric.

    c. The variation would be large. Since the climate supports swimming related activities year round, we expect the sales to be more or less evenly distributed over the year.

33. a. We expect one peak corresponding to the mode.

b. The distribution would be right-skewed because of the outliers at the high end.

c. The variation would be large, since there are huge outliers and many salaries lying between the high and median values. Salaries below median are probably close to it.

Further Applications

Smooth Distributions.

35. This distribution has two peaks and is considered to be bimodal. It is not symmetric with large variation.

37. This distribution has one peak. It is symmetric with moderate variation.

Unit 6B

Does It Make Sense?

7. Does not make sense. For example, a set of scores ranging from 10-20 has the same range as a set with scores from 20-30, but clearly the medians are different.

9. Makes sense. The low score appears to be an outlier in this case, but this set of values is certainly possible.

11. Makes sense. There should be greater variation for the group in which the children have many ages.

Basic Skills and Concepts

13. **Big Bank Verification.** The Big Bank mean of 7.2 minutes is obtained by dividing the sum of the numbers by 11. The median of 7.2 minutes is the number in the middle of the list arranged in ascending order.

Comparing Variations.

15. a. The mean of the Atlanta data is about 5.86 minutes, obtained by dividing the sum of the numbers by 11. The median of 5.5 minutes is the middle number when arranged in ascending order. The range is the difference between highest and lowest numbers = 8.0 − 4.0 = 4.0 minutes.

The mean of the Boston data is about 6.77 minutes obtained by dividing the sum of the numbers by 11. The median of 6.5 minutes is the number in the middle when arranged in ascending order. The range = 12.0 - 1.5 = 10.5 minutes.

b. Here are the five-number summaries followed by side-by-side boxplots.

	Atlanta	Boston
Low value	4	1.5
Lower quartile	5	5.0
Median	5.5	6.5
Upper quartile	7.0	9.5
High value	8.0	12.0

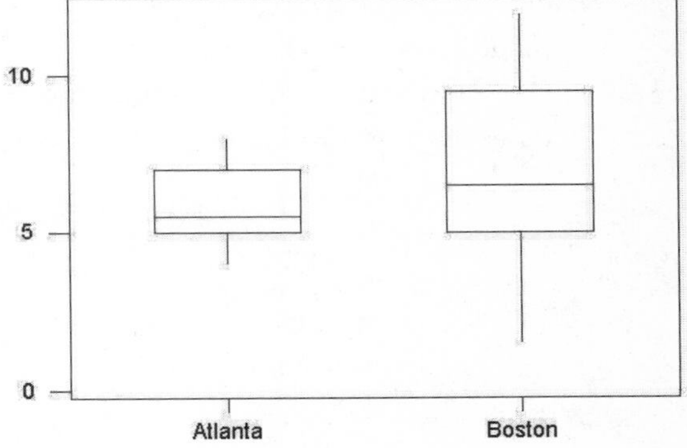

c. For each number in the set, the deviation is the difference between it and the mean (see Example 3). To find the standard deviation for the Atlanta data, sum the squares of the deviations to get 16.046, divide by one less than the number of numbers or 10, in this case, and then take the square root. This is the standard deviation and is about 1.267 minutes for the Atlanta data.

The standard deviation for the Boston numbers is obtained in the same way. The sum of the squares of the deviations is 105.682. After dividing by 10 and taking the square root, the standard deviation is seen to be about 3.251 minutes.

d. The range rule of thumb suggests that the standard deviation is about a quarter of the range. In the Atlanta case, that's 1 minute and for the Boston data it's about 2.6 minutes. Both turn out to underestimate the actual standard deviations.

e. The mean wait time in Boston was greater than in Atlanta and the distribution was more variable.

17. a. The mean of the First 7 data is about 58.29 years, obtained by dividing the sum of the numbers by 7. The median of 57 years is the middle number when arranged in ascending order. The range is 61 - 57 = 4 years.

The mean of the Last 7 data is about 57.43 years, obtained by dividing the sum of numbers by 7. The median of 56 years is the middle number when arranged in ascending order. The range is 69 - 46 = 23 years.

b. Here are the five-number summaries followed by the boxplots.

	First 7	Last 7
Low value	57	46
Lower quartile	57	52
Median	57	56
Upper quartile	61	64
High value	61	69

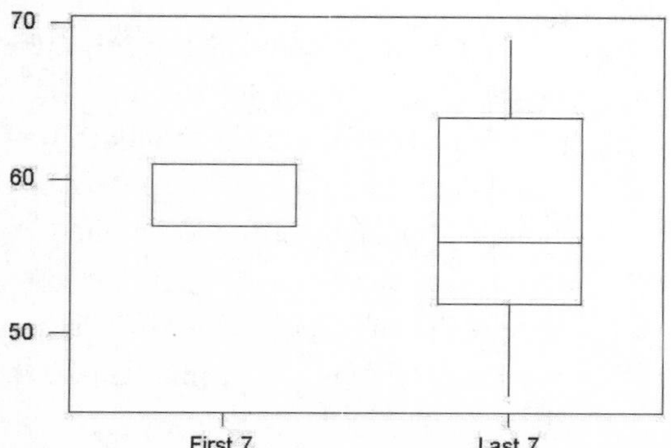

c. For each number in the set, the deviation is the difference between it and the mean (see Example 3). To find the standard deviation for the First 7 data, sum the squares of the deviations to get 21.43, divide by one less than the number of numbers, or 6 in this case, and then take the square root. This is the standard deviation and is about 1.89 years for the First 7 data.

The standard deviation for the Last 7 numbers is obtained in the same way. The sum of the squares of the deviations is 363.72. After dividing by 6 and taking the square root, the standard deviation is seen to be about 7.793 years.

d. The range rule of thumb suggests the standard deviation is about one quarter of the range. For the First 7 data this is 1 year and for the Last 7 data it is 5.75 years. Both underestimate the actual standard deviation.

e. The ages (at inauguration) of the First 7 U.S. presidents was on average no different than the Last 7, but the variation was much smaller.

Further Applications

Understanding Variation.

19. a. Here are the histograms for the four sets of data:

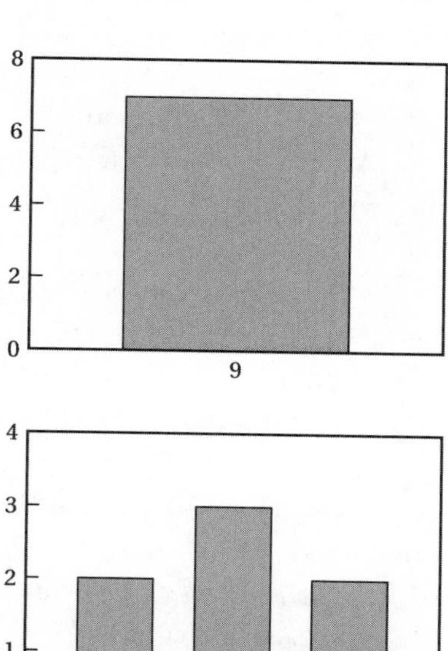

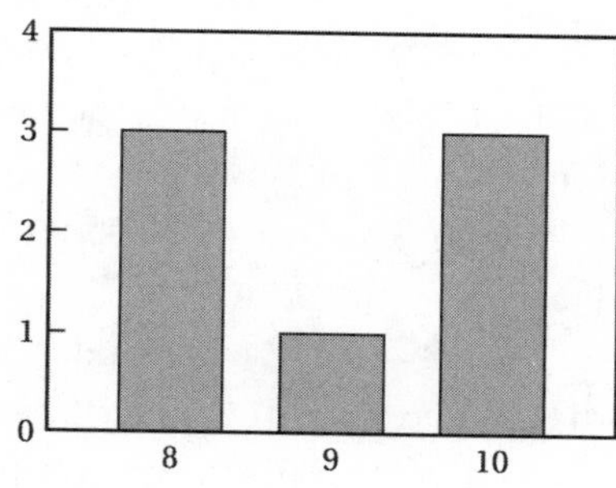

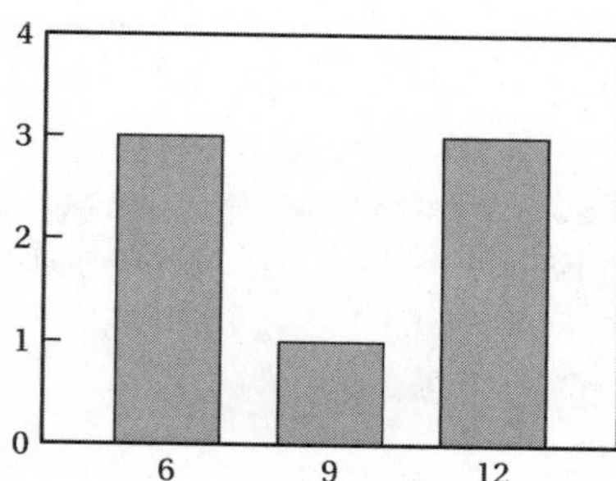

b. Here are the five-number summaries followed by the boxplots.

	Set 1	Set 2	Set 3	Set 4
Low value	9	8	8	6
Lower quartile	9	8	8	6
Median	9	9	9	9
Upper quartile	9	10	10	12
High value	9	10	10	12

c. For each number in the set, the deviation is the difference between it and the mean (see Example 3). To find the standard deviation for Set 1, sum the squares of the deviations to get 0, divide by one less than the number of numbers, or 6 in this case, and then take the square root. This is the standard deviation and is 0 for Set 1.

The standard deviation for the other sets are found in the same way. For Set 2, the sum of the squares of the deviations is 4. Dividing by 6 and taking the square root, you get about 0.8165. For Set 3, the sum of the squares of the deviations is 6. Dividing by 6 and taking the square root, you get 1. For Set 4, the sum of the squares of the deviations is 54. Dividing by 6 and taking the square root, you get 3.

d. The standard deviation is a measure of the deviation from the mean. There is no variation in Set 1, some variation in Sets 2 and 3, and a large variation in Set 4.

21. **Pizza Deliveries.** The means are nearly equal, but the variation is significantly greater for the second shop than the first. The first shop provides more reliable delivery.

23. **Portfolio Standard Deviation.** A lower

standard deviation means more certainty in the return and less risk.

25. **Batting Standard Deviation.** Batting averages are less varied today; players are more consistent. The mean, however, is unchanged, and consequently batting averages above 0.350 are less common.

Unit 6C

Does It Make Sense?

5. Makes sense. We expect heights to be normally distributed, and the values given seem quite reasonable.
7. Does not make sense. The given data would suggest that 16% of the babies are born with weights of less than zero, which is not possible.
9. Makes sense. This means she gave A grades for scores 2 or more standard deviations above the mean.

Basic Skills and Concepts

Normal Shape.

11. Both (a) and (c) are normal. (c) has the larger standard deviation.

Normal Distribution?

13. We expect these rental rates to be normally distributed because they should satisfy the four criteria listed in the text.
15. We expect these times to be normally distributed because they should satisfy the four criteria listed in the text.
17. We do not expect these waiting times to be normally distributed because the first criterion is not satisfied.
19. **The 68-95-99.7 Rule.**

a. 68% of the scores lie within one standard deviation of the mean. That is, 68% lie between 100-20 and 100+20, or 80 and 120. The remaining 32% are evenly split below and above 80 and 120; ie, 16% lie below 80 and 16% lie above 120. Therefore, 68% + 16% = 84% of the scores lie below 120.

b. 95% of the scores lie within two standard deviations of the mean. That is, 95% of the scores lie between 100-40 and 100+40, or 60 and 140. The remaining 5% lie evenly distributed below and above 60 and 140; ie, 2.5% lie below 60 and 2.5% lie above 140. Therefore, 95% + 2.5% = 97.5% of the scores lie below 140.

c. As indicated in (a), 16% of the scores lie below 80.

d. As indicated in (b), 2.5% of the scores lie below 60.

e. As indicated in (a), 16% of the scores lie above 120.

f. As indicated in (b), 2.5% of the scores lie above 140.

g. Since 16% of the scores lie below 80 (see(c)), the rest, or 84% lie above 80.

h. As shown in (a), 68% of the scores lie between 80 and 120.

Standard Scores.

21. If we are to use the table, we first need the standard score, $\frac{75-67}{8} = 1$. Looking this up in the table, we get a percentile of 84.13. This means that 84.13% of the scores lie below 75. Therefore, the rest, or 16%, of the scores are above 75. (Compare this with the 68-95-99.7 Rule. We know that 68% of the data lies between 67-8=59 and 67+8=75. The remaining 32% lies evenly distributed below 59 and above 75. Therefore, about 16% of the scores are above 75.)
23. Since the standard deviation is 8, then $67 - 2 \times 8 = 67 - 16 = 51$ is the failing score. The standard score for two standard deviations below the mean is -2 and the percentile is 2.28; ie, about 2.28% of students failed.
25. The standard score for 67 is $\frac{67-67}{8} = 0$. Notice that the standard score for the mean is always 0.
27. The standard score for 58 is $\frac{58-67}{8} = \frac{-9}{8} = -1.125$. Notice that standard scores for numbers below the mean are always negative.

Standard Scores and Percentiles.

29. a. The standard score is z = 1; from the table,

this corresponds to the 84.13 percentile.

b. The standard score is z = -1.5; from the table, this corresponds to the 6.68 percentile.

c. The standard score is z = -2; from the table, this corresponds to the 2.28 percentile.

Percentile Scores.

31. a. From the table, the 94th percentile corresponds to a standard score of z = 1.6; the data value lies 1.6 standard deviations above the mean.

b. From the table, the 6th percentile corresponds to a standard score of z = -1.6; the data value lies 1.6 standard deviations below the mean.

c. From the table, the 14th percentile corresponds to a standard score of z = -1.1; the data value lies 1.1 standard deviations below the mean.

Further Applications

Pregnancy Due Dates.

33. About 68% of births occur within 1 standard deviation of the mean; ie, within 15 days of the due date.

35. As noted in exercise 33, 68% of births occur within 15 days of the due date and so the remaining 32% are equally divided outside that time period. Therefore, 16% of births occur more than 15 days after the due date. It is not advisable to schedule an important meeting at that time.

37. **Heights.**

a. A height of 65 inches has a standard score of $z = \frac{65-63.6}{2.5} = 0.56$ This score corresponds to the 71st percentile.

b. A height of 63 inches has a standard score of $z = \frac{63-63.6}{2.5} = -0.24$ This score corresponds to the 40th percentile.

c. A height of 62.5 inches has a standard score of $z = \frac{62.5-63.6}{2.5} = -0.44$ This score corresponds to the 33rd percentile.

d. A height of 63.8 inches has a standard score of $z = \frac{63.8-63.6}{2.5} = 0.08$ This score corresponds to the 53rd percentile.

39. **Is It Likely?** This scenario is not possible. If it were true, then 68% of the first graders would weigh between 8 and 68 pounds–within 1 standard deviation of the mean–with half of the remaining 32% weighing less than 8 pounds.

GRE Scores.

41. A GRE score of 650 yields a standard score of $z = \frac{650-497}{115} \approx 1.3304$. From the table, this corresponds to the 91st percentile; ie, 91% of students scored below 650, and the remaining 9% scored above it.

Unit 6D

Does It Make Sense?

9. Makes sense. The statement tells us that there was not a large enough difference in the cure numbers for the old and new drugs for us to believe that the new drug really had an effect.

11. Does not make sense. The margin of error depends only on the sample size, so if both surveys used the same sample size they should both have the same margin of error. (The precise formula shows a dependence on the response proportion as well, but that was also the same in this question and so had no effect.)

13. Makes sense. The null hypothesis sounds perfectly reasonable in this case, and the alternative hypothesis does indeed describe the alternative in the event that the null hypothesis is false.

Basic Skills and Concepts

Subjective Significance.

15. While it is possible to observe only 10 tails in a hundred tosses of a fair coin, this represents such a large deviation from the mean of 50, that it is more likely that the coin is not fair. Thus, the observed outcome is statistically significant.

17. An 85% free throw shooter can expect to get about 85% of 30, or about 25 hits. Since 24 hits is quite near this value, the outcome is not statistically significant.

19. All else being equal, if 145 guns were bought in several dozen gun shops, one would not expect more than half of them to come from the same shop. This is unlikely to happen by chance alone, so it is statistically significant.

21. **Human Body Temperature.** We are told that if we assume a value of 98.6°F for the mean body temperature, then the probability that the mean for 106 individuals is 98.62°F or less is 1 in a million, or 0.000001. Since this is well below 0.01 and 0.05, it is significant at both the 0.01 and 0.05 levels. Thus, we can be reasonably confident that the accepted value for the mean human body temperature is wrong.

23. **SAT Preparation.** We are told that if we assume that the preparation course has no effect, then the probability of getting observed improvement in the SAT mean is 0.08. While this is unlikely, it is not below either the 0.01 or 0.05 levels and so it is not significant. Therefore, we cannot conclude with any confidence that the preparation course is effective at improving SAT scores.

Margin of Error.

25. For a poll of 1012 people, the margin of error is $\frac{1}{\sqrt{1012}} \approx 0.0314 = 3.14\%$. So the 95% confidence interval is 32-3.14% to 32+3.14%, or 28.86% to 35.14%. In other words, we can be 95% confident that the true proportion of Americans that keep a dog for protection is between roughly 29% and 35%.

27. For a poll of 513 people, the margin of error is $\frac{1}{\sqrt{513}} \approx 0.0442 = 4.42\%$. So the 95% confidence interval is 69-4.42% to 69+4.42%, or 64.58% to 73.42%. This means that we can be 95% confident that the true proportion of people who have flown in the last year and were satisfied with airline service is between roughly 65% and 73%.

29. For a poll of 1012 people, the margin of error is $\frac{1}{\sqrt{1012}} \approx 0.0314 = 3.14\%$. So the 95% confidence interval is 62-3.14% to 62+3.14%, or 58.86% to 65.14%. This means that we can be 95% confident that the true proportion of American workers age 18 or over who have Internet access at work and use it for personal reasons at least once a day is between roughly 59% and 65%.

31. For a poll of 1012 people, the margin of error is $\frac{1}{\sqrt{1012}} \approx 0.0314 = 3.14\%$. So the 95% confidence interval is 37-3.14% to 37+3.14%, or 33.86% to 40.14%. This means that we can be 95% confident that the true proportion of women who would prefer to spend their leisure time working on a home improvement project is between roughly 34% and 40%.

Formulating Hypotheses.

33. *Null hypothesis*: mean SAT score = 500.
Alternative hypothesis: mean SAT score is greater than 500.
Rejecting the null hypothesis means that there is evidence that SAT scores in the school are greater than 500. Failing to reject the null hypothesis means that there is insufficient evidence to conclude that SAT scores in the school are greater than 500.

35. *Null hypothesis*: amount of preservative = advertised amount.
Alternative hypothesis: amount of preservative exceeds the advertised amount .
Rejecting the null hypothesis means that there is evidence that the amount of preservative exceeds the advertised amount. Failing to reject the null hypothesis means that there is insufficient evidence to conclude that the amount of preservative exceeds the advertised amount.

37. *Null hypothesis*: yield = 540 bushels per acre.
Alternative hypothesis: yield exceeds 540 bushels per acre.
Rejecting the null hypothesis means that there is evidence that the yield exceeds 540 bushels per acre. Failing to reject the null hypothesis means that there is insufficient evidence to conclude that the yield exceeds 540 bushels per acre.

Hypothesis Tests.

39. *Null hypothesis*: mean annual mileage of cars in the fleet = 11,725 miles.
    Alternative hypothesis: mean annual mileage of cars in the fleet exceeds 11,725 miles.
    Since the probability that the owner had a sample with mean at least 12,000 is 0.01, there is strong evidence to reject the null hypothesis.
41. *Null hypothesis*: mean stay = 2.1 days.
    Alternative hypothesis: mean stay exceeds 2.1 days.
    The probability of observing a mean of at least 2.3 days is 0.17. This is greater than 0.05 so there is no evidence to reject the null hypothesis.
43. *Null hypothesis*: mean income = $40,000.
    Alternative hypothesis: mean income exceeds $40,000.
    The probability of observing a mean which is at least $41,182 is 0.007 which is less than 0.01. There is strong evidence to reject the null hypothesis.

Further Applications

45. **Nielsen Ratings.** For a sample of 13,000 people, the margin of error is $\frac{1}{\sqrt{13{,}000}} \approx 0.0088 =$ 0.88%. So the 95% confidence interval is 35-0.88% to 35+0.88%, or 34.12% to 35.88%. This means that we can be 95% confident that the true proportion of the TV audience who watched NFL Monday Night Football was between about 34.1% and 35.9%.
47. **Better Margin of Error.** For a sample of n people, the margin of error is roughly $\frac{1}{\sqrt{n}}$ and for a sample of 4n people the margin of error is $\frac{1}{\sqrt{4n}} = \frac{1}{2\sqrt{n}}$. So to halve the margin of error, one should quadruple the sample size.
49. **Gallup Description.**
    A sample of 1019 people has a margin of error $\frac{1}{\sqrt{1019}} \approx 0.0313 = 3.13\%$. So the given margin of error of 3% is consistent with the sample size.

Unit 7A

Does It Make Sense?

7. Makes sense. The outcomes that represent the event of 1H, 3T are HTTT, THTT, TTHT, and TTTH.
9. Makes sense. This is a subjective probability, and there is no reason to doubt this subjective estimate.
11. Does not make sense. The probabilities of winning and not winning must total to exactly 1.

Basic Skills and Concepts

Review of the Multiplication Principle.

13. There are 8 color selections to be made, and 3 style selections, so the total number of choices of car is $8 \times 3 = 24$.
15. There are 3 modes (AM, FM1, or FM2) for each button, and 6 buttons, so the total number of radio stations you can preset is $3 \times 6 = 18$.
17. There are 8 colors for each pattern, and 4 patterns, so the total number of wallpaper styles available is $8 \times 4 = 32$.
19. There are 6 TV sets, and 5 VCR players, so the total number of TV/VCR systems you can assemble is $6 \times 5 = 30$.

Theoretical Probabilities.

21. Each possible last digit represents an outcome, so there are 10 possible outcomes. It's reasonable to assume that these are equally likely outcomes. Only one of these—namely the digit 0—represents an event of interest, so the probability of meeting somebody with a phone number that ends in 0 is $\frac{1}{10} = 0.1$.
23. Each possibility {BB,BG,GB,GG} represents an outcome—e.g., BG denotes a boy followed by a girl—so there are 4 possible outcomes. If we assume that these are equally likely outcomes, then since only one of these—namely, GG—represents an event of interest, the probability of a randomly selected two-child family having two girls is $\frac{1}{4} = 0.25$.
25. There are 36 equally likely outcomes, namely $\{(1,1),(1,2),\ldots,(1,6),(2,1),(2,2),\ldots, (6,6)\}$, where, e.g., (2,1) denotes 2 on the first die and 1 on the second die. Since rolling a sum of 5 corresponds to one of the 4 outcomes $\{(1,4),(2,3),(3,2),(4,1)\}$, the probability of rolling a sum of 5 on a roll of two dice is $\frac{4}{36} \approx 0.111$.
27. There are 22 possible outcomes, since there are 22 pairs of socks. Assuming these are equally likely outcomes, 6 of these (the blue ones) are of interest, so the probability of selecting a pair of blue socks from the drawer is $\frac{6}{22} \approx 0.2727$.

Empirical Probabilities.

29. Based on the observation of 12 correct forecasts out of the last 30, the empirical probability of his next forecast being correct is $\frac{12}{30} = 0.4$.
31. Based on the observation of hitting 86% of the past free throws, so far this year, the empirical probability of her next free throw being successful is 0.86.
33. Based on the 34 observed correct diagnoses out of 100, the empirical probability of his diagnosis being correct is $\frac{34}{100} = 0.34$.

Subjective Probability.

35. Answers will vary.

Event Not Occurring.

37. The probability of rolling a 4 with a fair die is $\frac{1}{6}$, and so the probability of not rolling a 4 is $1 - \frac{1}{6} = \frac{5}{6} \approx 0.833$.
39. The probability that a 76% free shooter will be successful on his next free throw is 0.76, so the probability that he will miss his next free throw is $1 - 0.76 = 0.24$.
41. There are 36 equally likely outcomes, $\{(1,1),(1,2),\ldots, (1,6),(2,1),(2,2), \ldots,(6,6)\}$, and rolling a sum of 7 corresponds to one of the 6 outcomes $\{(1,6),(2,5),(3,4),(4,3),(5,2), (6,1)\}$, so that the probability of rolling a sum of 7 is $\frac{6}{36}$, and the probability of not rolling a sum of 7 is $1 - \frac{6}{36} = \frac{30}{36} \approx 0.833$.
43. The probability of rolling an odd number with a fair die is $\frac{3}{6}$, since 3 outcomes (namely 1, 3, or 5) out of 6 equally likely ones are of interest. The probability of not rolling an odd number is

$1 - \frac{3}{6} = \frac{3}{6} = 0.5.$

Probability Distributions.

45. Using the multiplication rule, there are 2^4 possibilities, all equally likely with probability $\frac{1}{16}$. The table below lists the number of heads, the corresponding events, and their probabilities.

Number of Heads	Events	Probability
0	TTTT	$\frac{1}{16} = 0.0625$
1	HTTT,THTT, TTHT,TTTH	$\frac{4}{16} = 0.25$
2	HHTT,HTHT,HTTH, THTH,THHT,TTHH	$\frac{6}{16} = 0.375$
3	HHHT,HHTH, HTHH,THHH	$\frac{4}{16} = 0.25$
4	HHHH	$\frac{1}{16} = 0.0625$

The Odds.

47. When rolling a fair die, the probability of A (the event of getting a 1 or a 2) is $\frac{2}{6} = \frac{1}{3}$, the probability of not A is $1 - \frac{1}{3} = \frac{2}{3}$, and so the odds of getting a 1 or a 2 are:

$$\text{Odds for A} = \frac{\text{P(A)}}{\text{P}(\sim \text{A})} = \frac{\frac{1}{3}}{\frac{2}{3}} = \frac{1}{2},$$

or, 1 to 2. The odds against A are the reverse, or 2 to 1.

49. When rolling a fair die, the probability of A (the event of getting a 5 or a 6) is $\frac{2}{6} = \frac{1}{3}$, the probability of not A is $1 - \frac{1}{3} = \frac{2}{3}$, and so the odds of getting a 5 or a 6 are:

$$\text{Odds for A} = \frac{\text{P(A)}}{\text{P}(\sim \text{A})} = \frac{\frac{1}{3}}{\frac{2}{3}} = \frac{1}{2},$$

or, 1 to 2. The odds against A are the reverse, or 2 to 1.

Gambling Odds.

51. Odds of 3 to 4 mean that for every \$4 you bet, you will gain \$3. Betting \$20 is equivalent to making five \$4 bets, so you will gain five times \$3, namely \$15.

53. **Gender Politics.** There are 100 possible outcomes, and since we meet a delegate at random, we will assume that these are equally likely outcomes. Since there are $28 + 16 + 4 = 48$ men present, the probability that the delegate will be a man is $\frac{48}{100}$, and hence the probability the delegate will not be a man is $1 - \frac{48}{100} = \frac{52}{100} = 0.52$. There are $21 + 28 = 49$ Republicans present, and so the probability that the delegate will be a Republican is $\frac{49}{100}$, and hence the probability the delegate will not be a Republican is $1 - \frac{49}{100} = \frac{51}{100} = 0.51$.

55. **Fair Coins?** In the table, the empirical probabilities were calculated by dividing the number of occurrences by the total number of events (coin tosses).

Number of Heads	Empirical Probability	Theoretical Probability
0	0.26	0.125
1	0.495	0.375
2	0.245	0.375
3	0	0.125

The coins appear to be unfair. There should be about 125 occurrences of 0 heads and 3 tails, since the probability of this is $\frac{1}{8} = 0.125$.

57. **Deceptive Odds.** Since P(A) = 0.99, then P(not A)= 0.01, and

$$\text{Odds for A} = \frac{\text{P(A)}}{\text{P(not A)}} = \frac{0.99}{0.01} = \frac{99}{1},$$

or, 99 to 1. Meanwhile, since P(B) = 0.96, then P(not B)= 0.04, and

$$\text{Odds for B} = \frac{\text{P(B)}}{\text{P(not B)}} = \frac{0.96}{0.04} = \frac{24}{1},$$

or, 24 to 1. A small shift in probability (relatively speaking) lead to a large change (by a factor of 4) in the odds; alternatively, two events with radically different odds can have deceptively similar probabilities.

59. **Three-Coin Experiment.** Solutions will vary.

Unit 7B

Does It Make Sense?

5. Makes sense. You cannot get both heads and tails on the same toss, so its probability is 0. You must get either heads or tails on a toss, so its probability is 1.

7. Does not make sense. The first probability is an or probability, while the second is an and probability, so they are different.
9. Does not make sense. This is the mistake made by the Chevalier de Mere.

Basic Skills and Concepts

And **Probabilities.**

11. These events are independent. The probability that all three tickets are winners is the product of the probabilities that any one ticket is a winner, i.e., $\frac{1}{10} \times \frac{1}{10} \times \frac{1}{10} = 0.001$.
13. These events are dependent. The probability that all three people selected are Americans is the probability that the first one is an American, times the probability that the second one is an American given that the first one is an American, times the probability that the third one is an American given that the first two are Americans, i.e.,
$$\frac{9}{21} \times \frac{8}{20} \times \frac{7}{19} \approx 0.0632.$$
15. These events are independent. The probability that all five of your best friends have telephone numbers ending in 1 is the probability that the first one does, times the probability that the second one does, times the probability that the third one does, times the probability that the fourth one does, times the probability that the fifth one does, i.e.,
$$\frac{1}{10} \times \frac{1}{10} \times \frac{1}{10} \times \frac{1}{10} \times \frac{1}{10} = 0.00001.$$
17. These events are independent. The probability that all five of the next births are girls is the probability that the first one is, times the probability that the second one is, times the probability that the third one is, times the probability that the fourth one is, times the probability that the fifth one is, i.e.,
$$\frac{1}{2} \times \frac{1}{2} \times \frac{1}{2} \times \frac{1}{2} \times \frac{1}{2} = 0.03125.$$

Either/Or Probabilities.

19. These events are non-overlapping, and the probability of rolling either a 1 or a 2 is the sum of the individual probabilities, i.e., $\frac{1}{6} + \frac{1}{6} = \frac{1}{3} \approx 0.333$.
21. These events are non-overlapping, and the probability of getting a sum of either 7 or 8 is the sum of the individual probabilities, which were found in Example 8 in Unit 7A in the text. We get $\frac{6}{36} + \frac{5}{36} = \frac{11}{36} \approx 0.306$.
23. These events are overlapping, and the probability of selecting either a woman or a Democrat is the sum of the individual probabilities minus the probability of selecting a female Democrat, i.e., $\frac{25+25}{100} + \frac{25+25}{100} - \frac{25}{100} = \frac{75}{100} = 0.75$.
25. These events are overlapping, and the probability of drawing either a king or a heart is the sum of the individual probabilities minus the probability of drawing both, i.e., $\frac{4}{52} + \frac{13}{52} - \frac{1}{52} = \frac{4}{13} \approx 0.308$.

At Least Once Problems.

27. The probability of getting at least one 6 in five rolls of a single die is 1 minus the probability of getting no 6s in five rolls, namely,
$$1 - \left(\frac{5}{6}\right)^5 \approx 0.598.$$
29. The probability of getting at least one head when tossing three coins is 1 minus the probability of getting no heads in three tosses, namely,
$$1 - \left(\frac{1}{2}\right)^3 = 0.875.$$
31. The probability of getting rain at least once in five days is 1 minus the probability of not getting rain on each of the five days, namely,
$$1 - (1 - 0.2)^5 \approx 0.672.$$
33. The probability of drawing at least one king in 20 draws is 1 minus the probability of not drawing a king on each of the 20 draws, namely,
$$1 - \left(1 - \frac{4}{52}\right)^{20} \approx 0.798.$$

Further Applications

35. **Probability and Court.**

a. These events are overlapping, and the probability that a randomly selected defendant either pled guilty or was sent to prison is the sum of the individual probabilities minus the probability that the person pled guilty and was sent to prison, i.e.,

$$\frac{392+564}{1028}+\frac{392+58}{1028}-\frac{392}{1028}=\frac{507}{514}\approx 0.986.$$

b. These events are overlapping, and the probability that a randomly selected defendant either pled not guilty or was not sent to prison is the sum of the individual probabilities minus the probability that the person pled not guilty and was not sent to prison, i.e.,

$$\frac{58+14}{1028}+\frac{564+14}{1028}-\frac{14}{1028}=\frac{159}{257}\approx 0.619.$$

37. **Polling Calls.**

a. These events are dependent if the pollster makes a point to eliminate people already called, since the probability that the first person called is a Republican is $\frac{25}{45}$, and the probability that the second person called is also a Republican is $\frac{24}{44}$. If calls are made without regard to who has already been called, the events would be independent. The former is the more likely scenario.

b. Assuming dependence, the probability that the first two calls are to Republicans is

$$\frac{25}{45}\times\frac{24}{44}\approx 0.303$$

c. Assuming independence, the probability that the first two calls are to Republicans is

$$\frac{25}{45}\times\frac{25}{45}\approx 0.309$$

d. The answers are very close (this is because the list of names is fairly large, the difference gets less noticeable for very long lists but is significant for very short ones).

39. **Better Bet for the Chevalier.** The probability of rolling at least one double-6 in 25 tries is

$$1-\left(1-\frac{1}{36}\right)^{25}\approx 0.506,$$

which is just over 50%. Hence, had he made his bet for 25 rather than 24 rolls, he would have had a slight edge, and over time he would have won money.

41. **Miami Hurricanes.**

a. Given the historical record, the empirical probability that Florida is hit by a hurricane next year is $\frac{1}{40}=0.025$.

b. The probability that Florida is hit by a hurricane in two consecutive years is is $\frac{1}{40}\times\frac{1}{40}=0.000625$.

c. The probability that Florida is hit by a hurricane at least once in the next ten years is

$$1-\left(1-\frac{1}{40}\right)^{10}\approx 0.224.$$

Unit 7C

Does It Make Sense?

7. Makes sense. This just means you can expect to lose 85 cents on each ticket, on average, if you purchase a lot of them.
9. Does not make sense. Every particular outcome is equally likely.
11. Does not make sense. The past pulls are independent of the next pull. This is just a variation on the gambler's fallacy.

Basic Skills and Concepts

13. **Understanding the Law of Large Numbers.** You shouldn't expect to get exactly 5000 heads, no more than you expect to get exactly one head it you toss a fair coin twice. The law of averages tells us that the more often we toss, the closer the proportion of heads will approach 0.5, so we do expect to get approximately 5000 heads.
15. There is only 1 way, out of 8 equally likely outcomes, to toss three heads in three tosses of a fair coin, so the probability of tossing three heads in three tosses of a fair coin is $\frac{1}{8}$, and

the probability of not tossing three heads is $\frac{7}{8}$. Hence, the expected value of the game is

$$(\$5 \times \frac{1}{8}) + (-\$1 \times \frac{7}{8}) = -\$0.25,$$

i.e., you expect to lose a quarter per game on average. While the outcome of one game cannot be predicted, over 100 games, you should expect to lose.

17. Note that rolling two even numbers with two fair dice means getting one of the 9 outcomes {(2,2), (2,4), (2,6), (4,2), (4,4), (4,6), (6,2), (6,4), (6,6)}, and so the probability of rolling two even numbers is $\frac{9}{36} = \frac{1}{4}$, and the probability of not rolling two even numbers is $\frac{3}{4}$. Hence, the expected value of the game is

$$(\$5 \times \frac{1}{4}) + (-\$1 \times \frac{3}{4}) = \$0.50,$$

i.e., you expect to win 50 cents per game on average. While the outcome of one game cannot be predicted, over 100 games, you should expect to win.

Insurance Claims.

19. There are four events here, each with a probability and value to the company: a policy purchase, a \$20,000 claim, a \$50,000 claim and a \$100,000 claim. Thus, the expected value to the insurance company of each policy is

$$(\$1000 \times 1) + (-\$20,000 \times \frac{1}{100}) +$$

$$(-\$50,000 \times \frac{1}{200}) + (-\$100,000 \times \frac{1}{500})$$

$=$ \$350. If the company sells 100,000 policies, its expected profit is $100,000 \times \$350 = \$35,000,000$.

21. **Expected Wait.** Since you arrive randomly, the actual wait time is between 0 and 30 mins, and is just as likely to be under 5 minutes as over 25 minutes. It seems reasonable to argue that the wait time has a symmetric distribution, with range 0 to 30, and mean (and median) equal to 15 minutes.

23. **Gambler's Fallacy and Coins.**

a. Heads has clearly come up 47% of the time in the first 100 tosses. You have won \$47 but had to pay \$53, so you are down \$6.

b. Since heads has come up 48% of the time in the first 300 tosses, and 48% is closer to 50% than 47%, this is indeed consistent with the long term percentage of heads predicted by the law of averages. However, at this stage you have won $\$1 \times 48\% \times 300 = \$144$ and had to pay $\$1 \times 52\% \times 300 = \$156$, and so you are down $\$156 - \$144 = \$12$.

c. You need 200 heads in 400 tosses to break even and you already have 48% of 300 = 144 heads. So you need 56 heads in the next 100 tosses. This is certainly possible, although not particularly likely!

d. If you are still behind after 400 tosses, you are not likely to recover your losses. Even though the percentage of heads is likely to approach 50% eventually, the excess of tails over heads—which is measured directly by your losses—does not necessarily shrink to zero.

25. **Can You Catch Up?**

a. On the 101st toss, the chances of a head is $\frac{1}{2}$, as is the chances of a tail. The former will raise the tail excess to 17, the latter will decrease it to 15, and we have just seen that these are equally likely to happen.

b. An argument similar to that in (a) above shows that on any subsequent toss, the chances of the tail excess growing is the same as the chances of it shrinking.

c. If you continue to bet, then as just seen in (b) above, your tail excess is as likely to be above 16 as is it below 16, and so your losses are as likely to exceed those already incurred by 100 tosses as they are to grow smaller. This illustrates the gambler's fallacy, as it shows that is not the case that a run of bad luck must be followed by good luck.

27. **Coin Streak.** The probability of getting 10 consecutive heads in 10 tosses is $(\frac{1}{2})^{10}$, which

is quite small. However, getting 10 consecutive heads in 1000 tosses is more likely and would only be surprising if you had considerably more tails than heads in 1000 tosses. In that case, you might suspect the coin of not being "fair" (in favor of tails) and so 10 heads in a row would be more unlikely. Generally, the number of patterns that appear in a very large sequence can easily be greater than in a smaller one.

29. **House Edge in Blackjack.**

a. There are two possible outcomes in a single game, a loss for you (house win), with probability 0.507, and win for you (house loss), with probability $1 - 0.507 = 0.493$. Your expected value if you bet \$1 is

$$(-\$1 \times 0.507) + (\$1 \times 0.493) = -\$0.014,$$

i.e., a 1.4 cent loss. Since this is also the house's win, per dollar gambled, the casino's edge is 0.014.

b. If you played 100 games of blackjack, then you expect to lose $100 \times \$0.014 = \$1.40$.

c. If you played 100 games of blackjack, betting \$5 per game, then your losses, like your bets, would increase by a factor of 5, and from (b) above we see that you expect to lose $5 \times \$1.40 = \$7$.

d. If patrons bet \$1,000,000 on blackjack, then since the casino expects to make 1.4 cents per dollar gambled, overall they expect to make $1,000,000 \times \$0.014 = \$14,000$.

Further Applications

Powerball.

31. There are ten events here, each with a probability and value to you: buying a lottery ticket, winning the \$30 million jackpot, a \$100,000 win, a \$5000 win, two different \$100 wins, two different \$7 wins, a \$4 win and a \$3 win.
Thus, your expected win for each ticket purchased is

$$(-\$1 \times 1) + (\$30,000,000 \times \frac{1}{80,089,128}) +$$
$$(\$100,000 \times \frac{1}{1,953,393}) + (\$5000 \times \frac{1}{364,042}) +$$
$$(\$100 \times \frac{1}{8879}) + (\$100 \times \frac{1}{8466}) +$$
$$(\$7 \times \frac{1}{207}) + (\$7 \times \frac{1}{605}) + (\$4 \times \frac{1}{188}) +$$
$$+(\$3 \times \frac{1}{74}) = -\$0.43,$$

i.e., you expect to lose 43 cents per ticket. Over the course of a year, your expected loss is about $365 \times \$0.43 = \$157$.

Big Game.

33. There are ten events here, each with a probability and value to you: buying a lottery ticket, winning the \$3 million jackpot, a \$150,000 win, a \$5000 win, a \$150 win, a \$100 win, two different \$5 wins, a \$2 win and a \$1 win. Thus, your expected win for each ticket purchased is

$$(-\$1 \times 1) + (\$3,000,000 \times \frac{1}{76,275,360}) +$$
$$(\$150,000 \times \frac{1}{2,179,296}) + (\$5000 \times \frac{1}{339,002}) +$$
$$(\$150 \times \frac{1}{9686}) + (\$100 \times \frac{1}{7705}) +$$
$$(\$5 \times \frac{1}{220}) + (\$5 \times \frac{1}{538}) +$$
$$(\$2 \times \frac{1}{102}) + (\$1 \times \frac{1}{62}) = -\$0.78,$$

i.e., you expect to lose 78 cents per ticket. Over the course of a year, your expected loss is about $365 \times \$0.78 = \$284.70$.

35. **Extra Points in Football.** If the team opts for trying to score 1 extra point, there are two events: success (with probability 0.94) and failure (with probability 0.06). The expected number of points is

$$(1 \times 0.94) + (0 \times 0.06) = 0.94.$$

If the team opts for trying to score 2 extra points, there are two events: success (with probability 0.37) and failure (with probability 0.63). The expected number of points is

$$(2 \times 0.37) + (0 \times 0.63) = 0.74.$$

Based on these expected values, it makes more sense to go for the first option in most cases, since on average more extra points will be won. However, if the team were one point behind, and the game were nearly over, it might be worth going for 2 extra points, which could clinch victory.

37. **Household Size.** If we interpret the expected number of people in an American household to mean the expected value of the size of a randomly selected American household, then we can argue that according to the given categories, there are three possible events. The first is that the household selected has 1 or 2 occupants, with value 1.5 persons, which happens with probability 0.57, the second is that the household selected has 3 or 4 occupants, with value 3.5 persons, which happens with probability 0.32, and the third is that the household selected has 5 or more occupants, with value 6 persons, which happens with probability 0.11. Hence, the expected number of people in an American household is

$$(1.5 \times 0.57) + (3.5 \times 0.32) + (6 \times 0.11),$$

which comes out to about 2.635 people.

39. **Psychology of Expected Values.**

a. Let's analyze Decision 1 first. For Option A, the expected value is

$$\$1,000,000 \times 1 = \$1,000,000.$$

For Option B, the expected value is

$$(\$2,500,000 \times 0.10) + (\$1,000,000 \times 0.89) +$$
$$(\$0 \times 0.01) = \$1,140,000.$$

Now let's analyze Decision 2. For Option A, the expected value is

$$(\$1,000,000 \times 0.11) + (\$0 \times 0.89) = \$110,000.$$

For Option B, the expected value is

$$(\$2,500,000 \times 0.10) + (\$0 \times 0.90) = \$250,000.$$

b. The survey responses for Decision 2 are consistent with the expected values, but those for Decision 1 are not.

c. In the case of Decision 1, the certainty of Option A (a large sum of money!) may have attracted people. The even larger sum of money mentioned in Option B may have seemed like a remote possibility, having only a 10% chance of being won, and people may have been put off by the small risk of gaining nothing, although one's expected gain is in fact greater with this option.

In the case of Decision 2, the allure of the \$2.5 million in Option B, whose probability of being won is only marginally lower that the chances of winning the \$1 of Option A, may have been a factor. As it happens, people's instincts here steer them towards a higher expected gain.

Unit 7D

Does It Make Sense?

5. Does not make sense. In fact, it's not true - consider tobacco, alcohol, or automobiles as examples of successful products that have each been responsible for millions of deaths.
7. Does not make sense. Life expectancy is an average for many people, and not applicable to a single individual.

Basic Skills and Concepts

Automobile Safety.

9. The 2000 fatality rate in deaths per 100 million vehicle-miles traveled was

$$\frac{41,821 \text{ fatalities}}{2.7 \text{ trillion vehicle} - \text{miles}}$$
$$\approx 1.5 \times 10^{-8} \frac{\text{fatalities}}{\text{vehicle} - \text{mile}}$$
$$= 1.5 \frac{\text{fatalities}}{100 \text{ million vehicle} - \text{miles}}.$$

11. The 2000 fatality rate in deaths per 100,000 licensed drivers was

$$\frac{41,821 \text{ fatalities}}{185 \text{ million licensed drivers}}$$
$$\approx 2.26 \times 10^{-4} \frac{\text{fatalities}}{\text{licensed drivers}}$$

$$= 22.6 \frac{\text{fatalities}}{100,000 \text{ licensed drivers}}.$$

13. **Airline Safety.** The 1999 commercial aviation accident rate per 100,000 flight hours was

$$\frac{52 \text{ accidents}}{16.5 \text{ million flight hours}}$$
$$\approx 3.2 \times 10^{-6} \frac{\text{accidents}}{\text{flight hour}}$$
$$= 0.32 \frac{\text{accidents}}{100,000 \text{ flight hours}},$$

and the 1999 commercial aviation fatality rate in deaths per 100,000 flight hours was

$$\frac{11 \text{ deaths}}{16.5 \text{ million flight hours}}$$
$$\approx 6.7 \times 10^{-7} \frac{\text{deaths}}{\text{flight hours}}$$
$$= 0.067 \frac{\text{deaths}}{100,000 \text{ flight hours}}.$$

The 1999 commercial aviation accident rate per billion miles flown was

$$\frac{52 \text{ accidents}}{6.8 \text{ billion miles flown}}$$
$$\approx 7.6 \frac{\text{accidents}}{\text{billion miles flown}},$$

and the 1999 commercial aviation fatality rate in deaths per billion miles flown was

$$\frac{11 \text{ deaths}}{6.8 \text{ billion miles flown}}$$
$$\approx 1.6 \frac{\text{deaths}}{\text{billion miles flown}}.$$

The 1999 commercial aviation accident rate per 100,000 departures was

$$\frac{52 \text{ accidents}}{8.2 \text{ million departures}}$$
$$\approx 6.3 \times 10^{-6} \frac{\text{accidents}}{\text{departure}}$$
$$= 0.63 \frac{\text{accidents}}{100,000 \text{ departures}},$$

and the 1999 commercial aviation fatality rate in deaths per 100,000 departures was

$$\frac{11 \text{ deaths}}{8.2 \text{ million departures}}$$
$$\approx 1.3 \times 10^{-6} \frac{\text{deaths}}{\text{departure}}$$
$$= 0.13 \frac{\text{deaths}}{100,000 \text{ departures}}.$$

Cause of Death.

15. Based on the data, the empirical probability of death by septicemia is $\frac{30,680}{281,000,000} \approx 0.000109$, or about 1 in 9160. For death by diabetes it's $\frac{68,399}{281,000,000} \approx 0.000243$, or about 1 in 4100. The risk of death by diabetes is more than twice the risk of death by septicemia.

17. The death rate due to kidney disease, based on the data, is

$$\frac{35,525 \text{ deaths}}{281 \text{ million people}} \approx 1.26 \times 10^{-4} \frac{\text{deaths}}{\text{person}}$$
$$= 12.6 \frac{\text{deaths}}{100,000 \text{ people}}.$$

19. The death rate due to stroke, based on the data, is

$$\frac{167,366 \text{ deaths}}{281 \text{ million people}} \approx 5.96 \times 10^{-4} \frac{\text{deaths}}{\text{person}}$$
$$= 59.6 \frac{\text{deaths}}{100,000 \text{ people}}.$$

Hence, in a city of 500,000, we'd expect about 5×59.6, or 298, deaths due to stroke.

Mortality Rates.

21. The death rate for 50- to 55-year-olds is about 5 deaths per 1000 people. Hence, assuming there are 15.8 million people in this age group, about $15,800,000 \times \frac{5}{1000} = 79,000$ of them would be expected to die in a year.

23. The life expectancy of 50-year-olds is about 30 years, and so the average 50-year-old could expect to live to the age of 80.

25. There are two possible outcomes per insured 50-year-old: no claim on the $200 policy, and death, with a $50,000 pay out to the beneficiaries. Thus, the expected gain for the insurance company per insuree is:

$$(\$200 \times 1) + (-\$50,000 \times \frac{5}{1000}) = -\$50,$$

which is a loss. For 1 million insured 50-year-olds, the loss will be $50 million.

Further Applications

27. **High/Low U.S. Birth Rates.**

a. Since 46,128 births occurred in Utah in one year, this translates to

$$\frac{47,368 \text{ births}}{365 \text{ days}} \approx 130 \frac{\text{births}}{\text{day}}.$$

Since 13,603 births occurred in Maine in the same year, this translates to

$$\frac{13,603 \text{ births}}{365 \text{ days}} \approx 37 \frac{\text{births}}{\text{day}}.$$

b. The birth rate in Utah was

$$\frac{47,368 \text{ births}}{1.8 \text{ million people}} \approx 2.63 \times 10^{-2} \frac{\text{births}}{\text{person}}$$

$$= 26.3 \frac{\text{births}}{1000 \text{ people}}.$$

The birth rate in Maine was

$$\frac{13,605 \text{ births}}{1.3 \text{ million people}} \approx 1.0 \times 10^{-2} \frac{\text{births}}{\text{person}}$$

$$= 10 \frac{\text{births}}{1000 \text{ people}}.$$

29. **U.S. Birth and Death Rates.**

a. If the birth rate was 14.8 per 1000 people, that translates into $1000 \times 14.8 = 14,800$ per million, and hence $281 \times 14,800 = 4,158,800$, or about 4.2 million, births in the U.S. overall.

b. If the death rate was 8.6 per 1000 people, that translates into $1000 \times 8.6 = 8600$ per million, and hence $281 \times 8600 = 2,416,600$, or about 2.4 million, deaths in the U.S. overall.

c. Since 4,158,800 people were born in the U.S. in 2000, and 2,416,600 died, by subtracting we estimate that the population rose by 1,793,800, or about 1.8 million.

d. Since about 3,000,000 people were added to the U.S. population in 2000, and an estimated 1,793,800 of these were due to births and deaths alone, by subtracting we estimate that there were about 1,206,200 immigrants. The proportion of the population growth due to immigration was $\frac{1,206,200}{3,000,000} \approx 0.40 = 40\%$.

Unit 7E

Does It Make Sense?

5. Makes sense. This is indeed a case where the permutations formula is applicable.
7. Makes sense. This is a permutations problem, and the answer, ${}_{25}P_9 \approx 741$ billion, is indeed far to large to ever have every order tried out.
9. Makes sense. The first probability is a "some" coincidence, which has a higher probability than the "particular" coincidence that someone will share your last name.

Basic Skills and Concepts

Review of Factorials.

11. $7! = 7 \times 6 \times 5 \times 4 \times 3 \times 2 \times 1 = 5040$.
13. $\frac{7!}{4!3!} = \frac{7\times6\times5\times4\times3\times2\times1}{(4\times3\times2\times1)(3\times2\times1)} = \frac{7\times6\times5}{3\times2\times1} = 35$.
15. $\frac{12!}{8!(12-8)!} = \frac{12\times11\times10\times9\times8\times7\times6\times5\times4\times3\times2\times1}{(8\times7\times6\times5\times4\times3\times2\times1)(4\times3\times2\times1)} = \frac{12\times11\times10\times9}{4\times3\times2\times1} = 495$.
17. $6! = 6 \times 5 \times 4 \times 3 \times 2 \times 1 = 720$.
19. $\frac{6!}{4!3!} = \frac{6\times5\times4\times3\times2\times1}{(4\times3\times2\times1)(3\times2\times1)} = \frac{6\times5}{3\times2\times1} = 5$.
21. $\frac{11!}{4!(11-4)!} = \frac{11\times10\times9\times8\times7\times6\times5\times4\times3\times2\times1}{(4\times3\times2\times1)(7\times6\times5\times4\times3\times2\times1)} = \frac{11\times10\times9\times8}{4\times3\times2\times1} = 330$.

Counting Possibilities.

23. This is arrangement with repetition, and so we have $10^4 = 10,000$ different four-digit addresses using the 10 available digits.
25. This is arrangement without repetition, i.e., permutations, and so we have $6 \times 5 \times 4 \times 3 \times 2 = 720$ different five-letter passwords using the available 6 letters.
27. This is combinations, as we are only interested in the makeup of the subcommittee, order plays no role. So we have ${}_{10}C_5$, which comes out to 252, different five-person subcommittees, using the ten available people.
29. This is combinations, as we are only interested in the makeup of the selection of compact disks taken, order plays no role. So we have ${}_{10}C_6$, which comes out to 210, different six-disk selections, using the ten available disks.

31. This is arrangement with repetition, and so we have $26^5 = 11,881,376$ different five-letter words.
33. This is arrangement with repetition, and so we have $4^3 = 64$ different three-letter words using the available four letters.
35. This is combinations, as we are only interested in the makeup of the subcommittee, order plays no role. So we have ${}_{12}C_4 = 495$ different five-person subcommittees, using the ten available people.
37. This is two arrangements with repetition—one for letters and another for numerals. The letters can be arranged in $26^3 = 17,576$ ways, and the numerals can be arranged in $10^3 = 1000$ ways. By the multiplication principle, we have $17,576 \times 1000 = 17,576,000$ different license plates.

Birthday Coincidences.

39. If you are one of 10 people at the party, then the probability that a particular other person present does not have your birthday is $\frac{364}{365}$. Hence, the probability that at least one other person has your birthday is 1 minus the probability that none do, namely:

$$1 - \left(\frac{364}{365}\right)^9 \approx 1 - 0.9756 = 0.0244.$$

The probability that at least one pair of guests share the same birthday—but not necessarily yours—is 1 minus the probability that none do, namely:

$$1 - \left(\frac{364 \times 363 \times 362 \ldots \times 356}{365^9}\right)$$
$$\approx 1 - 0.8831 = 0.1169.$$

So while there is only roughly a 2.4% chance that somebody else has the same birthday as you, there is almost a 12% chance that some two (or more) people present share a birthday.

Further Applications

41. **Ice Cream Shop.**

a. By the multiplication principle, we have $12 \times 6 = 72$ different sundaes.

b. This is arrangement with repetition, since we specify which flavor goes in which of three positions and the same flavor can be used more than once, and so we have $12^3 = 1728$ different triple cones.

c. This is arrangement without repetition, i.e., a permutation, since we specify which flavor goes in which of three positions and the same flavor may not be used more than once, and so we have $12 \times 11 \times 10 = 1320$ different triple cones this time.

d. This is combinations, as we are only interested in the makeup of the cone, order plays no role. So we have ${}_{12}C_3$, which comes out to 220, different triple cones, using the twelve available flavors.

43. **Pizza Hype.** This is combinations, as we are only interested in the makeup of the pizza, order plays no role. If Luigi uses N different pizza toppings, then we have ${}_NC_3 = 84$ different three-topping pizzas. We wish to know N: some trial and error leads to the discovery that $N = 9$. Similarly, if Ramona uses M different pizza toppings, then we have ${}_MC_2 = 45$ different two-topping pizzas. We wish to know M: some trial and error leads to the discovery that $M = 10$.

Counting and Probability.

45. There are ${}_{32}C_5 = 201,376$ ways to select 5 different numbers from the 32 available, and only 1 of these matches a particular randomly selected set. So the desired probability is $\frac{1}{201,376}$.
47. There are ${}_{52}C_5 = 2,598,960$ ways to select 5 cards from the 52 available. A-2-3-4 of hearts with any other card will count and there are 48 of these. Accounting for the 4 suits and the odd card, there are $4 \times 48 = 192$ such hands. So the desired probability is $\frac{192}{2,598,960} = \frac{4}{54,145}$.
49. There are ${}_{10}P_3 = 10 \times 9 \times 8 = 720$ ways to guess the top 3 winners (in order) from the 10

available, and only 1 of these guessed matches the actual list of top 3 winners, so the desired probability is $\frac{1}{720}$.

51. **Hot Streaks.**

a. The probability of winning five games in a row is $(0.48)^5$, or about $0.025 = 2.5\%$ (a 1 in 40 chance).

b. The probability of winning ten games in a row is $(0.48)^{10}$, or about $0.00065 = 0.065\%$ (a 1 in 1540 chance).

c. If an individual's chances of having a five-game hot streak is 2.5%, then out of 2000 players, we could expect $2.5\% \times 2000 = 50$ people to have a five-game hot streak.

d. If an individual's chances of having a ten-game hot streak is 0.065%, then out of 2000 players, we could expect $0.065\% \times 2000 = 1.3$ people to have a ten-game hot streak.

Unit 8A

Does It Make Sense?

5. Makes sense. Exponential growth is characterized the same percentage change in each unit of time.
7. Makes sense. Consider Los Angeles, for example.

Basic Skills and Concepts

Linear or Exponential?

9. This is linear growth; after three years the population would be $15,000 + (3 \times 505) = 16,515$ people.
11. This is exponential growth. After one month your food bill would have been higher by $0.30 \times \$100 = \$30$, making it \$130; and after a second month it would have risen an additional $0.30 \times \$130 = \$39$, making it \$169.
13. This is exponential decay. After one year the cost of a memory chip will drop $0.12 \times \$80 = \$9.60$, making the cost \$70.40; after a second year the cost will drop a further $0.12 \times \$70.40 \approx \$8.45$, to \$61.95.
15. This is linear growth; in three years your house will be worth $\$100,000 + (3 \times \$10,000) = \$130,000$.

Chessboard Parable.

17. Square 20 of the chessboard should hold $2^{19} = 524,288$ grains of wheat. At this point, there would be $2^{20} - 1 = 1,048,575$ grains of wheat on the board, weighing
$$1,048,575 \text{ grains} \times \frac{1 \text{ lb}}{7000 \text{ grains}},$$
or, about 150 lbs.
19. When the chessboard is full, there would be $2^{64} - 1 \approx 1.845 \times 10^{19}$ grains of wheat on it, weighing
$$1.845 \times 10^{19} \text{ grains} \times \frac{1 \text{ lb}}{7000 \text{ grains}} \approx 2.636 \times 10^{15} \text{ lbs},$$
or, dividing by 2000, about 1.3×10^{12} tons.

Magic Penny Parable.

21. After 15 days, you would have $2^{15} \times \$0.01 = \$327.68$.
23. A billion dollars is 100 billion cents, so we need to find the smallest N such that $2^N > 100,000,000,000$. Trying some values we find that $N = 10$ yields $2^N = 1024$; $N = 20$ yields $2^N = 1,048,576$; $N = 30$ yields $2^N = 1,073,741,824$; and $N = 40$ yields $2^N = 1,099,511,627,776$, So 30 is too small, and 40 works but may well be too large. Try $N = 35$, which yields 34,359,738,368, which is too small. Next, $N = 36$ yields 68,719,476,736, which is still too small, but $N = 37$ yields 137,438,953,472. Hence, about 37 days would elapse before you had your first billion dollars.

Bacteria in a Bottle.

25. At 11:50, which is 50 minutes after the bacteria started dividing, there are $2^{50} \approx 1.1259 \times 10^{15}$ bacteria in the bottle. Since the bottle is $\frac{1}{2}$ full 1 minute before 12:00, $\frac{1}{4}$ full 2 minutes before 12:00, $\frac{1}{8}$ full 3 minutes before 12:00, and so on, it must be $\frac{1}{2^{10}} = \frac{1}{1024}$ full 10 minutes before 12:00.
27. **Knee-Deep in Bacteria.** After two hours, the volume of the colony would be 1.3×10^{15} cubic meters (see text). To get the depth of the resulting layer, distributed evenly on the earth's surface, divide by the surface area of the earth, which was given as 5.1×10^{14} square meters. This yields
$$\frac{1.3 \times 10^{15} \text{ m}^3}{5.1 \times 10^{14} \text{ m}^2} = \frac{13 \times 10^{14} \text{ m}^3}{5.1 \times 10^{14} \text{ m}^2} \approx 2.55 \text{ m},$$
which is about 8.36 feet. This is a lot more than knee deep!

Further Applications

29. **Human Doubling.**

a.

Year	Population	Year	Population
2000	6.000×10^{9}	2550	1.229×10^{13}
2050	1.200×10^{10}	2600	2.458×10^{13}
2100	2.400×10^{10}	2650	4.915×10^{13}
2150	4.800×10^{10}	2700	9.830×10^{13}
2200	9.600×10^{10}	2750	1.966×10^{14}
2250	1.920×10^{11}	2800	3.932×10^{14}
2300	3.840×10^{11}	2850	7.864×10^{14}
2350	7.680×10^{11}	2900	1.573×10^{15}
2400	1.536×10^{12}	2950	3.146×10^{15}
2450	3.072×10^{12}	3000	6.291×10^{15}
2500	6.144×10^{12}		

b. If each person occupied 1 square meter of the 5.1×10^{14} square meters of the earth's surface area, then we would have 5.1×10^{14} people. From the table, this would happen sometime between 2800 and 2850. (Actually, it would happen sooner, since two thirds of the earth's surface is covered in water!)

c. If each person needs 10^4 square meters of the earth's surface to survive, then the number of people the earth could support can be found using unit analysis:

$$\frac{5.1 \times 10^{14}\ \text{m}^2}{10^4\ \text{m}^2/\text{person}} = 5.1 \times 10^{10}\ \text{people},$$

which is just over 50 billion people. From the table, this would happen soon after 2150, which is less than 150 years away!

d. If we had five times as much surface area at our disposal, then from (b) above, we would have enough room for $5 \times 5.1 \times 10^{14} = 2.55 \times 10^{15}$ people. This is smaller than the projected population for the year 3000, so we would *not* have enough room (never mind food!) for all of humanity in the solar system at that point.

Unit 8B

Does It Make Sense?

9. Does not make sense. It will double in 25 years and double again in the next 25 years, which means it will quadruple in 50 years.

11. Does not make sense. Half the remainder will be gone in the second 10-year period, so by the end of 20 years 1/4 of the original will still remain.

Basic Skills and Concepts

Logarithms.

13. False; 0.928 is between 0 and 1, so $10^{0.928}$ is between $10^0 = 1$ and $10^1 = 10$.

15. False; -5.2 is between -6 and -5, so $10^{-5.2}$ is between $10^{-6} = 0.000001$ and $10^{-5} = 0.0001$.

17. True; π is between 1 and 10, so $\log_{10}(\pi)$ is between $\log_{10}(1) = 0$ and $\log_{10}(10) = 1$.

19. True; 1,600,000 is between 1,000,000 and 10,000,000, and hence $\log_{10}(1,600,000)$ is between $\log_{10}(1,000,000) = 6$ and $\log_{10}(10,000,000) = 7$.

21. False; $\frac{1}{4} = 0.25$ is between 0.1 and 1, and so $\log_{10}(\frac{1}{4})$ is between $\log_{10}(0.1) = -1$ and $\log_{10}(1) = 0$.

23. a. Since $4 = 2^2$, we have $\log_{10}(4) = \log_{10}(2^2) = 2 \times \log_{10}(2) = 2 \times 0.301 = 0.602$.

b. Since $20,000 = 2 \times 10^4$, we have $\log_{10}(20,000) = \log_{10}(2 \times 10^4) = \log_{10}(2) + \log_{10}(10^4) = 0.301 + 4 = 4.301$.

c. Since $0.5 = 2^{-1}$, we have $\log_{10}(0.5) = \log_{10}(2^{-1}) = -1 \times \log_{10}(2) = -1 \times 0.301 = -0.301$.

d. Since $32 = 2^5$, we have $\log_{10}(32) = \log_{10}(2^5) = 5 \times \log_{10}(2) = 5 \times 0.301 = 1.505$.

e. Since $0.25 = 2^{-2}$, we have $\log_{10}(0.25) = \log_{10}(2^{-2}) = -2 \times \log_{10}(2) = -2 \times 0.301 = -0.602$.

f. Since $0.2 = 2 \times 10^{-1}$, we have $\log_{10}(0.2) = \log_{10}(2 \times 10^{-1}) = \log_{10}(2) + \log_{10}(10^{-1}) = 0.301 + (-1) = -0.699$.

Doubling Time.

25. Since the population increases by a factor of 2 in 3 hours, and 24 hours represents $\frac{24}{3} = 8$ doubling periods, it will increase by a factor of $2^8 = 256$ in 24 hours.

Since 1 week represents $\frac{7 \times 24}{3} = 56$ doubling periods, the population will increase by a factor of $2^{56} \approx 7.2 \times 10^{16}$ in 1 week.

27. Since the population increases by a factor of 2 in 22 years, it will quadruple ($2^2 = 4$) in 2 doubling periods, i.e., in 44 years.

29. Since the population increases by a factor of 2 in 20 years, and 12 years represents $\frac{12}{20} = 0.6$ doubling periods, it will increase by a factor of $2^{0.6}$. So, in 12 years there will be

$$15,600 \times 2^{0.6} \approx 23,645 \text{ people.}$$

Since 24 years represents $\frac{24}{20} = 1.2$ doubling periods, it will increase by a factor of $2^{1.2} \approx 2.29740$. So, in 24 years there will be

$$15,600 \times 2^{1.2} \approx 35,839 \text{ people.}$$

31. Since the number of cells increases by a factor of 2 in 1.5 months, and 3 years represents $\frac{3\times12}{1.5} = 24$ doubling periods, the number of cells will increase by a factor of $2^{24} = 16,777,216$ in 3 years. Thus, 1 cell grows to almost 17 million cells in 3 years.
Since 4 years represents $\frac{4\times12}{1.5} = 32$ doubling periods, the number of cells will increase by a factor of $2^{32} = 4,294,967,296$ in 4 years. Thus, 1 cell grows to over 4 billion cells in 4 years.

World Population.

33. Assuming the world population increases by a factor of 2 in 45 years, then since 2010 is 10 years after 2000, when the population was 6 billion people, and 10 years represents $\frac{10}{45} \approx 0.222$ doubling periods, the world population will increase by a factor of $2^{0.222} \approx 1.166$ to 6 billion $\times$ 1.166 $\approx$ 7.0 billion people by 2010.
Next, 2060 is 60 years after 2000, which is $\frac{60}{45} \approx 1.333$ doubling periods, so the world population will increase by a factor of $2^{1.333} \approx 2.520$ to 6 billion $\times$ 2.520 $\approx$ 15.1 billion people by 2060.
Finally, 2100 is 100 years after 2000, which is $\frac{100}{45} \approx 2.222$ doubling periods, so the world population will increase by a factor of $2^{2.222} \approx 4.665$ to 6 billion$\times$4.665 $\approx$ 28.0 billion people by 2100.

35. **Rabbits.**

M	Population at start of month	Population at end of month
1	$100 \times (1.07)^0 = 100$	$100 \times (1.07)^1 = 107$
2	$100 \times (1.07)^1 = 107$	$100 \times (1.07)^2 = 114$
3	$100 \times (1.07)^2 = 114$	$100 \times (1.07)^3 = 123$
4	$100 \times (1.07)^3 = 123$	$100 \times (1.07)^4 = 131$
5	$100 \times (1.07)^4 = 131$	$100 \times (1.07)^5 = 140$
6	$100 \times (1.07)^5 = 140$	$100 \times (1.07)^6 = 150$
7	$100 \times (1.07)^6 = 150$	$100 \times (1.07)^7 = 161$
8	$100 \times (1.07)^7 = 161$	$100 \times (1.07)^8 = 172$
9	$100 \times (1.07)^8 = 172$	$100 \times (1.07)^9 = 184$
10	$100 \times (1.07)^9 = 184$	$100 \times (1.07)^{10} = 197$
11	$100 \times (1.07)^{10} = 197$	$100 \times (1.07)^{11} = 210$
12	$100 \times (1.07)^{11} = 210$	$100 \times (1.07)^{12} = 225$
13	$100 \times (1.07)^{12} = 225$	$100 \times (1.07)^{13} = 241$
14	$100 \times (1.07)^{13} = 241$	$100 \times (1.07)^{14} = 258$
15	$100 \times (1.07)^{14} = 258$	$100 \times (1.07)^{15} = 276$

From the table, the doubling time is about 10 months, which agrees with the doubling time formula prediction of $\frac{70}{7} = 10$ months.

Doubling Time Formula.

37. The doubling time formula prediction for a 7% per year growth is $\frac{70}{7} = 10$ years; since the rate is less than 15%, the formula is valid. In 3 years, the CPI will increase by a factor of $1.07^3 \approx 1.23$.

39. The doubling time formula prediction for a 0.7% per month growth is $\frac{70}{0.7} \approx 100$ months (i.e., 8 years and 4 months). Since the rate is less than 15%, the formula is valid. In 1 year, prices will increase by a factor of $1.007^{12} \approx 1.09$. In 8 years, which is 96 months, they will increase by a factor of $1.007^{96} \approx 1.95$.

Half-Life.

41. Since 70 years is 2 half-lives, the amount of radioactive substance decreases by a factor of $(1/2)^2 = 1/4 = 0.25$, i.e., the amount present after 70 years is one fourth of the amount we started with. Since 140 years is 4 half-lives, the amount of radioactive substance decreases by a factor of $(1/2)^4 = 1/16 = 0.0625$, i.e., the amount present after 140 years is one sixteenth of the amount we started with.

43. Since 24 hours is 2 half-lives, the amount of the drug in the bloodstream decreases by a factor of $(1/2)^2 = \frac{1}{4} = 0.25$. Since 36 hours is 3 half-

lives, the amount of the drug decreases by a factor of $(1/2)^3 = \frac{1}{8} = 0.125$.

45. Since 40 years is 4 half-lives, the population decreases by a factor of $(1/2)^4 = 0.0625$, so after 40 years it will be 1 million $\times$ 0.0625 = 62,500 animals. Since 70 years is 7 half-lives, it decreases by a factor of $(1/2)^7$ and the population will be

$$1 \text{ million} \times (1/2)^7 \approx 7813 \text{ animals.}$$

47. Since 100 days is $\frac{100}{77}$ half-lives, the amount of Cobalt-56 decreases by a factor of about $(1/2)^{\frac{100}{77}} \approx 0.4065$, so the 1 kg will be reduced to about 0.41 kg.
Since 1 year is $\frac{365}{77}$ half-lives, the amount of Cobalt-56 decreases by a factor of about $(1/2)^{\frac{365}{77}} \approx 0.03741$, so the 1 kg will be reduced to about 0.037 kg.

Half-Life Formula.

49. The approximate half-life formula prediction for a 10% per year decay rate is $\frac{70}{10} = 7$ years. Since the rate is less than 15%, the formula is valid. In 100 years, the fraction of the forest remaining will be $(1/2)^{\frac{100}{7}} \approx 0.00005$, or about 1/20,000.

51. The approximate half-life formula prediction for a 7% per year decay rate is $\frac{70}{7} = 10$ years. Since the rate is less than 15%, the formula is valid. After 50 years, which is 5 half-lives, the elephant population will be reduced to $(1/2)^5 = 0.03125$ of its starting population. Multiplying by 10,000 we find that there would be about 313 elephants left.

Exact Formulas.

53. The approximate doubling time formula prediction for a 10% per year growth rate is $\frac{70}{10} = 7$ years. Using this, after 3 years, prices will be $2^{\frac{3}{7}} \approx 1.34590$ times their current level, so what costs \$1000 today should cost about \$1345.90 in 3 years.
The exact doubling time formula for a 10% per year growth rate is

$$\frac{\log_{10}(2)}{\log_{10}(1+0.10)} \approx 7.2725 \text{ years.}$$

Using this exact value, after 3 years, prices will be $2^{\frac{3}{7.2725}} \approx 1.331$ times their current level, so what costs \$1000 today should cost about \$1331 in 3 years.
Since the rate is less than 15%, the approximation formula is valid; as seen above, it gave fairly accurate results.

55. The approximate doubling time formula prediction for a 3% per year growth rate is $\frac{70}{3} \approx 23.33$ years. Using this, after 50 years, the population will be about $2^{\frac{50}{23.33}} \approx 4.42$ times its current level, so a nation of 100 million people today should have a population of about 442 million in 50 years.
The exact doubling time formula for a 3% per year growth rate is

$$\frac{\log_{10}(2)}{\log_{10}(1+0.03)} \approx 23.45 \text{ years.}$$

Using this exact value, after 50 years, the population would be $2^{\frac{50}{23.45}} \approx 4.38$ times its current level. Thus, a population of 100 million would grow to about 438 million in 50 years.
Since the rate is less than 15%, the approximation formula is valid; as seen above, it gave fairly accurate results.

Further Applications

57. **Plutonium on Earth.** Since 4.6 billion years is $\frac{4{,}600{,}000{,}000}{24{,}000} \approx 1.92 \times 10^5$ half-lives, the amount of Pu-2396 would have decreased by a factor of $(1/2)^{1.92\times10^5}$, which is close to zero, even when multiplied by 10 trillion tons! There would be so little left that no traces of it would be detectable today.

Unit 8C

Does It Make Sense?

7. Makes sense. This will indeed happen unless the growth rate falls dramatically.
9. Does not make sense. Carrying capacity depends on many factors.

11. Does not make sense. Logistic growth is quite rare. Overshoot and collapse, or more complex patterns, are far more common.

Basic Skills and Concepts

Varying Growth Rates.

13. For an annual growth rate of 0.9%, the approximate doubling time formula yields $\frac{70}{0.9} \approx 77.78$ years. Using this, the world population will be about 6 billion $\times\ 2^{\frac{50}{77.78}} \approx 9.4$ billion people by 2050.

15. For an annual growth rate of 1.6%, the approximate doubling time formula yields $\frac{70}{1.6} = 43.75$ years. Using this, the world population will be 6 billion $\times\ 2^{\frac{50}{43.75}} \approx 13.2$ billion people by 2050.

Birth and Death Rates.

17. a. The Czech Republic's net growth rate in 1975 was

$$\frac{19.6}{1000} - \frac{11.5}{1000} = \frac{8.1}{1000} = 0.0081.$$

For 1985, it was

$$\frac{14.5}{1000} - \frac{11.8}{1000} = \frac{2.7}{1000} = 0.0027.$$

For 1995, it was

$$\frac{9.3}{1000} - \frac{11.4}{1000} = -\frac{2.1}{1000} = -0.0021.$$

b. Between 1975 and 1995, the birth rate in the Czech Republic decreased dramatically, and the death rate was pretty constant. The population can be expected to decrease significantly over the next 20 years.

19. a. Sweden's net growth rate in 1975 was

$$\frac{12.8}{1000} - \frac{10.8}{1000} = \frac{2.0}{1000} = 0.0020.$$

For 1985, it was

$$\frac{11.8}{1000} - \frac{11.3}{1000} = \frac{0.5}{1000} = 0.0005.$$

For 1995, it was

$$\frac{11.7}{1000} - \frac{11.0}{1000} = -\frac{0.7}{1000} = 0.0007.$$

b. Between 1975 and 1995, the birth rate in Sweden decreased slightly, and the death rate increased slightly. The population can be expected to grow only a small amount over the next 20 years.

21. **Logistic Growth.** The actual growth rate when the population is 10 million is

$$0.03\left(1 - \frac{10 \text{ million}}{50 \text{ million}}\right) = 2.4\%.$$

When the population is 10 million the growth rate is

$$0.03 \times \left(1 - \frac{30 \text{ million}}{50 \text{ million}}\right) = 1.2\%.$$

When the population is 10 million the growth rate is

$$0.03 \times \left(1 - \frac{45 \text{ million}}{50 \text{ million}}\right) = 0.3\%.$$

Further Applications

U.S. Population.

Recall that the approximate doubling time formula for a growth rate P% is

$$T_{double} = \frac{70}{P}$$

23. For a growth rate of 0.7%, the approximate doubling time is $\frac{70}{0.7} = 100$ years. Thus, the U.S. population will be about

$$280 \text{ million} \times 2^{\frac{2050-2000}{100}} \approx 396 \text{ million}$$

in 2050 and

$$280 \text{ million} \times 2^{\frac{2100-2000}{100}} = 560 \text{ million}$$

by 2100.

25. For a growth rate of 1%, the approximate doubling time is $\frac{70}{1} = 70$ years. Thus, the U.S. population will be about

$$280 \text{ million} \times 2^{\frac{2050-2000}{70}} \approx 459 \text{ million}$$

in 2050 and

$$280 \text{ million} \times 2^{\frac{2100-2000}{70}} \approx 754 \text{ million}$$

by 2100.

27. **Population Growth in Your Lifetime.** The population estimates will vary depending on your age; what follows assumes that you were 16 years old in 2000. The growth rate is 1.4%.

When you are 50 years old, which will be in 2034, the world population will be 6 billion $\times (1.014)^{34} \approx 9.6$ billion people.

When you are 80 years old, which will be in 2064, the world population will be 6 billion $\times (1.014)^{64} \approx 14.6$ billion people.

When you are 100 years old, which will be in 2084, the world population will be 6 billion $\times (1.014)^{84} \approx 19.3$ billion people.

Carrying Capacity.

29. The base growth rate for the logistic model is given by

$$\frac{0.021}{(1-\frac{3\text{ million}}{8\text{ billion}})} \approx 0.0336,$$

which we now use to predict the growth rate for the growth rate for the current population of 6 billion:

$$0.0336 \times \left(1 - \frac{6\text{ billion}}{8\text{ billion}}\right) = 0.0084,$$

namely, 0.84%. This is significantly less than the actual current growth rate of 1.4%. The carrying capacity is too low for this logistic model to match reality.

31. The base growth rate for the logistic model is given by

$$\frac{0.021}{(1-\frac{3\text{ million}}{15\text{ billion}})} = 0.02625,$$

which we now use to predict the growth rate for the growth rate for the current population of 6 billion:

$$0.02625 \times \left(1 - \frac{6\text{ billion}}{15\text{ billion}}\right) \approx 1.58\%,$$

This is more than the actual current growth rate of 1.4%. The carrying capacity is too high for this logistic model to match reality.

33. **Growth Control Mediation.** For an annual growth rate of 2%, the approximate doubling time is $\frac{70}{2} = 35$ years. For an annual growth rate of 5%, the approximate doubling time would be about $\frac{70}{5} = 14$ years. The tables below gives the year, the growth factor, and the population for 2% and 5% growth rates, respectively. .

Year	Population at 2% growth
2000	$100,000 \times 2^{\frac{10}{35}} \approx 121,901$
2010	$100,000 \times 2^{\frac{20}{35}} \approx 148,599$
2050	$100,000 \times 2^{\frac{50}{35}} \approx 328,813$

Year	Population at 5% growth
2000	$100,000 \times 2^{\frac{10}{14}} \approx 142,857$
2010	$100,000 \times 2^{\frac{20}{14}} \approx 269,180$
2050	$100,000 \times 2^{\frac{50}{14}} \approx 1,950,422$

Unit 8D

Does It Make Sense?

5. Does not make sense. The scale is logarithmic, so it will do far more than twice the damage.
7. Does not make sense. pH measures acidity, and has nothing to do with the amount of the substance.

Basic Skills and Concepts

Earthquake Magnitudes.

9. An earthquake of magnitude 5 releases

$$E = (2.5 \times 10^4) \times 10^{1.5\times 5},$$

which is about 7.91×10^{11} joules.

11. An earthquake of magnitude 8.1 releases

$$E = (2.5 \times 10^4) \times 10^{1.5\times 8.1},$$

which is about 3.53×10^{16} joules.

13. An earthquake of magnitude 7 releases

$$E = (2.5 \times 10^4) \times 10^{1.5\times 7},$$

which is about 7.91×10^{14} joules. The 1 megaton nuclear bomb which released 5×10^{15} joules was about 6.3 times more powerful.

The Decibel Scale.

15. Busy street traffic, which has a loudness of 80dB, is $10^8 = 100$ million times louder than the softest audible sound.

17. We need the loudness in decibels, so we use the formula

$$\text{loudness in dB} =$$
$$10\log_{10}\left(\frac{\text{intensity of sound}}{\text{intensity of softest audible sound}}\right),$$

which in this case becomes

$$\text{loudness in dB} = 10\log_{10}(45 \text{ million}).$$

This is about 77 dB.

19. Recall that

$$\frac{\text{intensity of sound}}{\text{intensity of softest audible sound}} =$$
$$10^{\frac{\text{loudness in dB}}{10}}.$$

Hence, a 35 dB sound is $10^{\frac{35}{10}}$, or, about 3162, times more intense than the softest audible sound. Similarly, a 10 dB sound is $10^{\frac{10}{10}} = 10$ times more intense than the softest audible sound. Dividing, we see that a 35 dB sound is about 316 times more intense than a 10 dB sound.

Inverse Square Law.

21. One meter away is 5 times closer to the speaker than 5 meters away from the speaker. So the sound is $5^2 = 25$ times more intense at 1 meter away than at 5 meters away.

23. Twenty meters away is twice as close as 40 meters away from the speaker. So the sound is $2^2 = 4$ times more intense at 20 meters from the speaker than at 40 meters from the speaker.

pH Scale.

25. Each increase of 1 unit on the pH scale means that a solution becomes 10 times more basic because the hydrogen ion concentration decreases by a factor of 10, so an increase of 2 units results in the solution becoming (100 times) more basic, with the hydrogen ion concentration decreasing by a factor of 100. Alternatively, an increase from a pH of 4 to a pH of 6 results in the hydrogen ion concentration decreasing from

$$[H^+] = 10^{-4}$$

moles per liter to

$$[H^+] = 10^{-6}$$

moles per liter. Note that the hydrogen ion concentration decreases by a factor of 100.

27. A pH of 8.5 results in a hydrogen ion concentration of

$$[H^+] = 10^{-8.5},$$

or about 3.2×10^{-9} moles per liter.

29. The pH of a solution with a hydrogen ion concentration of $0.1 = 10^{-1}$ moles per liter is $-\log_{10}(10^{-1}) = 1$. Since this is less than 7, the solution is an acid.

31. The hydrogen ion content of the acid rain is $[H^+] = 10^{-3}$, while the hydrogen ion content of ordinary rain is $[H^+] = 10^{-6}$. So the acid rain is $\frac{10^{-3}}{10^{-6}} = 10^3 = 1000$ times more acidic.

Further Applications

Logarithmic Thinking.

33. This is a very minor earthquake, and we'd expect few effects.

35. This is unbelievably basic, even more so than household ammonia, and hence extremely toxic. We'd expect serious effects.

37. A shout that registers 90 dB would be inaudible in the presence of sirens at 100dB.

39. **Sound and Distance.**

a. At 1 meter away, the intensity of the street noise is 10^8 times louder than the softest audible sound. At 1 meter away, the sound is $100^2 = 10^4$ times more intense than at 100 meters away. So at 100 meters away, then sound has an intensity of $\frac{10^8}{10^4} = 10^4$ louder than the softest audible sound. This is about the same as background noise in the average home.

b. You need to be far enough away so that the sound is less than 120 dB, so you need to know how much more intense the 135 db level is than the 120 dB level.

$$\frac{10^{\frac{135}{10}}}{10^{\frac{120}{10}}} = 10^{1.5} \approx 32$$

Using the Inverse Square Law, we see that the distance from the speakers should be at least $sqrt(32) \times 10 \approx 57$ meters.

c. Since you are 8 times farther away from either of them than they are from each other, the sound that reaches you is 64 times less intense; i.e., if x is the decibel level, then

$$10^{\frac{x}{10}} = 10^{\frac{20}{10}} \div 64 = 1.5625$$

Taking logarithms and multiplying both sides by 10, we have

$$x = 10 \times \log_{10} 1.5665 \approx 1.94\text{db}.$$

The microphone will have to boost the intensity by a factor of about

$$\frac{10^{\frac{60}{10}}}{10^{\frac{1.94}{10}}} = 10^{5.806} \approx 640,000.$$

41. **Toxic Dumping in Acidified Lakes.**

a. With a pH of 4, the lake initially has in a hydrogen ion concentration of 10^{-4} moles per liter.

b. If the lake initially had a pH of 7, its hydrogen ion concentration would be 10^{-7} moles per liter. The amount of hydrogen ions in the lake would be

$$10^8 \text{ gal} \times \frac{3.785 \text{ l}}{1 \text{ gal}} \times \frac{10^{-7} \text{ moles}}{1 \text{ l}},$$

which is 37.85 moles.

Meanwhile, 100,000 gallons of pollutant with a pH of 2, containing 10^{-2} moles of hydrogen ions per liter, contain

$$10^5 \text{ gal} \times \frac{3.785 \text{ l}}{1 \text{ gal}} \times \frac{10^{-2} \text{ moles}}{1 \text{ l}},$$

which is about 3785 moles of hydrogen ions.

To find the hydrogen ion concentration after the pollution, we divide the total amount of ions by the total volume of liquid:

$$\frac{3785 \text{ moles} + 37.85 \text{ moles}}{3.785 \times 10^8 \text{ l} + 3.785 \times 10^5 \text{ l}}$$

which is 10^{-5} moles per liter. (The lake now has a pH of 5.)

c. If the lake initially had a pH of 4, its hydrogen ion concentration would be 10^{-4} moles per liter. The amount of hydrogen ions in the lake would be

$$10^8 \text{ gal} \times \frac{3.785 \text{ l}}{1 \text{ gal}} \times \frac{10^{-4} \text{ moles}}{1 \text{ l}},$$

which is 37,850 moles.

As seen in (b) above, 100,000 gallons of pollutant with a pH of 2 contains about 3785 moles of hydrogen ions, and hence the hydrogen ion concentration after the pollution is

$$\frac{37,850 \text{ moles} + 3785 \text{ moles}}{3.785 \times 10^8 \text{ l} + 3.785 \times 10^5 \text{ l}}$$

which is 1.1×10^{-4} moles per liter. The pH of the lake is now $-\log_{10}(1.1 \times 10^{-4})$, which is about 3.96.

d. A test with a sensitivity of 0.1 on the pH scale could detect the dumping of chemicals in case (b), in which the pH drops from 7 to 5, but in case (c) the change in pH from 4 to 3.96 is too small to be noticed by the EPA.

Unit 9A

Does It Make Sense?

5. Makes sense. Climate modeling is a great example of the importance of mathematical models.
7. Does not make sense. The domain covers the independent variable, which in this case is running speed, not heart rate.

Basic Skills and Concepts

Coordinate Plane Review.

9.

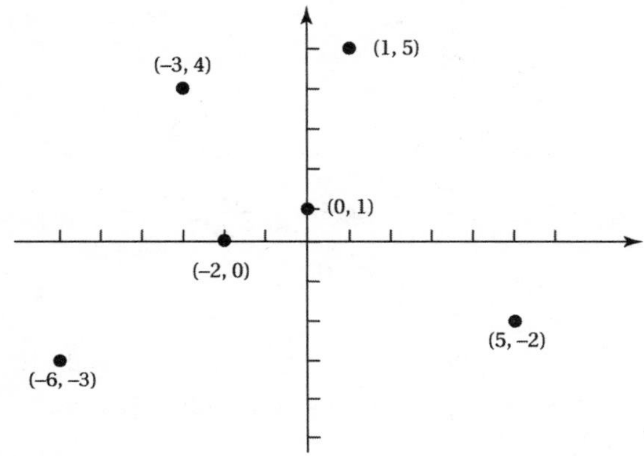

Related Quantities.

11. As the weight of the bag of apples increases, the price of the bag also increases.
13. As the price of a product increases, the demand (the number of items that can be sold) generally decreases.
15. If you coast down a hill on a skateboard, the steeper the hill, the faster you will coast.
17. If the tax rate increases, the amount of revenue generated will also increase (assuming overall sales do not decrease).

Further Applications

19. **Pressure Function.**

a. The pressure at altitudes of 8000 ft, 17,000 ft and 25,000 ft are approximately 23 inches, 16 inches and 12 inches of mercury, respectively.

b. The altitudes at which the pressure is 27 inches, 20 inches and 12 inches of mercury are approximately 4000 ft, 12,000 ft and 25,000 ft, respectively.

c. It appears that the pressure reaches 5 inches of mercury at an altitude of about 50,000 ft. The pressure approaches zero, but theoretically never reaches zero.

Functions from Graphs.

21. a. The independent variable is time, measured in years, and the dependent variable is world population. The domain is the years between 1950 and 2000. The range is all populations between about 2.5 billion and 6 billion.

b. The function shows a steadily increasing world population between 1950 and 2000.

Functions from Data Tables.

23. a. The variables are (time, temperature) or (date, temperature). The domain is all days over the course of a year. The range is temperatures between 38°F and 85°F.

b.

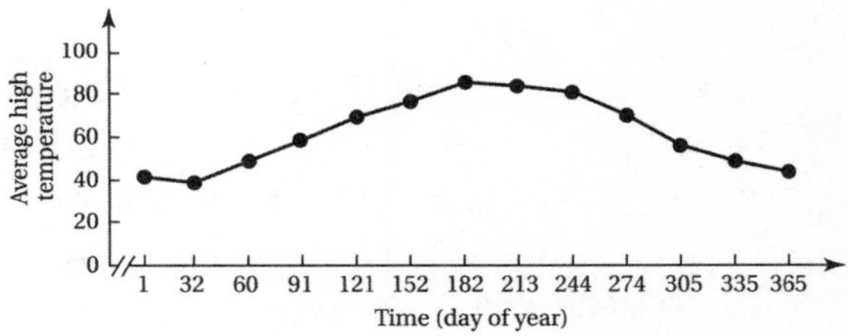

c. The temperature increases during the first half of the year and then decreases during the second half of the year.

25. a. The variables are (year, tobacco production). The domain is all years between 1975 and 1990. The range is the set of ten data values for tobacco produced.

b.

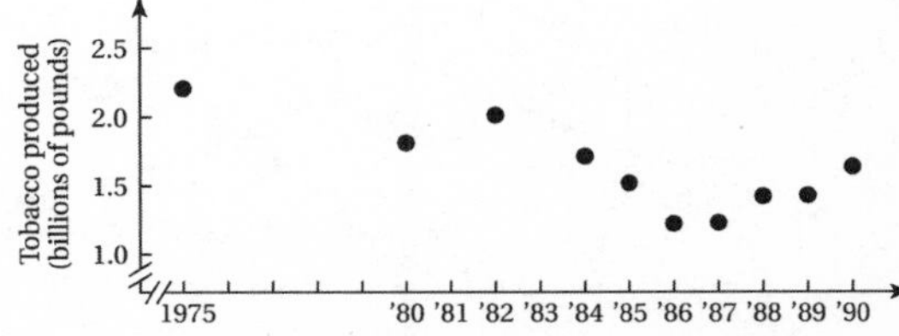

Because the data give yearly figures for production, it would not be appropriate to fill in the graph between the data points.

c. Tobacco production generally declined from the mid 70s to the mid 80s, but increased between then and 1990.

Rough Sketches of Functions.

27. a. The domain of the function (altitude, temperature) is all altitudes of interest; say, 0 ft to 15,000 ft (or 0 m to 4000 m). The range is all temperatures associated with the altitudes in the domain; the interval 0°C to 30°C covers all temperatures of interest.

b. Temperature declines as altitude increases.

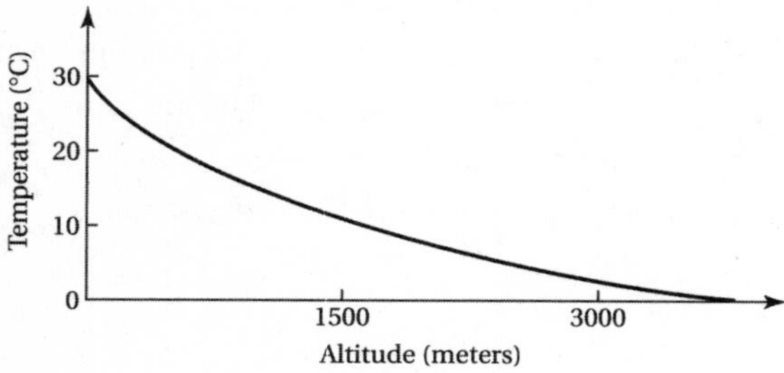

c. With some reliable data, this graph is a good model.

29. a. The domain of the (blood-alcohol content, reflex time) function consists of all possible blood-alcohol levels expressed as percentages; for example, numbers between 0% and 0.25% would be appropriate. The range would consist of the reflex times associated with those blood-alcohol levels.

b. Reflex time increases with blood-alcohol content.

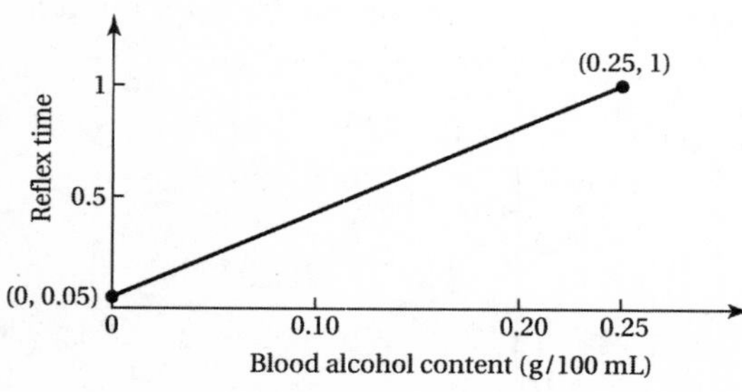

c. The validity of this graph as a model of alcohol impairment will depend on how accurately reflex times can be measured.

31. a. The domain of the function (time of day, traffic flow) consists of all times over a full day; it could be all numbers between 0 hours and 24 hours or all times between, say, 6:00 a.m on Monday and 6:00 a.m on Tuesday. The range consists of all traffic flows (in units of number of cars per minute) at the times during the day.

b. We would expect light traffic flow at night, medium traffic flow during the midday hours, and heavy traffic flow during the two rush hours.

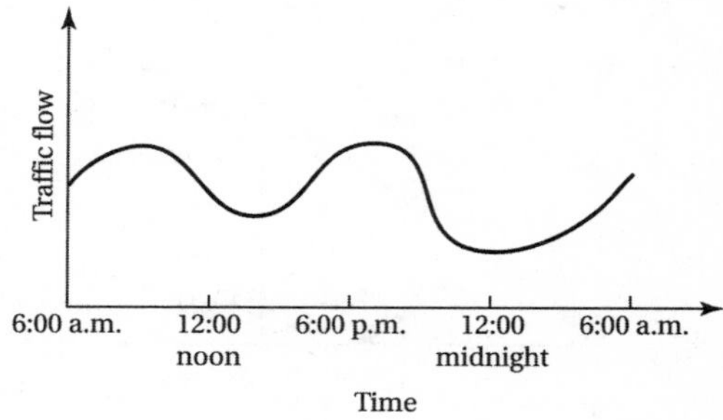

c. The graph of this function would be a good model only if based on reliable data.

33. a. The domain of the function (time, world record in 100-meter dash) consists of all years from 1970 to 2004. The range consists of the world records for the 100-meter dash at all times between 1970 and 2004.

b. This is a decreasing function; record times cannot increase, although they may be constant for a time.

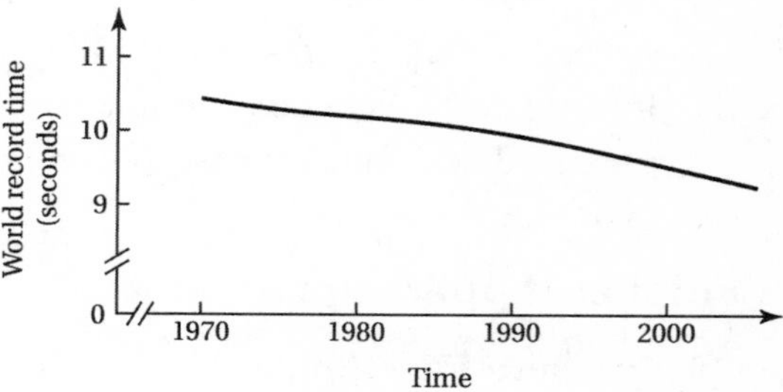

c. Some research would be needed to find the exact records and the days on which they were lowered. But the graph would show a slow decrease (from about 10.2 seconds to 9.8 seconds for men, and from about 11.0 seconds to 10.4 seconds for women) over this period of time.

35. a. The domain of the function (time, population of China) is all years from 1900 to 2004. The range consists of the populations of China during those years, roughly 400 million to 1.2 billion.

b. Many population graphs have this shape. (See 9C.)

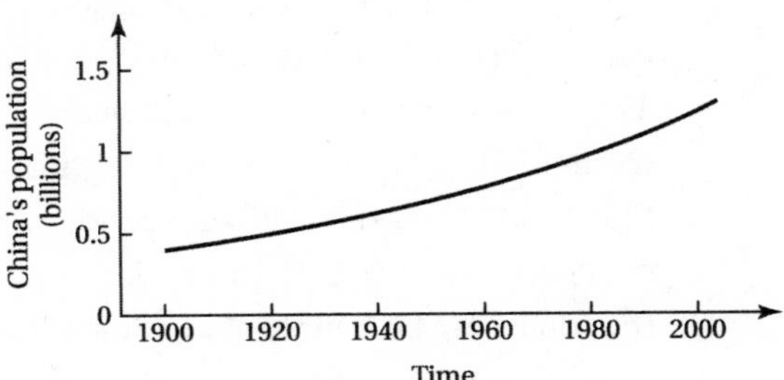

c. With accurate yearly data, this graph would be a good model of population growth in China.

37. a. The domain of the function (angle of cannon, horizontal distance traveled by cannonball) is all cannon angles between 0° and 90°. The range would consist of all ranges (no pun intended) of the cannon, i.e., the horizontal distances traveled by the cannonball, for the various angles in the domain. It is well known that a projectile has maximum range when the angle is about 45°, so the graph below shows a peak at about 45°

b. What goes up, often comes down.

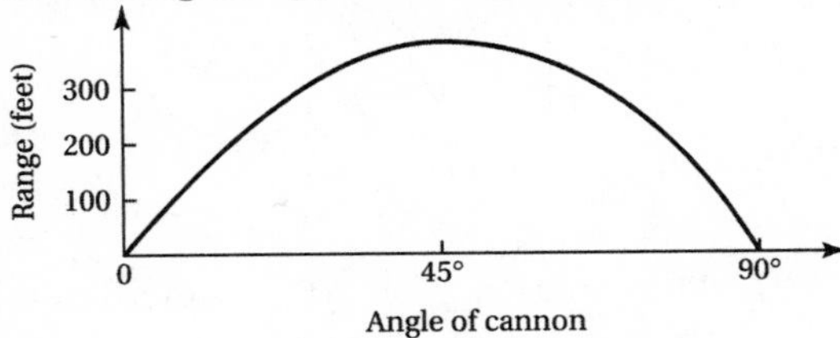

c. This is a good qualitative model.

Unit 9B

Does It Make Sense?

7. Does not make sense. A linear function has a straight line graph.

9. Makes sense. That's exactly what speed is: rate of change in distance with respect to time.

Basic Skills and Concepts

Linear Functions.

11. a. Rain depth increases with time.

b. Use any two points on the graph and measure the rise to run ratio. (Note: If (0,0) is on the graph, it is often a convenient choice.) Using (0,0) and (2, 2.4), the slope is estimated as $\frac{2.5-0}{2-0} = \frac{5}{4} = 1.25$ inches per hour.

c. Good model if rainfall rate is constant for four hours.

13. a. On a long trip, distance from home decreases with time.

b. Use any two points on the graph and measure the rise to run ratio. Using (0,500) and (0,7), the slope is $\frac{500-0}{0-7} \approx -71.43$ miles per hour. (The negative means that the distance from home is decreasing.)

c. Good model if speed is constant for eight hours.

15. a. Shoe size increases with the height of the individual.

b. Using (0,1) and (40,6), the slope is estimated as $\frac{6-1}{40-0} = \frac{5}{40} = 0.125$ sizes per inch.

c. The model is a rough approximation at best.

Rate of Change Rule.

17. The water depth decreases with respect to time at a rate of 0.25 inch per hours. The rate of change is -0.25 in./hr. In 6.5 hours, the water depth decreases 1.625 inches. In 12.5 hours, the water depth decreases 3.125 inches.

19. The tree diameter increases by 0.2 inch per year. The rate of change is 0.2 inch per year. In 4.5 years, the tree diameter increases 0.9 inch. In 20.5 years, the tree diameter increases 4.1 inches.

21. The snow depth increases by 4 inches per hour. The rate of change is 4 inches per hour. In 5.5 hours, the snow depth will increase by 22 inches. In 7.8 hours, the snow depth will increase by 31.2 inches.

Linear Equations.

23. The independent variable t is time measured in years; we assume $t = 0$ represents today. The dependent variable p is price. The equation of the price function is $p = 12,000 + 1200t$.
    The price of the car in 2.5 years would be found by substituting $t = 2.5$ into the equation for the price, yielding $p = \$15,000$. This function doesn't give a good model of car prices.
25. The variables are (snow depth, maximum speed), or (d, s), where snow depth is measured in inches and maximum speed is measured in mph. The equation for the function is $s = 30 - 0.5d$.
    The plow has zero maximum speed when $30 - 0.5d = 0$, which leads to $d = 60$ inches. Hence, when the snow depth reaches 5 feet, the plow will be unable to move.
    The plowing rate most likely is not a constant, so this model is an approximation.
27. The variables are (time, rental cost), or (t, r) where t is measured in minutes. Since each 5 minutes costs \$3, each minute costs \$3/5 = \$0.60, and so the equation for the function is $r = 5 + 0.60t$.
    The number of minutes you can rent for \$15 is found by solving $5 + 0.60t = 15$ for t. This yields $t = 16.67$ minutes, or 16 minutes and 40 seconds. (If the computer can only be rented out in 5 minute increments, at \$3 each, clearly we'd have to settle for 15 minutes, which would use up $5 + 0.6 \times 15 = \$14$ of the allotted \$15.)
    This function gives a very good model of rental costs, provided all of the costs are quoted correctly.

Equations from Two Data Points.

29. We seek a function (age, height), or (a, h), which gives height in inches as a function of age in years (with $a = 0$ corresponding to the moment of birth).
    We know that $h = 20$ when $a = 0$, i.e., the point (0,20) lies on the graph. To find the slope we use the additional point (10,48) corresponding to the fact that at age 10 years you were 4 feet (i.e., 48 inches) tall. The slope is therefore $\frac{48-20}{10-0} = 2.8$. Thus, we have $h = 20 + 2.8a$.
    Substituting $a = 2, 6, 20$ and 50 years, respectively, yields $h = 25.6, 36.8, 76.0$ and 160.0 inches. Clearly this model is accurate for small ages only!
31. If P denotes the profit and n denotes the number of tickets sold, then $P = -350 + 5n$.
    The break even point occurs when $P = 0$, so setting $-350 + 5n = 0$ and solving for n we find that $n = 70$ tickets. This means that 70 people must buy raffle tickets to break even.
33. If V denotes the depreciated value after t years, then $V = 1000 - 50t$.
    Setting $V = 0$, and solving for t, we find that the value depreciates to \$0 when 20 years has elapsed.

Further Applications

Algebraic Linear Functions.

35. The equation $y = 2x + 6$ describes a line with y-intercept (0, 6) and slope 2.

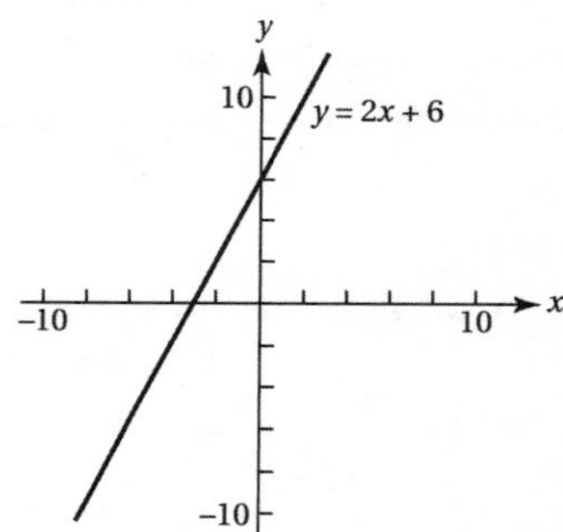

37. The equation $y = -5x - 5$ describes a line with y-intercept (0, −5) and slope −5.

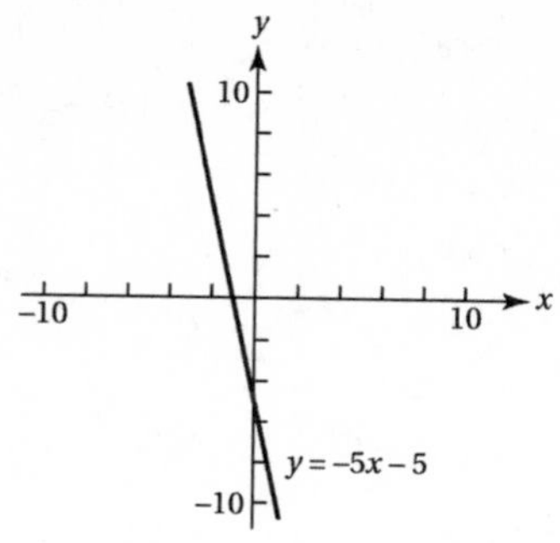

39. The equation $y = 3x - 6$ describes a line with y-intercept (0, −6) and slope 3. See next figure.
41. The equation $y = -x + 4$ describes a line with y-intercept (0, 4) and slope −1.See next figure.

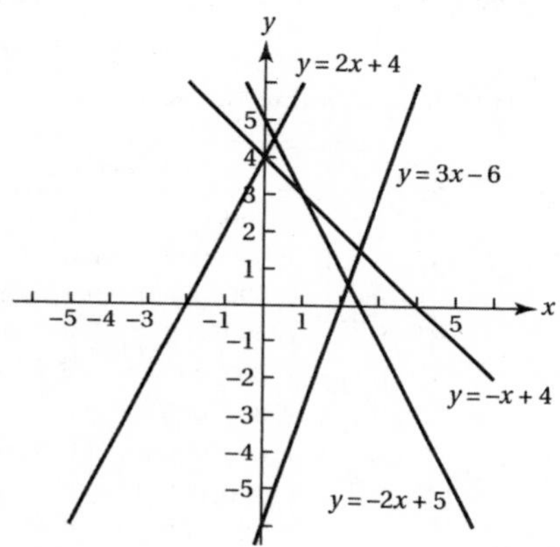

Linear Graphs.

43. The variables are (time, distance).

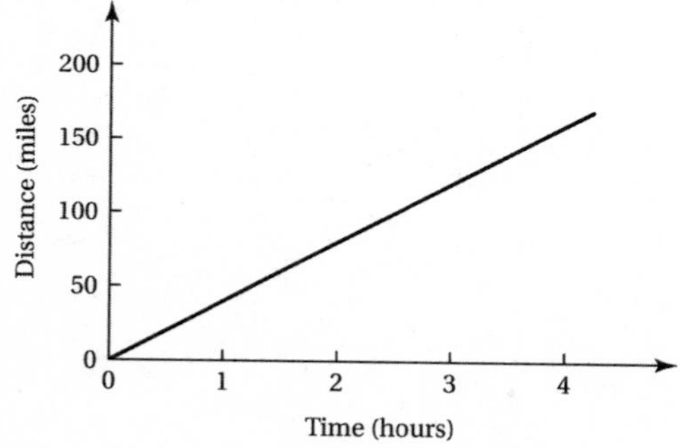

In 2.6 hours, the distance traveled is 104 miles. Provided the speed is really a constant, this linear equation gives a good model of the trip.

45. The variables are (number of posters, cost).

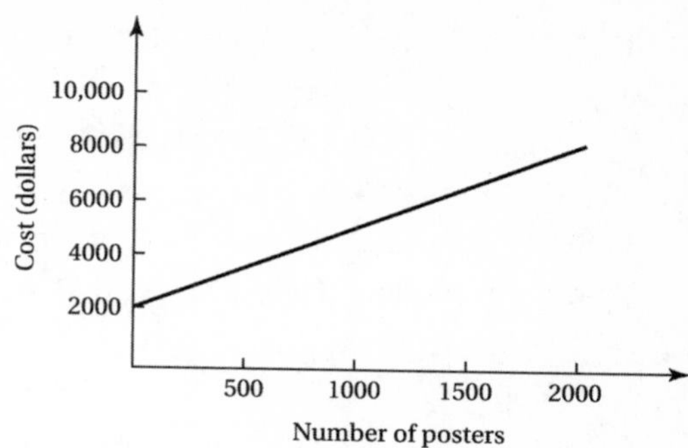

The cost of printing 2000 posters is $8000. This function probably gives a fairly realistic estimate of printing costs.

47. The variables are (time, cost).

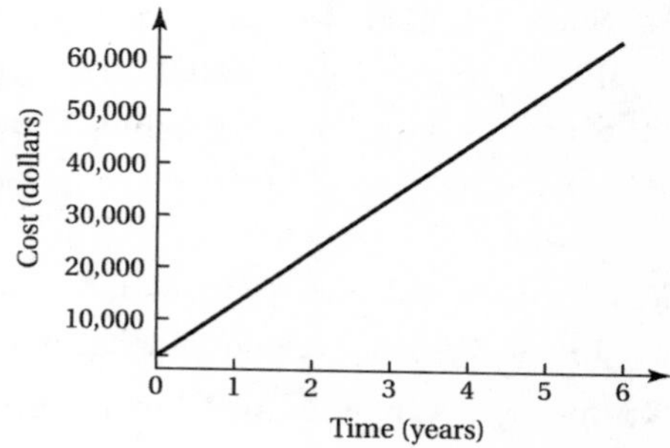

The cost of six years of school is $62,000. Provided costs do not change during the six-year period, this function is an accurate model of the cost.

Unit 9C

Does It Make Sense?

7. Does not make sense. This is not at all how exponential growth works.
9. Makes sense. This is indeed how bones are dated.

Basic Skills and Concepts

Review of Logarithms.

11. We have $2^x = 23$. Take logarithms to get $\log_{10}(2^x) = \log_{10}(23)$ and use the log rule to get $x \log_{10}(2) = \log_{10}(23)$ Divide by $\log_{10}(2)$ to get $x = \frac{\log_{10}(23)}{\log_{10}(2)} \approx 4.5236$

13. Since $3^{2x} = 12$, take logarithms to get $\log_{10}(3^{2x}) = \log_{10}(12)$, i.e., $2x\log_{10}(3) = \log_{10}(12)$. Dividing by $2\log_{10}(3)$ we get $x = \frac{\log_{10}(12)}{2\log_{10}(3)} \approx 1.1309$.

15. Since $3^x = 15$, take logarithms to get $\log_{10}(3^x) = \log_{10}(15)$ or $x\log_{10}(3) = \log_{10}(15)$. Dividing by $\log_{10}(3)$ we get $x = \frac{\log_{10}(15)}{\log_{10}(3)} \approx 2.4650$.

17. Since $2^{x/3} = 20$, take logarithms to get $\log_{10}(2^{x/3}) = \log_{10}(20)$ or $\frac{x}{3}\log_{10}(2) = \log_{10}(20)$. Multiplying by 3 and then dividing by $\log_{10}(2)$ we get $x = \frac{3\log_{10}(20)}{\log_{10}(2)} \approx 12.9658$.

19. Since $\log_{10}(x) = 1.5$, we have $10^{\log_{10}(x)} = 10^{1.5}$ or $x = 10^{1.5} \approx 31.6228$.

21. Since $\log_{10}(x) = -1.5$, we have $10^{\log_{10}(x)} = 10^{-1.5}$ or $x = 10^{-1.5} \approx 0.03162$.

23. Since $2\log_{10}(x) = 8$, divide by 2 to get $\log_{10}(x) = 4$, then $10^{\log_{10}(x)} = 10^4$ or $x = 10,000$.

25. Since $\log_{10}(3+x) = 1$, we have $10^{\log_{10}(3+x)} = 10^1$ or $3 + x = 10$, and hence $x = 7$.

Exponential Growth and Decay Laws.

27. a. $Q = 85,000 \times 1.024^t$, where Q is the population of the town, and t is the time (in years) since 1998.

b. When $t = 0$, the population is 87,000.

Year	Population
1	$85,000 \times 1.024^1 = 87,040$
2	$85,000 \times 1.024^2 = 89,129$
3	$85,000 \times 1.024^3 = 91,268$
4	$85,000 \times 1.024^4 = 93,458$
5	$85,000 \times 1.024^5 = 95,701$
6	$85,000 \times 1.024^6 = 97,998$
7	$85,000 \times 1.024^7 = 100,350$
8	$85,000 \times 1.024^8 = 102,759$
9	$85,000 \times 1.024^9 = 105,225$
10	$85,000 \times 1.024^{10} = 107,750$

c. The graph appears linear because of the small growth rate over a relatively short period of time. Many functions look nearly linear close up.

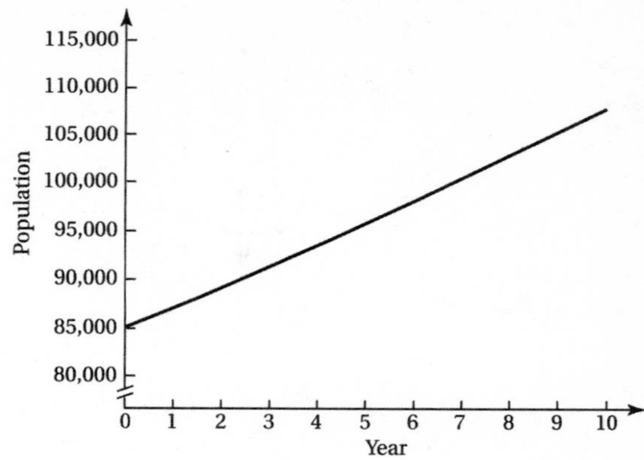

29. a. $Q = 1,000,000 \times 0.93^t$, where Q is the number of acres of old growth, and t is the time (in years) since the forest had 1 million acres.

b. When $t = 0$, the number of acres of old growth is 1,000,000.

Year	Acres
1	$1,000,000 \times 0.93^1 = 930,000$
2	$1,000,000 \times 0.93^2 = 864,900$
3	$1,000,000 \times 0.93^3 = 804,357$
4	$1,000,000 \times 0.93^4 = 748,052$
5	$1,000,000 \times 0.93^5 = 695,688$
6	$1,000,000 \times 0.93^6 = 646,990$
7	$1,000,000 \times 0.93^7 = 601,701$
8	$1,000,000 \times 0.93^8 = 559,582$
9	$1,000,000 \times 0.93^9 = 520,411$
10	$1,000,000 \times 0.93^{10} = 483,982$

c. The annual rate of decline, 7%, is nearly three times that in Problem 27 and you can begin to see more curve in the graph.

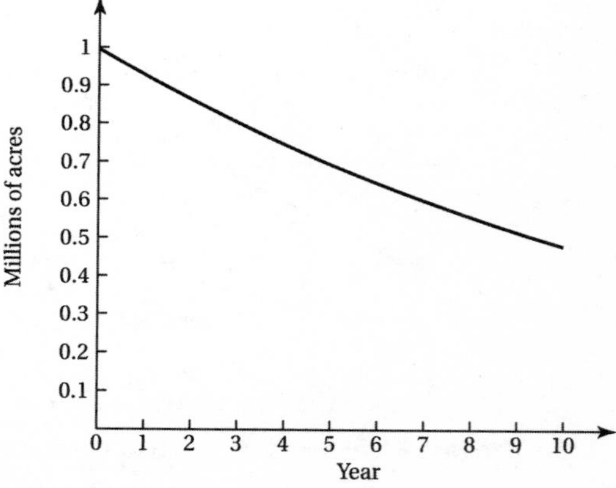

31. a. $Q = 125,000 \times 1.07^t$, where Q is the average price of a home, and t is the time (in years)

since 1995.

b. When $t = 0$, the average home price was \$125,000.

Year	Price
1	$\$125,000 \times 1.07^1 = \$133,750$
2	$\$125,000 \times 1.07^2 = \$143,113$
3	$\$125,000 \times 1.07^3 = \$153,130$
4	$\$125,000 \times 1.07^4 = \$163,850$
5	$\$125,000 \times 1.07^5 = \$175,319$
6	$\$125,000 \times 1.07^6 = \$187,591$
7	$\$125,000 \times 1.07^7 = \$200,723$
8	$\$125,000 \times 1.07^8 = \$214,773$
9	$\$125,000 \times 1.07^9 = \$229,807$
10	$\$125,000 \times 1.07^{10} = \$245,894$

c. The value is increasing.

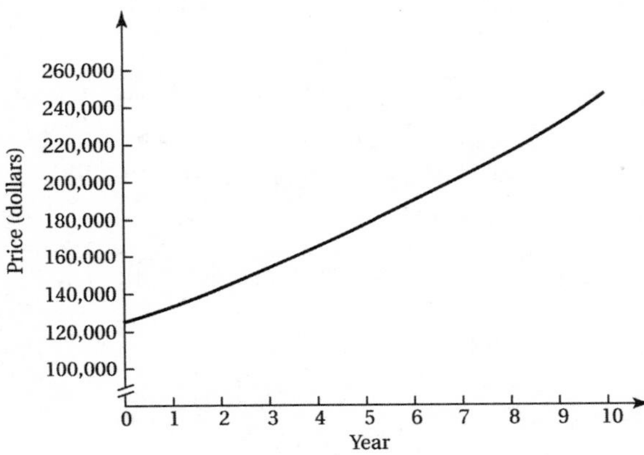

33. a. $Q = \$2000 \times 1.05^t$, where Q is your monthly salary, and t is the time (in years) since your salary was \$2000.

b. When $t = 0$, your salary was \$2000.

Year	Monthly Salary
1	$\$2000 \times 1.05^1 = \$2100.00$
2	$\$2000 \times 1.05^2 = \$2205.00$
3	$\$2000 \times 1.05^3 = \$2315.25$
4	$\$2000 \times 1.05^4 = \$2431.01$
5	$\$2000 \times 1.05^5 = \$2552.56$
6	$\$2000 \times 1.05^6 = \$2680.19$
7	$\$2000 \times 1.05^7 = \$2814.20$
8	$\$2000 \times 1.05^8 = \$2954.91$
9	$\$2000 \times 1.05^9 = \$3102.66$
10	$\$2000 \times 1.05^{10} = \$3257.79$

c. Congratulations! Your salary is increasing.

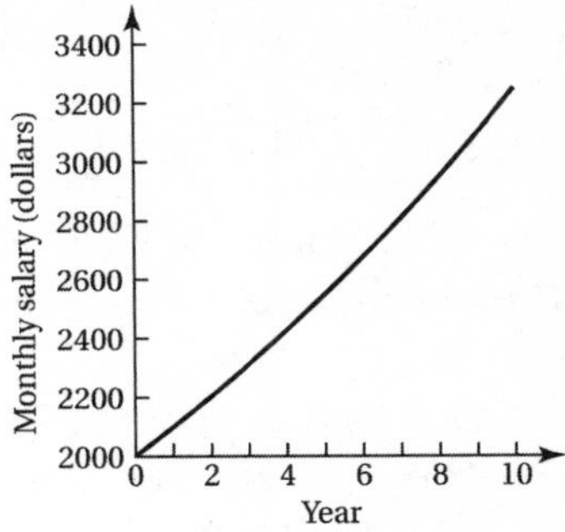

Further Applications

Annual versus Monthly Inflation.

35. A monthly inflation rate of 0.6% implies that after 12 months a price $\$Q$ will grow to $\$Q \times 1.006^{12} = \$Q \times 1.0744$, and so the annual inflation rate is 7.44%.

37. **Hyperinflation in Brazil.** A monthly inflation rate of 80% implies that after 12 months a price $\$Q$ will grow to

$$\$Q \times 1.80^{12} \approx \$Q \times 1156.83$$

and so the annual inflation rate is about 115,683%: things cost 1157 times what they cost a year earlier.

Since 1 day is 1/30 of a month, and after 1/30 of a month a price $\$Q$ will grow to

$$\$Q \times 1.80^{(1/30)} \approx \$Q \times 1.01979$$

the daily inflation rate was about 1.98%.

39. **Extinction by Poaching.** An annual decay rate of 10% implies that after t years a population of 1000 animals is reduced to $Q = 1000 \times 0.90^t$. We need to find for what value of t we get $Q = 30$, the level of extinction. Set $1000 \times 0.90^t = 30$ and solve for t.

Divide by 1000 so that $0.90^t = 0.03$, then take logarithms to get $\log_{10}(0.90^t) = \log_{10}(0.03)$, i.e., $t \log_{10}(0.90) = \log_{10}(0.03)$. Dividing by $\log_{10}(0.90)$ we arrive at

$$t = \frac{\log_{10}(0.03)}{\log_{10}(0.90)} \approx 33.28 \text{ years.}$$

41. **Valium Metabolism.** The amount of Valium present in the bloodstream (in milligrams) is given by

$$Q = 20 \times \left(\frac{1}{2}\right)^{\frac{t}{36}},$$

where t is the time in hours after midnight.

a. By noon, when $t = 12$, we have

$$Q = 20 \times \left(\frac{1}{2}\right)^{\frac{12}{36}} \approx 15.9 \text{ milligrams.}$$

b. We need to find the value of t for which $Q = 0.10 \times 20 = 2$ milligrams. So we set $20 \times (\frac{1}{2})^{\frac{t}{36}} = 2$, and solve for t.

First, divide by 20 and rewrite as $0.50^{\frac{t}{36}} = 0.1$. Take logarithms to get $\log_{10}(0.50^{\frac{t}{36}}) = \log_{10}(0.1)$, i.e., $\frac{t}{36}\log_{10}(0.50) = \log_{10}(0.1) = -1$. Multiplying by 36, and then dividing by $\log_{10}(0.50)$ yields

$$t = \frac{-36}{\log_{10}(0.50)} \approx 119.59 \text{ hours.}$$

or about 120 hours.

Radiometric Dating.

43. The current amount Q of uranium-238 present in the rock is given in terms of the original amount Q_0 present via the formula:

$$Q = Q_0 \times \left(\frac{1}{2}\right)^{\frac{t}{4.5}},$$

where t is time in billions of years.

a. If 85% of the original uranium-238 remains at time t, this means that

$$0.85 \times Q_0 = Q_0 \times \left(\frac{1}{2}\right)^{\frac{t}{4.5}},$$

and so, dividing by Q_0 and switching sides,

$$\left(\frac{1}{2}\right)^{\frac{t}{4.5}} = 0.85.$$

We must solve this equation for t.

Taking logarithms we get $\log_{10}(0.50^{\frac{t}{4.5}}) = \log_{10}(0.85)$, i.e., $\frac{t}{4.5}\log_{10}(0.50) = \log_{10}(0.85)$. Multiplying by 4.5, and then dividing by $\log_{10}(0.50)$, we find that

$$t = \frac{4.5\log_{10}(0.85)}{\log_{10}(0.50)} \approx 1.06 \text{ billion years.}$$

b. We repeat the calculations done in (a) with 55% in place of 85%, i.e., we solve

$$\left(\frac{1}{2}\right)^{\frac{t}{4.5}} = 0.55.$$

for t.

Proceeding as in (a), we eventually get

$$t = \frac{4.5\ \log_{10}(0.55)}{\log_{10}(0.50)} \approx 3.88 \text{ billion years.}$$

45. **Radioactive Waste.** The current density Q of the substance is given in terms of the density Q_0 of the substance 45 years ago via the formula:

$$Q = Q_0 \times \left(\frac{1}{2}\right)^{\frac{t}{20}},$$

where t is time in years, with $t = 0$ corresponding to 45 years ago. If a density of 2 milligrams per square meter is detected today, this means that

$$2 = Q_0 \times \left(\frac{1}{2}\right)^{\frac{45}{20}},$$

and so,

$$Q_0 = \frac{2}{(\frac{1}{2})^{\frac{45}{20}}} \approx 9.5 \text{ mg/m}^2.$$

47. **Rising Costs.** For an annual inflation rate of 3%, a cart of groceries that cost \$100 in 1995 would have cost $\$100 \times 1.03^5 = \$115.93$ in 2000.

Unit 10A

Does It Make Sense?

11. Does not make sense. Two lines intersect at most once.
13. Makes sense. A room is often shaped like a rectangular prism, and it would have three dimensions.
15. Does not make sense. A basketball is spherical, or nearly so.

Basic Skills and Concepts

Angles and Circles.

17. An angle of $(\frac{360}{3})^\circ = 120^\circ$ subtends $\frac{1}{3}$ of a circle.

19. An angle of $(\frac{360}{20})^\circ = 18^\circ$ subtends $\frac{1}{20}$ of a circle.

21. An angle of $(\frac{360}{90})^\circ = 4^\circ$ subtends $\frac{1}{90}$ of a circle.

Fractions of Circles.

23. An angle of 1° subtends $\frac{1}{360}$ of a circle.
25. An angle of 15° subtends $\frac{15}{360} = \frac{1}{24}$ of a circle.
27. An angle of 60° subtends $\frac{60}{360} = \frac{1}{6}$ of a circle.
29. An angle of 180° subtends $\frac{180}{360} = \frac{1}{2}$ of a circle.

Circle Practice.

31. The circumference is $2\pi(6) \approx 37.7$ meters, and the area is $\pi(6)^2 \approx 113.10\text{ m}^2$.
33. The circumference is $\pi(25) \approx 78.5$ centimeters, and the area is $\pi(\frac{25}{2})^2 \approx 490.9\text{ cm}^2$.
35. The circumference is $\pi(9) \approx 28.3$ mm, and the area is $\pi(\frac{9}{2})^2 \approx 63.6\text{ mm}^2$.

Perimeters and Areas.

37. The perimeter is $4 \times 12 = 48$ miles. The area is $12 \times 12 = 144$ square miles.
39. The perimeter is $(2 \times 20) + (2 \times 10) = 60$ feet. The area is $20 \times 5 = 100\text{ ft}^2$..
41. The perimeter is $(2 \times 8) + (2 \times 2) = 20$ meters. The area is $8 \times 2 = 16\text{ m}^2$.

Triangle Geometry.

43. The perimeter is $6 + 8 + 10 = 24$. The area is $\frac{1}{2}(6)(8) = 24$.
45. The perimeter is $9 + 9 + 15 = 33$. The area is $\frac{1}{2}(15)(4) = 30$.
47. **Window Space.** The perimeter is the sum of the lengths of the straight sides and the semicircle ends: $2 \times 4 + 2\pi(1.5) \approx 17.4$ feet. The area is the sum of the rectangular middle and the semicircular ends: $3 \times 4 + \pi(1.5)^2 \approx 19.07\text{ ft}^2$.
49. **Building Stairs.** The area to be covered is triangular, with base equal to 12 feet and height equal to 14 feet, so its area is $\frac{1}{2} \times 12 \times 14 = 84\text{ m}^2$.
51. **Parking Lot.** The area is $230 \times 120 = 27,600$ square yards.

Three-Dimensional Objects.

53. The pool has volume $50\text{ m} \times 25\text{ m} \times 2\text{ m} = 2500\text{ m}^3$.
55. The duct's volume is $\pi(25)(\frac{10}{12})^2 \approx 54.54\text{ ft}^3$. Its surface area is $2\pi(25)(\frac{10}{12}) \approx 130.90\text{ ft}^2$, that being how much paint is needed.
57. The circumference of the can is greater, being $\pi \approx 3.1416$ times the diameter of one of the balls, since the height of the can is only 3 times that diameter.
59. **Water Reservoir.** The capacity of the reservoir is $300 \times 100 \times 15 = 450,000$ cubic meters. If the reservoir is 70% full, it is 30% empty. Therefore, it will require $0.30 \times 450,000 = 135,000$ cubic meters to refill it.
61. **Tree Volumes.** Calculate both volumes using the formula $V = \pi r^2 h$. The first tree has volume $\pi(1.5)^2(50) = 112.5\pi$ cubic feet. The second tree has volume $\pi(0.75)^2(80) = 45\pi$ cubic feet. Thus, the first tree is the larger.

Architectural Model.

63. The surface area of the actual concert hall will be $25^2 = 625$ times greater than the surface area of the scale model.
65. The height of the actual office complex will be 50 times greater than the height of the scale model.
67. The actual office complex will require $50^3 = 125,000$ times more marbles than the scale model.

Tripling Your Size.

69. Your waist size has increased by a factor of 3.
71. Your weight, which is proportional to your volume, has increased by a factor of $3^3 = 27$.

Comparing People.

73. For example, if you have a 32 inch waist, then Sam has a $32 \times 1.10 = 35.2$ inch waist.

Squirrels or People?

75. Squirrels have a much higher surface area to volume ratio than humans.

Earth and Moon.

77. Surface area to volume ratio of the Moon is 4 times that of the Earth because the diameter is $\frac{1}{4}$ that of Earth.
79. **Comparing Balls.** The formulas necessary are $A = 4\pi r^2$ and $V = \frac{4}{3}\pi r^3$. For the smaller ball, the surface area is $4\pi(2)^2 \approx 50.3\text{in}^2$ and the volume is $\frac{4}{3}\pi(2)^3 \approx 33.5\text{in}^3$. The ratio of surface area to volume is about $\frac{50.3}{33.5} \approx 1.5$.
For the larger ball, the surface area is $4\pi(6)^2 = 452.4\text{in}^2$ and the volume is $\frac{4}{3}\pi(6)^3 \approx 904.8\text{in}^3$. It has an area to volume ratio of about $\frac{452.4}{904.8} \approx 0.5$.
Thus, the smaller ball has the larger ratio.
In general, the ratio of surface area to volume for a sphere is
$$\frac{4\pi r^2}{\frac{4}{3}\pi r^3} = \frac{3}{r}$$
In other words, the larger the radius, the smaller the ratio.

Further Applications

81. **Dimension.**
a. Three dimensions are needed to describe the book; namely, length, width and thickness.
b. Two dimensions are needed to describe the cover of the book; namely, length and width.
c. One dimension is needed to describe the edge of the book; namely, its length.
d. The tip of a corner of the book, or a period in the text, are examples of aspects of the book that represent zero dimensions.

83. **Perpendicular and Parallel.** The third line would necessarily be perpendicular to both lines.

85. **Human Lung.**
a. The total surface area of the air sacs is approximately 300 million times the surface area of a single $\frac{1}{3}$ mm diameter sphere. Each such sphere has radius $\frac{1}{6}$ mm. The combined surface area of the air sacs is
$$4\pi(\frac{1}{6})^2 \text{ mm}^2 \times 3 \times 10^8 \approx 1.05 \times 10^8 \text{ mm}^2,$$
or about 105 square meters.
The total volume of the air sacs is approximately 300 million times the volume of a single $\frac{1}{3}$ mm diameter sphere. Each such sphere has radius $\frac{1}{6}$ mm, and the total volume is
$$\frac{4}{3}\pi(\frac{1}{6})^3 \text{ mm}^3 \times 3 \times 10^8 \approx 5.8 \times 10^6 \text{ mm}^3,$$
or about 0.006 of a cubic meter.
b. If a single sphere has radius R mm and volume 5.82×10^6 mm^3, then we wish to find R so that
$$\frac{4}{3}\pi R^3 = 5.82 \times 10^6$$
Solving for R (multiply both sides by $\frac{3}{4\pi}$ and take the cube root), we find that the radius would be about 111.6 mm, i.e, about 11.2 centimeters (over 4 inches). The surface area of such a sphere would be
$$4\pi(111.6)^2 \approx 1.57 \times 10^5 \text{ mm}^2.$$
The air sacs have $\frac{1.05\times10^8}{1.57\times10^5} \approx 669$ times more area than a single sphere with the same volume. The human body would be hard pressed to accommodate a sphere of this size as part of the lungs! Even if it could, it could not facilitate the requisite amount of air exchange.
c. If a single sphere has radius R mm and surface area 1.05×10^8 mm^2, then we wish to find R so that
$$4\pi R^2 = 1.05 \times 10^8 \text{ mm}^2$$

Solving for R (divide both sides by 4π and take the square root), we find that the radius would be about 2886 mm, i.e, about 2.9 meters. For their volume, the air sacs have a very large surface area. Certainly the human body could not accommodate a sphere of radius 2.9 meters (9.5 feet).

87. **The Chunnel.** The volume of the tunnels is 3 times half the volume of a cylinder of radius 0.004 km and height 50 km, i.e.,

$$\frac{3}{2} \times \pi(50)(0.004)^2 \text{ km}^3 \approx 0.0038 \text{ km}^3,$$

or 3.8 million cubic meters. It is reasonable to assume that additional earth was removed in the building of the tunnels!

Unit 10B

Does It Make Sense?

9. Does not make sense. This location is in the southern hemisphere where it is summer in December.
11. Makes sense. A road with a 5% grade is not very steep.
13. Makes sense. This is a property of similar triangles.

Basic Skills and Concepts

Angle Conversions I.

15. $26.5^\circ = 26^\circ + 0.5^\circ \times \frac{60'}{1^\circ} = 26^\circ\ 30'$
17. $15.0161^\circ = 15^\circ + 0.0161^\circ \times \frac{60'}{1;o}$
$= 15^\circ + 0.966' = 15^\circ + 0.966' \times \frac{60''}{1'} \approx 15^\circ\ 0'\ 58''$
19. $126.9972^\circ = 126^\circ + 0.9972 \times \frac{60'}{1^\circ}$
$= 126^\circ + 59.8260' = 126^\circ\ 59' + 0.8320 \times \frac{60''}{1'}$
$\approx 126^\circ\ 59'\ 50''$

Angle Conversions II.

21. $10^\circ\ 15' = 10^\circ + (\frac{15}{60})^\circ = 10.25^\circ$
23. $36^\circ\ 45'\ 8'' = 36 + \frac{45}{60} + \frac{8}{3600}$
$= 36 + 0.75 + 0.0022 = 36.7522^\circ$
25. $1^\circ\ 1'\ 1'' = 1 + \frac{1}{60} + \frac{1}{3600} \approx 1.0169^\circ$
27. **Minutes in a Circle.** A full circle measures 360° and each degree measures $60'$. So there are $360^\circ \times \frac{60'}{1^\circ} = 21,600'$ in a circle.

Latitude and Longitude.

29. The latitude and longitude of Sydney, Australia is 33° S 151° E.
31. The location opposite would have longitude 180° away and the opposite direction from the equator. Thus, the location opposite 210° N, 158° W is 21° S and (180 − 158)° E, or 21° S and 22° E.
33. Buenos Aires at 34° 35′ S is farther south of the equator than Capetown at 15° 25′ S. Thus, Buenos Aires is farther from the North Pole.
35. There is a $43 - 26 = 17^\circ$ difference. Since each degree corresponds to about 70 miles, the cities are $17 \times 70 = 1190$ miles apart.

Angular Size.

For problems 37-40, recall the formulas from page 596 of the text.

37. The angular size of the quarter at 10 yards (360 inches) is $1 \times \frac{360}{2\pi \times 360} \approx 0.1592^\circ$ or about $10'$.
39. The diameter of the Sun is the physical size, $0.5 \times \frac{2\pi \times 1.5 \times 10^8}{360} \approx 1.3$ million km.

Slope, Pitch, Grade.

41. The slope of the roof is $\frac{1}{3} > \frac{3}{10}$.
43. The grade of the railroad track is $\frac{1}{20} = 5\% > 4\%$.
45. **Slope of a Roof.** The slope is $\frac{5}{12}$. Since the vertical rise is 5 in. for every horizontal 12 in., the total rise is $5 \times 10 = 50$ in.
47. **Pitch of a Roof.** The angle is 45°. It is possible to have a 7 in 6 roof, though local regulations may prohibit such a steep roof.
49. **Grade of a Road.** The grade is the slope in percentage form: $\frac{10}{120} \approx 8.3\%$.

Map Distances.

For problems 51-56, note that the walking distance is always the sum of the horizontal and vertical distances between the points, whereas the straight-line distance is always obtained using Pythagoras' Theorem. Also, each horizontal block is $\frac{1}{8} = 0.125$ miles and each vertical block is $\frac{1}{5} = 0.2$ miles.

51. a. The horizontal distance is 6 blocks $= 6(0.125) = 0.75$ miles. The vertical distance is 1 block $= 0.2$ miles. Thus the walking distance between the bus stop and the library is $0.75 + 0.2 = 0.95$ miles.
   b. $\sqrt{0.75^2 + 0.2^2} \approx 0.78$ miles.

53. a. The horizontal distance is $1(0.125) = 0.25$ miles and the vertical distance is $3(0.2) = 0.6$ miles. Thus, the walking distance from the bus stop to the theater is $0.25 + 0.6 \approx 0.85$ miles.
   b. $\sqrt{0.25^2 + 0.6^2} \approx 0.65$ miles.

55. a. The horizontal distance is $3(0.125) = 0.375$ miles. The vertical distance is $3(0.2) = 0.6$ miles. Thus, the walking distance from the grocery store to the library is $0.375 + 0.6 = 0.975$ miles.
   b. $\sqrt{0.375^2 + 0.6^2} \approx 0.71$ miles

Acreage Problems.

In problems 57-60, we use the formula for the area of a triangle: $A = \frac{1}{2}bh$. We assume that the missing side is h in each case and is rounded to the nearest foot.

57. By Pythagoras, the height of the triangle is $\sqrt{600^2 - 125^2} \approx 587$ feet. The area is approximately $0.5(125)(587) = 36,688$ ft^2, or

$$\frac{36,688 \text{ ft}^2}{43,560 \frac{\text{acres}}{\text{ft}^2}} \approx 0.84 \text{ acres.}$$

59. By Pythagoras, the height is $\sqrt{400^2 - 60^2} \approx 396$ feet. The area is approximately $0.5(60)(396) = 11,864$ ft^2, or

$$\frac{11,864 \text{ ft}^2}{43,560 \frac{\text{acres}}{\text{ft}^2}} \approx 0.27 \text{ acres.}$$

Determining Similarity.

61. They appear to be similar since the smaller appears to be a scaled down version of the larger.

63. These are not similar. The have the same height but different bases.

Analyzing Similar Triangles.

65. The scale factor between sides is $\frac{5}{10} = \frac{1}{2}$. Then, x is half of 8, or 4, and y is half of 6, or 3.

67. The scale factor between the sides is $\frac{60}{40} = 1.5$. Then, $x = 1.5(10) = 15$ and $y = \frac{50}{1.5} = 33.3$.

Solar Access.

Problems 69-72 use the relationship from page 601 of the text.

69. The fence height is 12, the house shadow length is $20 + 40 = 60$, and the fence shadow length is 20. Then $\frac{h}{12} = \frac{60}{20} = 3$, so $h = 36$ feet.

71. The fence height is 12, the house shadow length is $20 + 20 = 40$, and the fence shadow length is 20. Then $\frac{h}{12} = \frac{40}{20} = 2$, so $h = 24$ feet.

Optimizing Area.

73. A circular enclosure with a perimeter of 120 meters would have a radius of $\frac{120}{2\pi} \approx 19.10$ meters and an area of approximately $\pi(19.10)^2 \approx 1146$ m^2. A square with perimeter 120 meters would measure 30 meters on each side and would have an area of $30^2 = 900$ m^2.

75. A circular enclosure with a perimeter of 450 meters would have a radius of $\frac{450}{2\pi} \approx 71.62$ meters and an area of approximately $\pi(71.62)^2 \approx 16,1145$ m^2. A square with perimeter 450 meters would measure $\frac{450}{4} = 112.5$ meters on each side and would have an area of $(112.5)^2 = 12,656$ m^2.

77. **Designing Cans.** We need to compare total cost for each can. Since the unit costs are measured in \$ per square inch, we will need areas. Each end has an area of πr^2 and each side has an area of $2\pi rh$. The total cost is the cost of the two ends plus the cost of the middle. For the first can, the cost is

$$\$1 \times 2\pi(3)^2 + \$0.50 \times 2\pi(3)(4) = \$94.25.$$

For the second can, we have a cost of

$$\$1 \times 2\pi(4)^2 + \$0.50 \times 2\pi(3)(4) = \$138.23.$$

Thus, the second can costs more to manufacture.

79. **Designing Cardboard Boxes.** Since each side of the box has the same unit cost, the most economical design will be a cube. Since the volume is 6 cubic feet, each side measures

$\sqrt[3]{6} \approx 1.82$ feet. Each side has an area of approximately $1.82^2 \approx 3.3$ ft^2 and there are 6 so the total area is approximately 19.8 ft^2. Finally, the total cost is approximately $0.25 \times 19.8 = \$4.95$.

Further Applications

81. **Reading with the Hubble Space Telescope.** First, a conversion:

$$0.1'' = \frac{0.1}{3600} \approx (2.8 \times 10^{-5})^\circ$$

The physical size would have to be at least

$$2.8 \times 10^{-5} \times \frac{2\pi(350,000)}{360}\text{m} \approx 0.17\text{m}$$

or about 17 cm. If you aren't used to metric units yet, that's about 6.6 inches. You could not read a typical newspaper with the Hubble telescope.

83. **Baseball Geometry.** The sides of the diamond meet at right angles. Thus, the line from the catcher to second base is the hypotenuse of a right triangle whose sides are each 90 feet. The distance then is given by Pythagoras: $\sqrt{90^2 + 90^2} \approx 127$ feet.

85. **Travel Times.** Assume that you can walk about 2 mph and swim 1 mph. If you walk the whole way, the distance is $1.5 + 0.8 = 2.3$ miles and takes $\frac{2.3}{2} = 1.15$ hours. If you swim the whole way, the distance is $\sqrt{1.5^2 + 0.8^2} = 1.7$ miles and takes 1.7 hours. So, it will take longer if you swim.

87. **Water Bed Leak.**

a. The volume of water in the bed is $8 \times 7 \times 0.75 = 42$ cubic feet. In a room measuring $10 \times 8 = 80$ ft^2, the water would be $\frac{42}{80} = 0.525$ feet, or a little over 3 inches deep.

b. The weight is volume $\times$ density: $42 \times 64 = 2688$ pounds, over 2 tons.

89. **Optimal Fencing.** She needs $2(40) + 2(10) = 100$ meters of fencing which encloses $10 \times 40 = 400$ m^2. Given that the corral must be rectangular, the optimal solution is a square. In this case, each side would be $\sqrt{400} = 20$ meters and the perimeter would be $4 \times 20 = 80$ meters, 20% less than before.

91. **Optimal Cable.** The total cost can be calculated by adding the land and underwater costs. The land costs are $\$500 \times 3 = \$1500$. The underwater distance is given by Pythagoras: $\sqrt{1^2 + 2^2} \approx 2.236$ miles. The underwater cost is then about $\$1000 \times 2.236 = \$2236$ for a total cost of $1500 + 2236 = \$3736$.

Using the boss's suggestion, the land cost would be $\$500 \times 4 = \$2000$. The underwater distance would be $\sqrt{1^2 + 1^2} \approx 1.414$. The underwater cost would then be approximately $\$1000 \times 1.414 = \$1414$ for a total cost of $2000 + 1414 = \$3414$. This is less than your proposal. You may end up digging the ditches rather than planning them.

93. **Soda Can Design**. Solutions will vary.

95. **Sand Cones.**

a. If the height is one third of the radius and the height is 2 feet, then the radius is 6. The volume would be $\frac{1}{3}\pi \times 6^2 \times 2 \approx 75.36$ ft^3.

b. Whatever the height is, the radius of the base will be $3h$. In the formula, we have

$$1000 = \frac{1}{3}\pi(3h)^2 h = \frac{9\pi h^3}{3} = 3\pi h^3$$

To solve for h, divide by 3π and then take the cube root: $h = \sqrt[3]{\frac{1000}{3\pi}} \approx 4.73$ feet.

c. Answers will vary.

97. **The Great Pyramids of Egypt.**

a. Since a football field is 100 yards, or 300 feet long, and $\frac{481}{300} \approx 1.603$, the height of the Great Pyramid of Khufu is about 1.6 times greater than the length of a football field.

b. The pyramid's volume is about

$$1/3 \times (756)^2 \times 481 = 91,636,272 \text{ ft}^3,$$

or, dividing by 27, about 3,393,936 cubic yards.

c. Since each limestone block used has volume 1.5 cubic yards, the number of such blocks used to construct the pyramid was roughly $\frac{3,393,936}{1.5} = 2,262,624$.

d. At a rate of 2.5 minutes per block, it would have taken

$$2,262,624 \text{ blocks} \times 2.5\frac{\text{mins}}{\text{block}}$$

$$= 5,656,560 \text{ minutes}$$

to build the Great Pyramid. If the labor force worked 12 hours a day for 365 days a year, or $(60)(12)(365) = 262,800$ minutes per year, the total construction time comes out to be

$$\frac{5,656,560 \text{ mins}}{262,800 \text{ mins/year}} \approx 21.5\text{years},$$

which is close to the estimate from historical records. However, it is not obvious why Lehner's research team concluded that 10,000 workers would have sufficed, unless the 2.5 minutes per stone figure was based on such an assumption. The conclusion is that either there is missing information, or Lerner made an error.

e. Assuming the Eiffel Tower is a solid pyramid, its volume is

$$\frac{1}{3} \times (120)^2 \times 980 = 4,704,000\text{ft}^3.$$

Since $\frac{4,704,000}{91,636,272}$ is about 0.05, the volume of the Eiffel Tower is about 5% of the volume of the Great Pyramid.

Unit 10C

Does It Make Sense?

9. Makes sense. A rectangular patio is a regular non-fractal object that can be measured accurately with a yardstick.
11. Does not make sense. The usual area formulas do not apply to fractal objects.
13. Makes sense. Like the snowflake curve, the edge of a leaf has a fractal dimension between 1 and 2.

Basic Skills and Concepts

15. The dimension is 1 because when you reduce the length of the ruler by a factor of 3, the number of length elements increases by a factor of 3, and $3^1 = 3$. The object is ordinary (non-fractal).
17. The dimension is 3 because when you reduce the length of the ruler by a factor of 3, the number of volume elements increases by a factor of 27, and $3^3 = 27$. The object is ordinary (non-fractal).
19. The dimension is that number D such that $3^D = 12$, because when you reduce the length of the ruler by a factor of 3, the number of area elements increases by a factor of 12. Taking logarithms, and solving for D we find that

$$D = \frac{\log_{10}(12)}{\log_{10}(3)} \approx 2.262.$$

The dimension is about 2.262 and the object is a fractal.

21. The dimension is 1 because when you reduce the length of the ruler by a factor of 4, the number of length elements increases by a factor of 4, and $4^1 = 4$. The object is ordinary (non-fractal).
23. The dimension is 3 because when you reduce the length of the ruler by a factor of 4, the number of volume elements increases by a factor of 64, and $4^3 = 64$. The object is ordinary (non-fractal).
25. The dimension is that number D such that $4^D = 24$, because when you reduce the length of the ruler by a factor of 4, the number of area elements increases by a factor of 24. Taking logarithms, and solving for D we find that

$$D = \frac{\log_{10}(24)}{\log_{10}(4)} \approx 2.292.$$

The dimension is about 2.292 and the object is a fractal.

27. **The Quadric Koch Curve and Quadric Koch Island.**

a. Reducing the ruler size by a factor of R = 4, there are N = 8 times as many elements.

b. The dimension is that number D such that $4^D = 8$, from (a) above. Taking logarithms, and solving for D we find that the fractal dimension of the curve is

$$D = \frac{\log_{10}(8)}{\log_{10}(4)} = 1.5.$$

c. The objects that lead to the quadric island all have the same area because each time a piece of the boundary juts out (adding area) a corresponding piece juts in (removing the same amount of area). The length of the coastline of the quadric island is infinite.

Further Applications

29. **The Cantor Set.** Reducing the ruler size by a factor of 3, there are twice as many elements. Reducing the ruler size by a factor of 3 again, there are 4 length elements. So, the fractal dimension is that number D such that $3^D = 2$. Taking logarithms, and solving for D we find that

$$D = \frac{\log_{10}(2)}{\log_{10}(3)} \approx 0.631.$$

The fractal dimension of this set is less than 1 because there is "material missing" from a regular dimension 1 set.

31. **Fractal Dimensions for Fractal Objects.**

a. Using a 15-meter ruler resulted in just 1 length element, using a 1.5-meter ruler resulted in 20 length elements, and using a 15 centimeter (i.e., a 15-meter) ruler resulted in 400 length elements, so when you reduce the length of the ruler by a factor of 10, the number of length elements increases by a factor of 20. Hence, the dimension is that number D such that $10^D = 20$. Taking logarithms, we find that $\log_{10}(10^D) = \log_{10}(20)$, i.e., the fractal dimension of the stream frontage is $D = \log_{10}(20) \approx 1.301$.

b. Using a 10-centimeter ruler resulted in just 1 area element, using a 5-centimeter ruler resulted in 3 area elements, and using a 2.5 centimeter ruler resulted in 9 area elements, so when you reduce the length of the ruler by a factor of 2, the number of area elements increases by a factor of 3. Hence, the dimension is that number D such that $2^D = 3$. Taking logarithms, we find that $\log_{10}(2^D) = \log_{10}(3)$, i.e., $D\log_{10}(2) = \log_{10}(3)$. Dividing by $\log_{10}(2)$ we see that the fractal dimension of the leaf is

$$D = \frac{\log_{10}(3)}{\log_{10}(2)} \approx 1.585.$$

Although the leaf is a surface, with ordinary dimension 2, its fractal dimension is less than 2 because of the numerous holes in it: "material is missing."

c. Using a 10-meter ruler resulted in just 1 volume element, using a 5-meter ruler resulted in 6 volume elements, and using a 2.5-meter ruler resulted in 36 volume elements, so when you reduce the length of the ruler by a factor of 2, the number of volume elements increases by a factor of 6. Hence, the dimension is that number D such that $2^D = 6$. Taking logarithms, we find that $\log_{10}(2^D) = \log_{10}(6)$, i.e., $D\log_{10}(2) = \log_{10}(6)$. Dividing by $\log_{10}(2)$ we see that the fractal dimension of the rock is

$$D = \frac{\log_{10}(6)}{\log_{10}(2)} \approx 2.585.$$

Although the rock is a solid, with ordinary dimension 3, its fractal dimension is less than 3 because of the numerous holes in it: "material is missing." Its fractal dimension exceeds 2 because, despite the holes, it is more than 2 dimensional in the ordinary sense.

33. **Natural Fractals Through Branching.** The branching in many natural objects has the same pattern repeated on many different scales; this is the process by which self-similar fractals are generated. Euclidean geometry is not equipped to describe the repetition of patterns on many scales, but fractal geometry handles this sort of behavior well.

Unit 11A

Does It Make Sense?

7. Does not make sense. A higher pitch results from increasing the frequency of the vibration of the string, not the frequency at which it is plucked.
9. Makes sense. The frequencies on a musical scale are governed by the exponential growth laws.
11. Does not make sense. A phonograph record is an analog, not digital, recording. So digital methods cannot be used directly on a phonograph record.

Basic Skills and Concepts

13. **Octaves.** To lower any tone by one octave, we half its frequency. So, starting with a tone with frequency 880 cps, we get a frequency of 440 cps for the tone one octave lower. We half the frequency again to go another octave lower, getting a frequency of 220 cps for the tone two octaves lower than the original, a frequency of 110 cps for the tone three octaves lower than the original, and a frequency of 55 cps for the tone four octaves lower than the original.
15. **Notes of a Scale.** Each half-step on a 12-tone scale corresponds to an increase in frequency by a factor of $f \approx 1.05946$. Hence, $Q \approx 390 \times 1.05946^n$ gives the frequency of a tone n half-steps above the G above middle C. Rounding to the nearest number, we obtain the frequencies in the following table:

Note	Frequency (cps)
G	390
$G^\sharp$	$390 \times 1.05946^1 \approx 413$
A	$390 \times 1.05946^2 \approx 438$
$A^\sharp$	$390 \times 1.05946^3 \approx 464$
B	$390 \times 1.05946^4 \approx 491$
C	$390 \times 1.05946^5 \approx 521$
$C^\sharp$	$390 \times 1.05946^6 \approx 552$
D	$390 \times 1.05946^7 \approx 584$
$D^\sharp$	$390 \times 1.05946^8 \approx 619$
$E^\sharp$	$390 \times 1.05946^9 \approx 656$
F	$390 \times 1.05946^{10} \approx 695$
$F^\sharp$	$390 \times 1.05946^{11} \approx 736$
G	$390 \times 1.05946^{12} \approx 780$

17. **Exponential Growth and Scales.**
$Q = 260 \times 1.05946^n$ gives the frequency of a tone n half-steps above middle C.
a. If $n = 5$ we get
$Q = 260 \times 1.05946^5 \approx 347$ cps.
b. Since a fifth corresponds to 7 half-steps, we set $n = 7$ and get
$Q = 260 \times 1.05946^7 \approx 390$ cps.
c. Since a fourth corresponds to 5 half-steps, an octave and a fourth accounts for $12+5 = 17$ half-steps, so we set $n = 17$ and get
$Q = 260 \times 1.05946^{17} \approx 694$ cps.
d. If $n = 36$ we get
$Q = 260 \times 1.05946^{36} \approx 2080$ cps.
e. Four octaves and 3 half-steps accounts for $4 \times 12 + 3 = 51$ half-steps, so we set $n = 51$ and get $Q = 260 \times 1.05946^{51} \approx 4946$ cps.
19. **Exponential Decay and Scales.**
To find the frequency of a note n half-steps above another note, we multiply by a factor of 1.05946^n, and to find the frequency of a note n half-steps below another note, we divide by a factor of 1.05946^n.
The frequency of the note 5 half-steps below the note with a frequency of 437 cps is $437/(1.05946)^5 \approx 327$ cps.
The frequency of the note 8 half-steps below the note with a frequency of 437 cps is $437/(1.05946)^8 \approx 275$ cps.

Further Applications

21. **Circle of Fourths.** Raising a note by one fourth, or five half-steps, increases the frequency by a factor of $2^{\frac{5}{12}} \approx 1.3348$. The circle passes through 12 notes. For example, starting at C the progression is: C - F - A# - D# - G# - C# - F# - B - E - A - D - G - C. Counting, we see that this sequence passes through 5 octaves.

Unit 11B

Does It Make Sense?

9. Does not make sense. Although it corresponds to a point at which parallel lines intersect, the

principal vanishing point does appear in a painting.

11. Makes sense. Principles of perspective accomplish this.
13. Makes no sense. A flat surface cannot be tiled with octagons without leaving spaces.

Basic Skills and Concepts

15. **Vanishing Points.**

a. A vanishing point of the picture is that point at which the edges of the road appear to meet. This vanishing point is not the principal vanishing point as defined in the text; that one corresponds to all lines that are parallel in the real scene and perpendicular to the canvas. The road in this scene is not perpendicular to the canvas.

b.

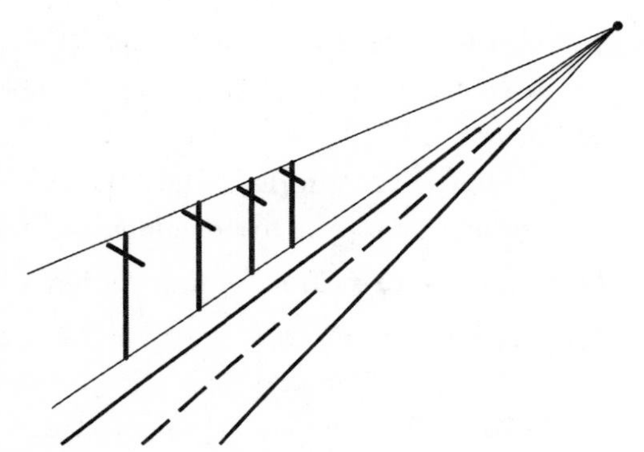

17. **Drawing with Perspective.**

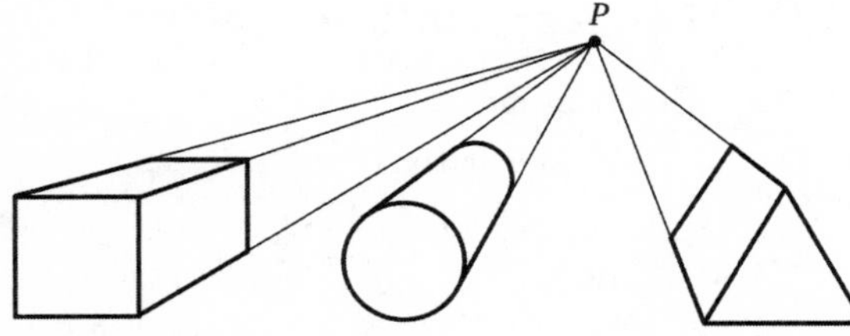

19. **Proportion and Perspective.**

a.

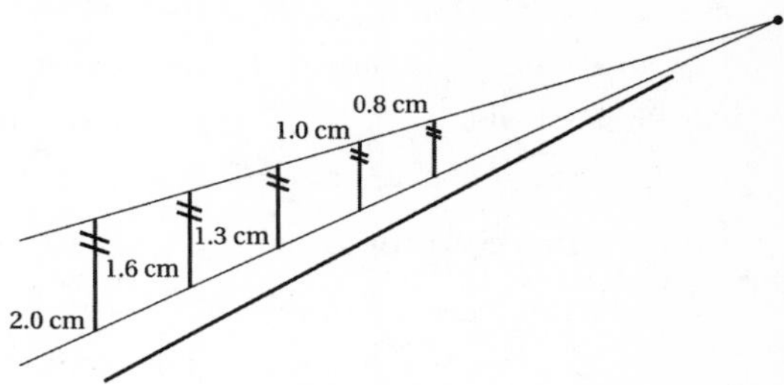

b. The ratios of the lengths of the two poles is $1.6/2.0 = 0.8$, and this ratio must be maintained for all successive poles spaced 2 cm apart. So the third pole has a height of $0.8 \times 1.6 = 1.28$ cm, the fourth pole has a height of $0.8 \times 1.28 = 1.024$ cm, and the fifth pole has a height of $0.8 \times 1.024 = 0.82$ cm.

c. No: if the poles are equally spaced in the drawing, then they would not be equally spaced in the real scene, or alternatively, if they are equally spaced in the real scene, then they would not appear to be equally spaced in the drawing.

21. **Symmetry in Letters.**

a. These letters have right/left symmetry: A, H, I, M, O, T, U, V, W, X and Y.

b. These letters have bottom/top symmetry: B, C, D, E, H, I, K, O and X.

c. These letters have both right/left and bottom/top symmetry: H, I, O and X.

d. The letters H, I, O and X have a rotational symmetry of 180°, since they have both right/left and bottom/top symmetry. The letters N, S and Z also have a rotational symmetry of 180°.

23. **Symmetries of Geometric Figures.**

a. An equilateral triangle has two rotational symmetries, corresponding to rotations of 120° and 240°.

b. A square has three rotational symmetries, corresponding to rotations of 90°, 180° and 270°.

c. A regular pentagon has four rotational symmetries, corresponding to rotations of 72°, 144°, 216° and 288°.

d. A regular polygon with n sides has $n-1$ rotational symmetries, corresponding to rotations through $(\frac{360}{n})^{\circ}$ degrees, and multiples of this angle by factors of 2, 3, 4, ..., $n-1$.

Identifying Symmetries.

25. It has reflection symmetries: it can be reflected across a vertical line through its center or a horizontal line through its center and its appearance remains the same. It has a rotational symmetry: if rotated though 180° its appearance remains the same.

27. It has rotational symmetry with angles of $(\frac{360}{6})^{\circ} = 60^{\circ}$, and multiples of 60° by factors of 2, 3, 4 or 5. It can also be reflected across six lines through its center and retain its appearance.

29.

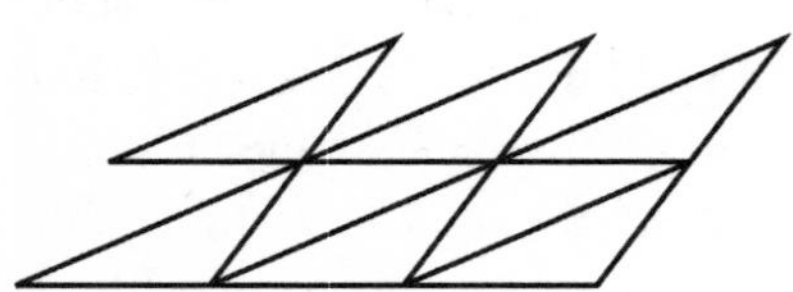

Tilings from Translating and Reflecting Triangles.

31.

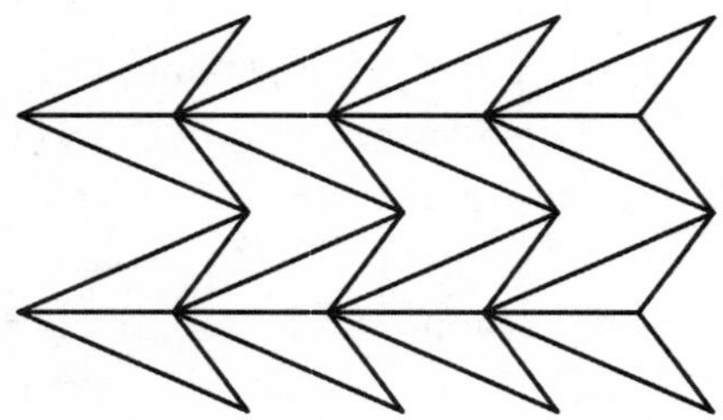

Tilings from Quadrilaterals.

33.

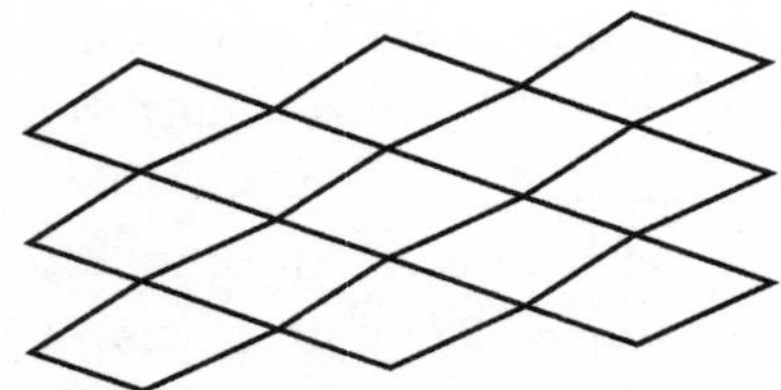

Further Applications

35. **Why Quadrilateral Tilings Work.** The angles around a point P are precisely the angles that appear inside of a single quadrilateral. Thus the angles around P have a sum of 360°, and the quadrilaterals around P fit together perfectly.

Unit 11C

Does It Make Sense?

7. Does not make sense. The golden ratio would not produce sticks of equal length.

9. Does not make sense. While circles have a lot of symmetry, they do not embody the golden ratio.

Basic Skills and Concepts

11. **Golden Ratio.** The longer segment should have length 2.47 inches, the shorter one 1.53 inches.

13. **Golden Rectangles.** Only the third and fifth rectangles appear to be golden rectangles.

Dimensions of Golden Rectangles.

15. If the other side is longer, it's $2.5 \times \phi \approx 2.5 \times 1.62 = 4.05$ meters long; if it's shorter, it's $2.5/\phi \approx 2.5/1.62 = 1.54$ meters long.

17. If the other side is longer, it's $0.12 \times \phi \approx 0.12 \times 1.62 = 0.19$ cm long; if it's shorter, it's $0.12/\phi \approx 0.12/1.62 = 0.074$ cm long.

Further Applications

19. **Finding ϕ.**

a. Starting with

$$\frac{L}{1} = \frac{L+1}{L},$$

we multiply across by L to get $L^2 = L + 1$, or $L^2 - L - 1 = 0$. Plugging in $\phi \approx 1.618034$ for L yields: $1.618034^2 - 1.618034 - 1 \approx 0$.

b. Applying the quadratic formula to the equation found in (a), we get

$$L = \frac{-(-1) \pm \sqrt{(-1)^2 - 4(1)(-1)}}{2}$$

$$= \frac{1 \pm \sqrt{5}}{2},$$

The plus sign yields about 1.618034, and the minus sign yields about −0.618034.

21. **Logarithmic Spirals.** Solutions will vary.
23. **Graphing Fechner's Data.** These are actually bar graphs, but very close to the histogram. The first one is most pleasing rectangle data.

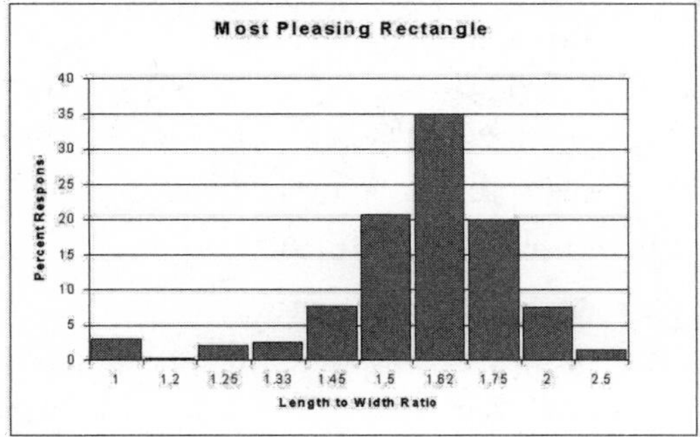

Here's the least pleasing rectangle data:

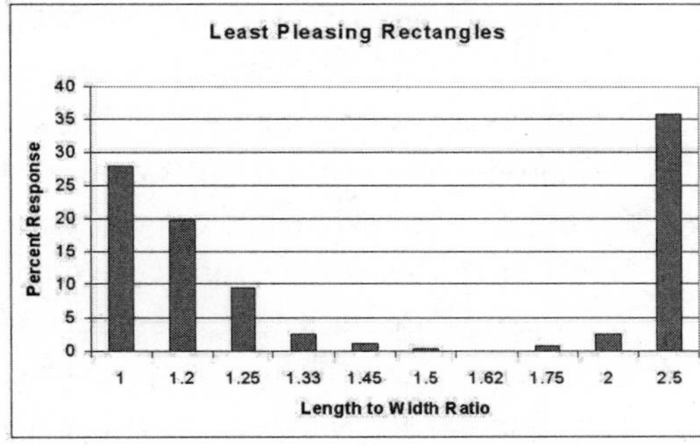

Unit 12A

Does It Make Sense?

9. Does not make sense At most one candidate can receive more than 50% of the vote.
11. Makes sense. One candidate can win a plurality but lose to another in a runoff.
13. Makes sense. Most presidential elections turn out this way.

Basic Skills and Concepts

15. **1876 Presidential Election.** To find a candidate's percent of the vote, divide the candidates votes by the total number of votes.

Total Popular Vote 8,430,783	Total Electoral Vote 369
Tilden 51.01%	Tilden 49.9%
Hayes 47.88%	Hayes 50.1%

Although Tilden narrowly won the popular vote, Hayes narrowly won the electoral vote and became President.

Close Presidential Elections.

17. To find a candidate's percent of the vote, divide the candidates votes by the total number of votes.

Total Popular Vote 8,891,088	Total Electoral Vote 369
Garfield 50.04%	Garfield 58.0%
Hancock 49.96%	Hancock 42.0%

Garfield narrowly won the popular vote and easily won the electoral vote to become President.

19. To find a candidate's percent of the vote, divide the candidates votes by the total number of votes.

Total Popular Vote 79,978,736	Total Electoral Vote 537
Carter 51.05%	Carter 55.3%
Ford 48.95%	Ford 44.7%

Carter narrowly won the popular vote and comfortably won the electoral vote to become President.

21. **Super Majorities.**

a. The percentage of shareholders favoring the merger is $10,580/15,890 = 66.58\%$ which is just shy of the required $2/3 = 66.67\%$ vote needed.

b. A 3/4 vote of a 15-member jury is at least 12 votes (since $0.75 \times 15 = 11.25$). Thus there will be no conviction.

c. A 3/4 super majority of the states is needed to amend the Constitution. In this case, 32 of the 50 states, or 64% of the states, support the amendment, so it fails to pass.

d. A $2/3 = 66.67\%$ vote is needed in both the House and the Senate to override a veto. The override gets a $68/100 = 68\%$ vote in the Senate and a $292/435 = 67.13\%$ vote in the House. So the veto can be overturned.

Preference Schedules.

23. a. A total of 66 votes were cast.

b. A received 8 first place votes, B received 20 first place votes, C received 16 first place votes, and D received 22 first place votes. Therefore, D is the plurality winner (but not by a majority).

c. From part (b), we see that B and D enter the runoff and the votes of A and C are redistributed. Now B receives $20 + 6 = 26$ votes and D receives the remainder, or 40, of the votes. Thus D is the winner of the top two runoff.

d. In the sequential runoff we eliminate only the candidate with the fewest first place votes at each stage. From part (b), we see that A is eliminated first. Redistributing A's votes, D receives A's 8 first place votes; so at this point B has 20 votes, C has 16 votes, and D has 30 votes. Now C is eliminated and the election is between B and D, as in part (c). The winner by sequential runoff is D.

e. For the Borda Count, we score 4 points for a first place vote, 3 points for a second place vote, 2 points for a third place vote, and 1 point for a fourth place vote. The point totals are as follows:

$$\text{A: } (20 \times 1) + (15 \times 3) + (10 \times 2) + (8 \times 4) + (7 \times 3) + (6 \times 3) = 156.$$
$$\text{B: } (20 \times 4) + (15 \times 1) + (10 \times 1) + (8 \times 1) + (7 \times 2) + (6 \times 2) = 139.$$
$$\text{C: } (20 \times 2) + (15 \times 2) + (10 \times 4) + (8 \times 2) + (7 \times 1) + (6 \times 4) = 157.$$
$$\text{D: } (20 \times 3) + (15 \times 4) + (10 \times 3) + (8 \times 3) + (7 \times 4) + (6 \times 1) = 208.$$

Note that the point total is 660, as it must be. We see that D is the winner by the Borda count.

f. Here are the results of the 6 pairwise races:

A over B, 46 to 20.
C over A, 36 to 30.
D over A, 52 to 14.
C over B, 39 to 27.
D over B, 40 to 26.
D over C, 50 to 16.

Thus A scores 1 point, B scores 0 points, C scores 2 points and D scores 3 points. D wins by the pairwise comparison method.

g. As the winner by all five methods, candidate D is clearly the winner of the election.

25. a. A total of 100 votes were cast.

b. A received 35 first place votes, B received 25 first place votes, and C received 40 first place votes. Therefore, C is the plurality winner (but not by a majority).

c. From part (b), we see that A and C enter the runoff and the votes of B are redistributed. Now A receives 20 votes and C receives the remainder, or 5, of the votes. A now has 55 votes and C has 45 votes. Thus A is the winner of the top two runoff.

d. With only three candidates, the sequential runoff method is the same as the top two runoff method.

e. For the Borda Count, we score 3 points for a first place vote, 2 points for a second place vote, and 1 point for a third place vote. The point totals are as follows:

A: $(30 \times 3) + (5 \times 3) + (20 \times 2) + (5 \times 1) + (10 \times 2) + (30 \times 1) = 200$.
B: $(30 \times 2) + (5 \times 1) + (20 \times 3) + (5 \times 3) + (10 \times 1) + (30 \times 2) = 210$.
C: $(30 \times 1) + (5 \times 2) + (20 \times 1) + (5 \times 2) + (10 \times 3) + (30 \times 3) = 190$.

Note that the point total is 600, as it must be. We see that B is the winner by the Borda count.

f. Here are the results of the 6 pairwise races:

B over A, 55 to 45.
A over C, 55 to 45.
B over C, 55 to 45.

Thus A scores 1 point, B scores 2 points, and C scores no points. B wins by the pairwise comparison method.

g. A wins by runoff, B wins by Borda count and pairwise comparisons, C is the plurality winner. There is not a clear winner.

27. a. A total of 90 votes were cast.

b. E wins by plurality with $\frac{40}{90} \approx 44\%$, but this is not a majority.

c. B and E received the most first-place votes, eliminating A, C, and D. Then E received 40 first place votes and B received $30+20 = 50$ first place votes (B is favored over E in the second and third columns), so B wins in a run-off.

d. A and C are eliminated with no first-place votes. D then is eliminated with only 20 first place votes. B then wins as above.

e. For the Borda Count, we score 3 points for a first place vote, 2 points for a second place vote, 1 point for a third place vote. The point totals are as follows:

A: $(40 \times 3) + (30 \times 2) + (20 \times 4) = 260$.
B: $(40 \times 2) + (30 \times 5) + (20 \times 3) = 290$.
C: $(40 \times 1) + (30 \times 4) + (20 \times 2) = 260$.
D: $(40 \times 4) + (30 \times 1) + (20 \times 5) = 290$.
E: $(40 \times 5) + (30 \times 3) + (20 \times 1) = 310$.

We see that E wins by the Borda count.

f.

A over B, 60 to 30
A over C, 60 to 30
D over A, 60 to 30
E over A, 70 to 20
B over C, 90 to 0
D over B, 60 to 30
B over E, 50 to 40
D over C, 60 to 30
C over E, 50 to 40
E over D, 70 to 20

D wins.

g. B and E both win by two methods; each has a strong claim to victory. There is no clear winner here.

29. **Condorcet Paradox.** We see that A wins over B, B wins over C, and C wins over A. This curious situation in which A is preferred to B is preferred to C is preferred to A is called the Condorcet Paradox or Voting Paradox.

Further Applications

31. **Three-Candidate Elections.**
   a. Fillipo wins a plurality, but not a majority.
   b. Imagine that there are 100 votes cast in the entire election. Then Earnest needs 13 votes to win (giving him a majority of votes). Thirteen votes represents $13/21 \approx 61.9\%$ of Davis' votes.
33. **Three-Candidate Elections.**
   a. The total number of votes cast is 870. King, who has the most votes, wins $360/870 = 41.4\%$ of the votes, which is a plurality, but not a majority.
   b. Lord needs at least 151 of Joker's votes to have a majority (at least 436) of the total votes cast.

First	A	A	C	C
Second	B	C	A	B
Third	C	B	B	A
	4	2	3	1

37. **Borda Question.** Each voter will award a first, second, third, fourth and fifth place vote. The points for these places total $5+4+3+2+1 = 15$ points. If there are 25 voters, there are $25 \times 15 = 375$ points.

Unit 12B

Does It Make Sense?

5. Makes sense. According to Fairness Criterion #2, Karen has a good point.
7. Does not make sense. According to Table 12.12, the plurality method satisfies Fairness Criterion 3.

Basic Skills and Concepts

9. **Plurality and Criterion 1.** Assume a candidate receives a majority. Then s/he is the only candidate to receive a plurality and wins by the plurality method. Thus criterion 1 is satisfied.
11. **Plurality and Criterion 2.** Solutions will vary. The following preference schedule is just one possible example.

First	B	A	C	C
Second	A	B	A	B
Third	C	C	B	A
	2	4	2	3

C is the plurality winner, but A beats C and B beats C in one-on-one races.

13. **Plurality and Criterion 4.** Candidate A would win by the plurality method. However if candidate C were to drop out of the election, then B would win by the plurality method. So Criterion 4 is violated.
15. **Runoff Methods and Criterion 1.** Assume a candidate receives a majority. In either runoff method, votes are redistributed as candidates are eliminated. But it is impossible for another candidate to accumulate enough votes to overtake a candidate who already has a majority.
17. **Sequential Runoff and Criterion 2.** By the sequential runoff method (which is the same as the top two runoff method with three candidates), candidate B is eliminated and C wins the runoff. However candidate B wins head-to-head races against A and C, so Criterion 2 is violated.
19. **Sequential Runoff and Criterion 3.** In the sequential runoff method, candidate B is eliminated first, then candidate A, making candidate C the winner. Now suppose that the 4 voters on the third ballot (ACB) move C up and vote for the ranking CAB. Now A is eliminated first and B wins the election. Thus Criterion 3 is violated.
21. **Sequential Runoff and Criterion 4.** Solutions will vary. The following preference schedule is just one possible example.

First	A	B	C
Second	B	A	B
Third	C	C	A
	4	3	5

After candidate B is eliminated, candidate A wins the runoff. However if candidate C were to drop out, B would win the election. So Criterion 4 is violated.

23. **Point System and Criterion 1.** Solutions will vary. The following preference schedule is just one possible example.

First	A	B	C
Second	B	C	B
Third	C	A	A
	4	2	1

Candidate A has a majority of the votes, but loses in a Borda count (A gets 15 points, B gets 16 points, and C gets 11 points).

25. **Point System and Criterion 2.** Solutions will vary. The following preference schedule is just one possible example.

First	A	D	C
Second	B	B	B
Third	C	A	D
Fourth	D	C	A
	4	8	3

Using the Borda count (with 3, 2, 1, and 0 points), A receives 20 points, B receives 30 points, C receives 13 points, and D receives 27 points, making B the winner by the Borda count. However D wins head-to-head races against all other candidates. Thus Criterion 2 is violated.

27. **Point System and Criterion 4.** Using the point system (with 2, 1, and 0 points), candidate A receives 11 points, candidate B receives 11 points, and candidate C receives 14 points. This makes candidate C the winner. However if candidate A were to drop from the race, then candidate B would receive 7 points and candidate C would receive 5 points (notice that the point values become 1 and 0 with only two candidates). Thus Criterion 4 is violated.

29. **Pairwise Comparisons and Criterion 1.** Assume candidate A wins a majority of the first place votes. Then in every head-to-head race with another candidate A must win (by a majority). Thus A wins every head-to-head race and is the winner by pairwise comparisons. Thus Criterion 1 is satisfied.

31. **Pairwise Comparison and Criterion 3.** Suppose candidate A wins by the pairwise comparison method, and in a second election that candidate switches places with candidate B and moves up in at least one ballot. A's position relative to B remains the same or improves. A's position and B's position relative to the other candidates remains the same. So A must win the second election.

33. **Pairwise Comparison and Criterion 4.** Solutions will vary. One solution is to take consider the preference schedule in Problem 32 if C is not a candidate. A wins over B, D, and E in pairwise comparison. If D drops out, there is no winner.

35. **Approval Voting.**
    a. Voting for only their first choices, candidate C wins by plurality with 42% of the vote.
    b. By an approval vote, $28\% + 29\% = 57\%$ of the voters approve of candidate A, $28\%+29\%+1\% = 58\%$ approve of candidate B, and 42% of the voters approve of candidate C. The winner by approval vote is candidate B.

Electoral Power.

For problems 37-41, the following table gives the electoral votes per person for each of the states. These figures were found by dividing the number of electoral votes by the state's population.

Alaska	4.78×10^{-6}
Illinois	1.69×10^{-6}
New York	1.63×10^{-6}
Rhode Island	3.82×10^{-6}

37. From the table, we see that voters in Alaska have more voting power than those in Illinois.
39. From the table, we see that voters in Rhode Island have more voting power than those in Illinois.
41. From least to greatest voting power, the ranking is: New York, Illinois, Rhode Island, Alaska.

Further Applications

Fairness Criteria.

43. A top two runoff would eliminate C and D. Candidate A would win the runoff, 23 votes to 18

votes. There is no majority winner, so Criterion 1 does not apply. Candidate A beats all other candidates one-on-one and is also declared winner by the top two runoff method; so Criterion 2 is satisfied. If candidate A is moved up in any of the rankings, it doesn't affect the outcome of the election, so Criterion 3 is satisfied. If either B, C, or D drops out of the race, the outcome is not changed. So in this case (but not in general), Criterion 4 is satisfied.

45. Candidate A wins by the point system with 83 points. There is no majority winner, so Criterion 1 does not apply. Candidate A beats all other candidates one-on-one and is also declared winner by the point system; so Criterion 2 is satisfied. The point system always satisfies Criterion 3. If either B, C, or D drops out of the race, the outcome is not changed. So in this case (but not in general), Criterion 4 is satisfied.
47. Candidate A wins by a plurality, but not by a majority. There is no majority winner, so Criterion 1 does not apply. Candidate E beats all other candidates in head-to-head races, but loses by the plurality method, so Criterion 2 is violated. The plurality method always satisfies Criterion 3. If B, C, or D were to drop out of the election, the outcome of A winning would change, so Criterion 4 is violated.
49. The candidates E, D, and B are eliminated sequentially leaving a final runoff between A and C, which candidate C wins. There is no majority winner, so Criterion 1 does not apply. Candidate E beats all other candidates in head-to-head races, but loses by the sequential runoff method, so Criterion 2 is violated. If candidate C is moved up in any of the rankings, the outcome is not affected, so Criterion 3 is satisfied. If candidate A were to drop out of the election, candidate D would win instead of C, so Criterion 4 is violated.
51. We have seen that candidate E beats all others in pairwise races and is the winner by the pairwise comparison method. There is no majority winner, so Criterion 1 does not apply. Candidate E beats all other candidates in head-to-head races, and wins by the pairwise comparison method, so Criterion 2 is satisfied. The pairwise comparison method always satisfies Criterion 3. It can be shown that if either candidate A, B, C, or D drops out of the race, then the winner is still E; so Criterion 4 is satisfied.

Unit 12C

Does It Make Sense?

9. Makes sense. If the number of staff support persons in a division depends on the number of employees in the division, an apportionment method should work.
11. Does not make sense. All apportionment methods have deficiencies and no single method is superior to the other methods.

Basic Skills and Concepts

13. **Representation in Congress.** The number of people per representative is $\frac{300,000,000}{435} = 689,655$. If the constitutional limit were observed, the number of representatives would be $\frac{300,000,000}{30,000} = 10,000$. One supposes they might wish for a larger facility.

State Representation.

For the following problems, recall that

$$\text{standard divisor} = \frac{281 \text{ million}}{435} = 646,000,$$

and

$$\text{standard quota} = \frac{\text{state population}}{\text{standard divisor}}.$$

15. For Connecticut, we have

$$\text{standard quota} = \frac{3,406,000}{646,000} = 5.27,$$

which is bigger than the 5 seats the state actually has, so Connecticut is under-represented in the House.

17. For Florida, we have

$$\text{standard quota} = \frac{15,982,000}{646,000} = 24.74,$$

which is smaller than the 25 seats the state actually has, so Florida is over-represented in the House.

19. **Standard Quotas in Business.** The total is $250+320+380+400 = 1350$. The standard divisor is then $\frac{1350}{35} = 38.57$. The standard quota (number of individuals / standard divisor) for each division is shown in the table below.

Division	I	II	III	IV
Number in division	250	320	380	400
Standard quota	6.48	8.30	9.85	10.37

21. **Hamilton's Method.** Using Hamilton's Method for the assignments, round each standard quota down to get $6+8+9+10 = 33$. Since divisions I and III have the highest remainders, the extra two technicians will be assigned to them. The table shows the final apportionment.

Division	I	II	III	IV
Number in division	250	320	380	400
Standard quota	6.48	8.30	9.85	10.37
Number assigned	7	8	10	10

Alabama Paradox.

23. The total population is $950 + 670 + 246 = 1866$, so with 100 seats to be apportioned, the standard divisor is $1866/100 = 18.66$. This is used to compute the standard quota, and hence the minimum quotas, in the table below. Hamilton's method applied to these three states yields:

State	A	B	C	Total
Pop.	950	670	246	1866
Std. Q.	50.91	35.91	13.18	100
Min. Q.	50	35	13	98
Frac. R.	0.91	0.91	0.18	2
Final A.	51	36	13	100

Assuming 101 delegates, Hamilton's method applied to these three states yields:

State	A	B	C	Total
Pop.	950	670	246	1866
Std. Q.	51.42	36.26	13.32	101
Min. Q.	51	36	13	100
Frac. R.	0.42	0.26	0.32	1
Final A.	52	36	13	101

No state lost seats as a result of the additional available seat, so the Alabama paradox does not occur here.

25. The total population is $770 + 155 + 70 + 673 = 1668$, so with 100 seats to be apportioned, the standard divisor is $1668/100 = 16.68$. This is used to compute the standard quota, and hence the minimum quotas, in the table below. Hamilton's method applied to these four states yields:

State	A	B	C	D	Total
Pop.	770	155	70	673	1668
Std. Q.	46.16	9.29	4.20	40.35	100
Min. Q.	46	9	4	40	99
Frac. R.	0.16	0.29	0.20	0.35	1
Final A.	46	9	4	41	100

Assuming 101 delegates, Hamilton's method applied to these four states yields:

State	A	B	C	D	Total
Pop.	770	155	70	673	1668
Std. Q.	46.62	9.39	4.24	40.75	101
Min. Q.	46	9	4	40	99
Frac. R.	0.62	0.39	0.24	0.75	2
Final A.	47	9	4	41	101

No state lost seats as a result of the additional available seat, so the Alabama paradox does not occur here.

Jefferson's Method.

27. The total population is $98+689+212 = 999$, so with 100 seats to be apportioned, the standard divisor is $999/100 = 9.99$. This is used to compute the standard quota, and hence the minimum quotas, in the table below. Using a modified divisor of 9.83 instead, we get the modified quotas listed, and the new minimum quotas.

State	A	B	C	Total
Pop.	98	689	212	999
Std. Q.	9.81	68.97	21.22	100
Min. Q.	9	68	21	98
Mod. Q.	9.97	70.09	21.57	101.63
N. Min. Q.	9	70	21	100

Since the new minimum quota successfully apportions all 100 seats, we can stop. Note, however, that the quota criterion is violated, because State B's standard quota is 68.97 yet it ends up being apportioned 70 seats.

29. The total population is 979, so with 100 seats to be apportioned, the standard divisor is $979/100 = 9.79$. This is used to compute the standard quota, and hence the minimum quotas, in the table below. Using a modified divisor of 9.60 instead, we get the modified quotas listed, and the new minimum quotas.

State	A	B	C	D	Total
Pop.	69	680	155	75	979
Std. Q.	7.05	69.46	15.83	7.66	100
Min. Q.	7	69	15	7	98
Mod. Q.	7.19	70.83	16.15	7.81	101.98
N. Min. Q.	7	70	16	7	100

Since the new minimum quota successfully apportions all 100 seats, we can stop. The quota criterion is satisfied.

31. **Webster's Method.** After trial and error, a modified divisor of 38.3 was found to work. The results are summarized in the table below.

Division	I	II	III	IV
Number in division	250	320	380	400
Modified quota	6.53	8.36	9.92	10.44
# assigned	7	8	10	10

33. **Hill-Huntington Method.** The modified divisor is 38.3 (see Problem 31.) Notice in the table below that the modified quota is higher than the geometric mean for divisions I and III. Therefore, those quotas should be rounded up.

Division	I	II	III	IV
Number in division	250	320	380	400
Modified quota	6.53	8.36	9.92	10.44
Geomtric mean	$\sqrt{6 \times 7}$ ≈ 6.48	$\sqrt{8 \times 9}$ ≈ 8.49	$\sqrt{9 \times 10}$ ≈ 9.49	$\sqrt{10 \times 11}$ ≈ 10.49
Number assigned	7	8	10	10

Further Applications

New States Paradox.

35. The total population is $1140 + 6320 + 250 = 7710$, so with 100 seats to be apportioned, the standard divisor is $7710/100 = 77.10$. This is used to compute the standard quota, and hence the minimum quotas, in the table below. Hamilton's method applied to these three states yields:

State	A	B	C	Total
Pop.	1140	6320	250	7710
Std. Q.	14.79	81.97	3.24	100
Min. Q.	14	81	3	98
Frac. R.	0.79	0.97	0.24	2
Final A.	15	82	3	100

With the addition of a new state D with population 500, for whom 5 new delegates are added, the new standard divisor is $\frac{7710+500}{100+5} \approx 78.19$. Hamilton's method applied to these four states yields:

State	A	B	C	D	Total
Pop.	1140	6320	250	500	8210
Std. Q.	14.58	80.83	3.20	6.39	105
Min. Q.	14	80	3	6	103
Frac. R.	0.58	0.83	0.20	0.39	2
Final A.	15	81	3	6	105

Even though 5 new seats were added with state D representation in mind, Hamilton's method actually assigned 6 seats to this state, 1 of them at the expense of State B. Since B lost a seat as a result of the additional seats for the new state, the New States paradox does occur here.

Comparing Methods.

37. a. The total population is $535 + 344 + 120 = 999$, so with 100 seats to be apportioned, the standard divisor is $999/100 = 9.99$. This is used to compute the standard quota, and hence the minimum quotas, in the table below. Hamilton's method applied to these three states yields:

State	A	B	C	Total
Pop.	535	344	120	999
Std. Q.	53.55	34.43	12.01	99.9
Min. Q.	53	34	12	99
Frac. R.	0.55	0.43	0.01	1
Final A.	54	34	12	100

b. Jefferson's method starts off like Hamilton's. As noted in (a), the standard divisor is 9.99, so we try lower modified divisors until the apportionment comes out just right. By trial and error, the modified divisor 9.90 is found to work, as documented in the last two rows of the table below. Note that this choice of modified divisor is not unique, other nearby values also work.

State	A	B	C	Total
Pop.	535	344	120	999
Std. Q.	53.55	34.43	12.01	99.9
Min. Q.	53	34	12	99
Mod. Q.	54.04	34.75	12.12	100.91
N. Min. Q.	54	34	12	100

c. Webster's method here requires us to find a modified divisor such that the corresponding modified quotas *round* (not truncate) to numbers which sum to the desired 100. Inspecting the tables in (a) or (b), we see that the standard divisor and standard quota are already adequate, as documented in the last row of the table below. Note that this choice of modified divisor is not unique, other nearby values also work.

State	A	B	C	Total
Pop.	535	344	120	999
Std. Q.	53.55	34.43	12.01	100
Min. Q.	53	34	12	99
Rou. Q.	54	34	12	100

d. The Hill-Huntington method here requires us to find a modified divisor such that the corresponding modified quotas *rounded relative to the geometric mean* yield numbers which sum to the desired 100. The standard divisor 9.99 fits the bill admirably, as documented in the last two rows of the table below. Note that this choice of divisor is not unique, other nearby values also work.

State	A	B	C	Total
Pop.	535	344	120	999
Std. Q.	53.55	34.43	12.01	100
Min. Q.	53	34	12	99
Geom. M.	53.50	34.50	12.49	-
Rou. Q.	54	34	12	100

The Geometric Means are for the whole numbers bracketing the standard quotas, namely, $\sqrt{53 \times 54} = 53.50$, $\sqrt{34 \times 35} = 34.50$, and $\sqrt{12 \times 13} = 12.49$. The modified quotas—in this case the standard quota—are compared to these, and hence 34.43 and 12.01 are rounded down to 34 and 12, respectively, whereas 53.55 is rounded up to 54. All told, for this example, the Hill-Huntington method worked out exactly the same as Webster's.

e. All four methods gave the same results.

39. a. The total population is $836 + 2703 + 2626 + 3835 = 10,000$, so with 100 seats to be apportioned, the standard divisor is $10,000/100 = 100$. This is used to compute the standard quota, and hence the minimum quotas, in the table below. Hamilton's method applied to these four states yields:

State	A	B	C	D	Total
Pop.	836	2703	2626	3835	10,000
Std. Q.	8.36	27.03	26.26	38.35	100
Min. Q.	8	27	26	38	99
Frac. R.	0.36	0.03	0.26	0.35	1
Final A.	9	27	26	38	100

b. Jefferson's method starts off like Hamilton's. As noted in (a), the standard divisor is 100, so we try lower modified divisors until the apportionment comes out just right. By trial and error, the modified divisor 98.3 is found to work, as documented in the last two rows of the table below. Note that this choice of modified divisor is not unique, other nearby values also work.

State	A	B	C	D	Total
Pop.	836	2703	2626	3835	10,000
Std. Q.	8.36	27.03	26.26	38.35	100
Min. Q.	8	27	26	38	99
Mod. Q.	8.50	27.50	26.71	39.01	101.73
N. Min. Q.	8	27	26	39	100

c. Webster's method here requires us to find a modified divisor such that the corresponding modified quotas *round* (not truncate) to numbers which sum to the desired 100. Inspecting the tables in (a) or (b), we see that neither the standard nor modified divisors and quotas there work, so we must try other modified divisors. By trial and error, we find that 99.5 is a suitable modified divisor, as documented in the last rows of the table below. Note that this choice of modified divisor is not unique, other nearby values also work.

State	A	B	C	D	Total
Pop.	836	2703	2626	3835	10,000
Std. Q	8.36	27.03	26.26	38.35	100
Min. Q.	8	27	26	38	99
Mod. Q.	8.40	27.17	26.39	38.54	100.50
Rou. Q.	8	27	26	39	100

d. The Hill-Huntington method here requires us to find a modified divisor such that the corresponding modified quotas *rounded relative to the geometric mean* yield numbers which sum to the desired 100. The standard divisor does not work here, nor does the modified divisor of (b), but the modified divisor 99.5 encountered in (c) turns out to be suitable, as documented in the last three rows of the table below. Note that this choice of divisor is not unique, other nearby values also work.

State	A	B	C	D	Total
Pop.	836	2703	2626	3835	10,000
Std. Q	8.36	27.03	26.26	38.35	100
Min. Q.	8	27	26	38	99
Mod. Q.	8.40	27.17	26.39	38.53	100.49
Geom. M.	8.49	27.50	26.50	38.50	-
Rou. Q.	8	27	26	39	100

The Geometric Means are for the whole numbers bracketing the modified quotas, namely, $\sqrt{8 \times 9} = 8.49$, $\sqrt{27 \times 28} = 27.50$, $\sqrt{26 \times 27} = 26.50$ and $\sqrt{38 \times 39} = 38.50$. The modified quotas are compared to these, and hence 8.40, 27.17 and 26.39 are rounded down to 8, 27 and 26, respectively, whereas 38.53 is rounded up to 39. All told, for this example, the Hill-Huntington method worked out exactly the same as Webster's.

e. The Jefferson, Webster and Hill-Huntington methods all gave the same result, so one could argue that these yield the best apportionment.

Non-House Apportionments.

41. a. The total population is $48 + 97 + 245 = 390$, so with 10 committee positions to be apportioned, the standard divisor is $390/10 = 39$. This is used to compute the standard quota, and hence the minimum quotas, in the table below. Hamilton's method applied to these three groups yields:

Group	Soc.	Pol.	Ath.	Total
Pop.	48	97	245	390
Std. Q.	1.23	2.49	6.28	10
Min. Q.	1	2	6	9
Frac. R.	0.23	0.49	0.28	1
Final A.	1	3	6	10

b. Jefferson's method starts off like Hamilton's. As noted in (a), the standard divisor is 39, so we try lower modified divisors until the apportionment comes out just right. By trial and error, the modified divisor 35 is found to work, as documented in the last two rows of the table below. Note that this choice of modified divisor is not unique, other nearby values also work.

Group	Soc.	Pol.	Ath.	Total
Pop.	48	97	245	390
Std. Q.	1.23	2.49	6.28	10
Min. Q.	1	2	6	9
Mod. Q.	1.37	2.77	7.00	11.14
N. Min. Q.	1	2	7	10

c. Webster's method here requires us to find a modified divisor such that the corresponding modified quotas *round* (not truncate) to numbers which sum to the desired 10. Inspecting the tables in (a) or (b), we see that neither the standard nor modified divisors and quotas there work, so we must try other modified divisors. This time, we find that 38 is a suitable modified divisor, as documented in the last rows of the table below. Note that this choice of modified divisor is not unique, other nearby values also work.

Group	Soc.	Pol.	Ath.	Total
Pop.	48	97	245	390
Std. Q.	1.23	2.49	6.28	10
Min. Q.	1	2	6	9
Mod. Q.	1.26	2.55	6.45	10.26
Rou. Q.	1	3	6	10

d. The Hill-Huntington method here requires us to find a modified divisor such that the corresponding modified quotas *rounded relative to the geometric mean* yield numbers which sum to the desired 10. The standard divisor 39 fits the bill admirably, as documented in the last two rows of the table below. Note that this choice of divisor is not unique, other nearby values also work.

Group	Soc.	Pol.	Ath.	Total
Pop.	48	97	245	390
Std. Q.	1.23	2.49	6.28	10
Min. Q.	1	2	6	9
Geom. M.	1.41	2.45	6.48	-
Rou. Q.	1	3	6	10

The Geometric Means are for the whole numbers bracketing the standard quotas, namely, $\sqrt{1 \times 2} = 1.41$, $\sqrt{2 \times 3} = 2.45$, and $\sqrt{6 \times 7} = 6.48$. The modified quotas are compared to these, and hence 1.23 and 6.28 are rounded down to 1 and 6, respectively, whereas 2.49 is rounded up to 3. All told, for this example, the

Hill-Huntington method worked out exactly the same as Webster's.

e. The Hamilton, Webster and Hill-Huntington methods all gave the same result, so one could argue that these yield the best apportionment.

43. a. The total "population" here is the total monthly gross sales, i.e., $2.5 + 7.6 + 3.9 + 5.5 = 19.5$ (in millions of dollars), so with 25 managers to be apportioned according to these sales, the standard divisor is $19.5/25 = 0.78$. This is used to compute the standard quota, and hence the minimum quotas, in the table below. Hamilton's method applied to these four stores yields:

Store	Bo.	D.	Br.	Ft. Co.	Total
Pop.	2.5	7.6	3.9	5.5	19.5
Std. Q.	3.21	9.74	5.00	7.05	25
Min. Q.	3	9	5	7	24
Frac. R.	0.21	0.74	0.00	0.05	1
Final A.	3	10	5	7	25

b. Jefferson's method starts off like Hamilton's. As noted in (a), the standard divisor is 0.78, so we try lower modified divisors until the apportionment comes out just right. By trial and error, the modified divisor 0.76 is found to work, as documented in the last two rows of the table below. Note that this choice of modified divisor is not unique, other nearby values also work.

Store	Bo.	D.	Br.	Ft. Co.	Total
Pop.	2.5	7.6	3.9	5.5	19.5
Std. Q.	3.21	9.74	5.00	7.05	25
Min. Q.	3	9	5	7	24
Mod. Q.	3.29	10.00	5.13	7.24	25.66
N. Min. Q.	3	10	5	7	25

c. Webster's method here requires us to find a modified divisor such that the corresponding modified quotas *round* (not truncate) to numbers which sum to the desired 25. Inspecting the tables in (a) or (b), we see that the standard divisor and standard quota are already adequate, as documented in the last row of the table below. Note that this choice of modified divisor is not unique, other nearby values also work.

Store	Bo.	D.	Br.	Ft. Co.	Total
Pop.	2.5	7.6	3.9	5.5	19.5
Std. Q.	3.21	9.74	5.00	7.05	25
Min. Q.	3	9	5	7	24
Rou. Q.	3	10	5	7	25

d. The Hill-Huntington method here requires us to find a modified divisor such that the corresponding modified quotas *rounded relative to the geometric mean* yield numbers which sum to the desired 25. The standard divisor 0.78 fits the bill admirably, as documented in the last two rows of the table below. Note that this choice of divisor is not unique, other nearby values also work.

Store	Bo.	D.	Br.	Ft. Co.	Total
Pop.	2.5	7.6	3.9	5.5	19.5
Std. Q.	3.21	9.74	5.00	7.05	25
Min. Q.	3	9	5	7	24
Geom. M.	3.46	9.49	5.48	7.48	-
Rou. Q.	3	10	5	7	25

The Geometric Means are for the whole numbers bracketing the standard quotas, namely, $\sqrt{3 \times 4} = 3.46$, $\sqrt{9 \times 10} = 9.49$, $\sqrt{5 \times 6} = 5.48$ and $\sqrt{7 \times 8} = 7.48$. The standard quotas are compared to these, and hence 3.21, 5.00 and 7.05 are rounded down to 3, 5 and 7, respectively, whereas 9.74 is rounded up to 10. All told, for this example, the Hill-Huntington method worked out exactly the same as Webster's.

e. All four methods gave the same results.

Unit 13A

Does It Make Sense?

11. Makes sense. A network could be used to represent which countries (vertices) trade with each other.
13. Does not make sense. An Euler circuit traverses each edge in a network exactly once, but may visit a vertex more than once.
15. Does not make sense. A minimum cost spanning tree will not give an optimal walking route.

Basic Skills and Concepts

17. **City Streets.**

a. Letting vertices represent intersections and edges represent streets, the network for the map is shown below. This network does not have an Euler circuit because there are vertices with an odd degree.

b. Letting vertices represent intersections and edges represent sidewalks, the network for the map would look the same as below except that every edge would be replaced by two edges (because every street has two sidewalks, one on each side). The network for sidewalks does have Euler circuits because every vertex has an even degree.

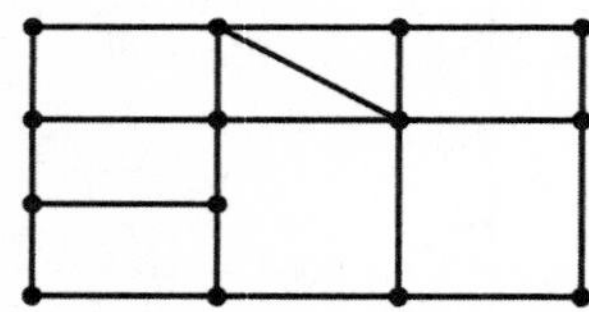

19. **Friendships and International Trade.** We can use vertices to represent the four people, Amy, Beth, Cate, and Daniel, and edges to represent the reciprocal relation "trades with." The resulting network is shown below.

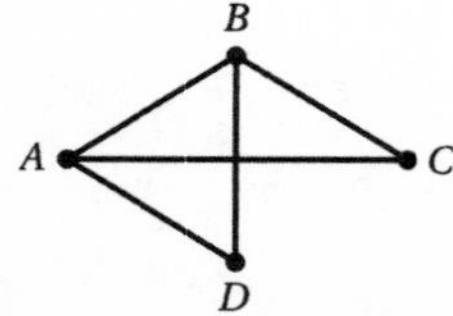

As with all networks, the precise shape makes no difference, what is important is the connections between the vertices. A similar network could be used to represent countries with edges standing for the relation "is a trading partner of;" this would display the trading relations between the countries.

21. **Euler Circuits.**

a. Letting vertices represent the town and the islands, and edges represent ferry routes, we need four vertices and five edges.

b. The network for the town is shown below.

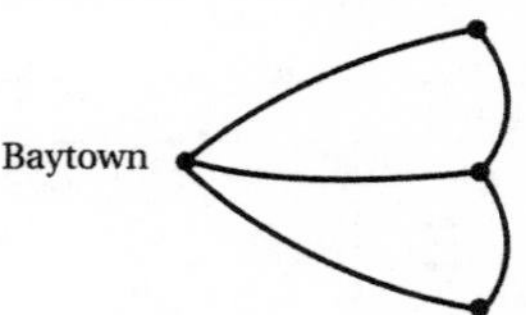

c. Since there is at least one vertex with an odd number of edges attached to it, the network has no Euler circuit.

23. **Checking Parking Meters.**
Letting vertices represent intersections and edges represent sidewalks, the network for the map is shown below.

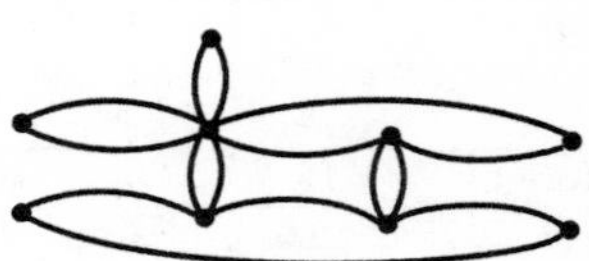

Every vertex has an even degree which tells us that an Euler circuit can be found. In fact, there are many Euler circuits.

Network Terminology.

25. a. The network has order 8 (a total of 8 vertices).

b. Vertices A, D, E, F, G, H have degree 3 and vertices B and C have degree 4.

c. The network has no special form.

d. As the network has vertices of odd degree, there are no Euler circuits.

27. a. The network has order 8.

b. Each of the vertices has degree 4.

c. The network has no special form.

d. Because all vertices have even degree, there

are Euler circuits.

e. Starting at an arbitrary vertex, say A, we can proceed to E, then B, F, C, G, D, H; then C, E, D, F; followed by A, G, B, H, and finally back to A.

29. a. The network has order 5.

b. Vertex A, has degree 1, vertices C and D have degree 2, vertex E has degree 3, and vertex B has degree 4.

c. The network has no special form.

d. As the network has vertices of odd degree, there are no Euler circuits.

Kruskal's Algorithm.

31. Kruskal's algorithm for finding the minimum cost spanning tree requires us first to list the edges in increasing order. The ordered vertices and their lengths are: AB (2), BC (2), BE (3), EF (3), BD (4), CF (4), DE (4). We now assemble these edges in order and stop when a spanning tree is reached. If we assemble the first five edges, AB, BC, BE, EF, and BD, we have a spanning tree that connects every vertex to every other vertex (notice that there are no closed loops). The length of the spanning tree is 14 and Kruskal's algorithm guarantees that it is the minimum cost spanning tree.

33. **Community Planning.** The goal is to find the minimum cost spanning tree for this network. Using Kruskal's algorithm, we first order the edges in increasing order: d (1), b (2), f (2), h (2), a (3), c (3), e (4), g (4). We can now assemble them in this order and stop when all of the vertices are connected. The first six edges, d, b, f, h, a, c, make a spanning tree (with no loops) with length 13. It is the minimum length spanning tree.

Further Applications

35. **Drawing Networks.** Examples of networks with the given properties are shown. They are by no means unique (many solutions are possible).

a.

b.

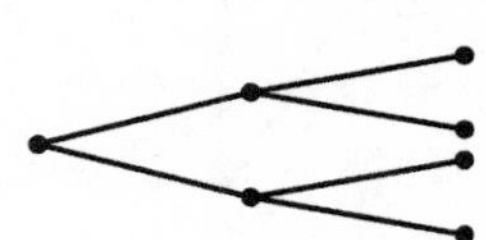

c.

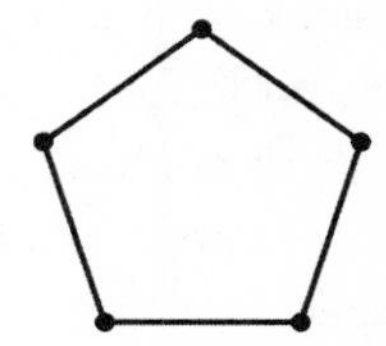

37. **Complete Network.** The complete network of order 5 is shown below. In this network, vertex 1 is connected to vertices 2, 3, 4, 5 (four edges); vertex 2 is also connected to vertices 3, 4, 5 (three more edges); vertex 3 is also connected to vertices 4, 5 (two additional edges); and vertex 4 is also connected to vertex 5 (one last edge). In total, we have $4 + 3 + 2 + 1 = 10$ edges.

If, in general, a complete network with n vertices has $n \times (n - 1)/2$ edges, then for $n = 5$ we'd have $5 \times 4/2 = 10$ edges, which agrees with what we discovered above.

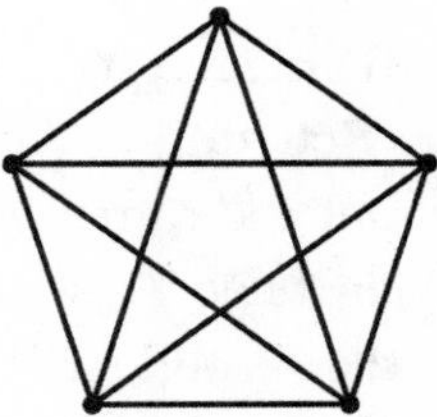

39. **Neighboring States.** The Tennessee network is shown below.

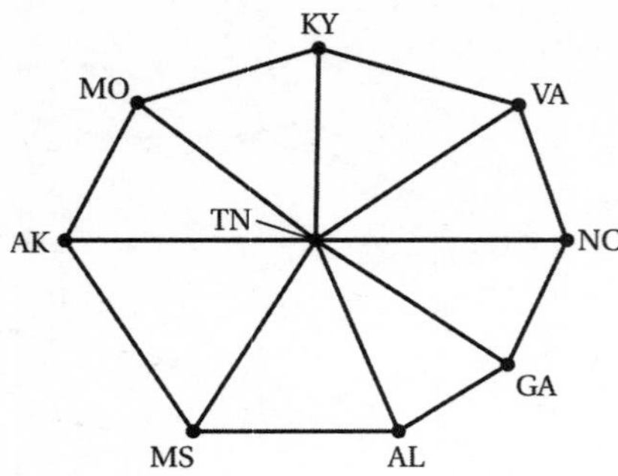

There is a vertex for each state and vertices are connected with an edge if the corresponding states are neighbors. The order of the network is nine (there are nine vertices) and the degree of the Tennessee vertex is eight since Tennessee has eight neighbors.

41. **Family Trees.**

a.

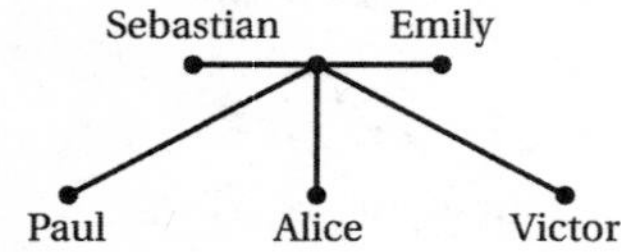

b.

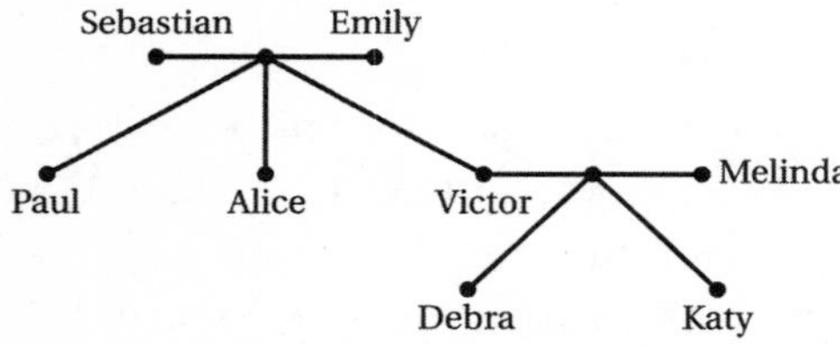

c. Solutions will vary.

43. **Soccer Schedule.** An edge in the network means that the corresponding teams play each other. The table below shows the games scheduled in the network.

—	A	B	C	D	E	F
A	—	X	X	X	X	
B	X	—	X		X	X
C	X	X	—	X		X
D	X		X	—	X	X
E	X	X		X	—	X
F		X	X	X	X	—

Unit 13B

Does It Make Sense?

5. Makes sense, provided he wants to visit each cousin exactly once and make the trip in the most efficient way possible.
7. Does not make sense. Unless he can work very quickly, it will take more than one night to test the 2520 circuits.

Basic Skills and Concepts

Practice with Hamiltonian Circuits.

9. The circuit shown is not a Hamiltonian circuit because it doesn't return to the starting point. It can be made into a Hamiltonian circuit by moving the vertical edge so it returns to the leftmost vertex instead of the topmost one.
11. The circuit shown is not a Hamiltonian circuit because it doesn't return to the starting point. It cannot be made into a Hamiltonian circuit.
13. **Number of Hamiltonian Circuits.** Recall that there are $(n-1)!/2$ Hamiltonian circuits in a complete network of order n.

a. In a complete network of order 8 there are $7!/2 = 5040/2 = 2520$ Hamiltonian circuits.

b. In a complete network of order 18 there are $17!/2$, or approximately 1.7784×10^{14}, Hamiltonian circuits.

c. From (a) above, we see that checking all the Hamiltonian circuits in a complete network of order 8 would require 2520 seconds, which, upon division by 60, comes out to exactly 42 minutes.
From (b) above, we see that checking all the Hamiltonian circuits in a complete network of order 18 would require 1.7784×10^{14} seconds. Recall that there are $60 \times 60 \times 24 \times 365 = 31,536,000$ seconds in a year. Dividing this into the number of seconds required, we find that it would take about 5.6 million years to check all of the circuits in the network.

15. **Traveling the National Parks.**

a. The network will look exactly like Figure 11.29 of the text except that the vertex for Zion will be missing along with all of the edges connected to it. The resulting network has four vertices and a total of six edges.

b. The leg from Bryce to Canyonlands is 136 miles, Canyonlands to Capitol Reef is 75 miles, Capitol Reef to Grand Canyon is 151 miles for a total of 362 miles. With the return to Bryce, the trip has length 470 miles.

c. Starting at Grand Canyon, the nearest neighbor method would send us to Bryce first at a distance of 108 miles. The next stop would be Capitol Reef, 69 miles away. The next stop would be Canyonlands , 75 miles away. To return to Grand Canyon, we need to travel another 202 miles. The total length is 454 miles.

d. Starting at Bryce, the nearest neighbor method would first send us to Capitol Reef, 69 miles away. The next stop would be Canyonlands , 75 miles away. The next stop would be Grand Canyon, 202 miles away. To return to Bryce, we need to travel another 108 miles. The total length is 454 miles. This is the same circuit that results from starting at the Grand Canyon as in part (c).

e. There are three different Hamiltonian circuits possible in this network of order four. They have lengths 454, 470, and 558. So we have found the Hamiltonian circuit with the shortest length in parts (c) and (d).

Solving Traveling Salesman Problems by Computer.

17. a. $\frac{(16-1)!}{2} = 6.5 \times 10^{11}$

b. $\frac{6.5\times10^{11}}{10^6} = 6.5 \times 10^5$ seconds or about 180 hours.

c. That's a little more than a week.

19. a. $\frac{(25-1)!}{2} = 3.1 \times 10^{23}$

b. $\frac{3.1\times10^{23}}{10^6} = 3.1 \times 10^{17}$ seconds or almost 9.8 billion years.

c. That's about twice the oldest estimate for the age of our solar system.

21. **A Traveling Salesperson Problem.** Notice that since the network is not complete—not every vertex is connected to every other vertex—it may not always be possible to apply the nearest neighbor method depending on the starting vertex. E.g., the nearest neighbor method does find the circuit FEABCDF which has length 23.

The circuit BCDFEAB is not produced by the nearest neighbor method, but by trial and error; it too has length 23. These two circuits appear to be the shortest possible.

Further Applications

23. **Car Shuttles.** There are three different Hamiltonian circuits in this network. The nearest neighbor method gives the circuit ACBDA which has length 15.

The other two possible circuits, ACDBA with length 14 and ABCDA with length 17, can be found by trial and error. The shortest route for Abe is ACDBA. All of the drivers would use the same route.

25. **Overnight Delivery.** The time savings with the new route is 890 hours less 860 hours, i.e., 30 hours. At \$15,000 per hour, this savings amounts to $30 \times \$15,000 = \$450,000$. In a year, the savings would be $365 \times \$450,000 = \$164,250,000$.

Unit 13C

Does It Make Sense?

7. Does not make sense. Vacations are usually sequential affairs in which one stop/city occurs at a time. Critical path analysis applies to situations that require concurrent tasks.

9. Does not make sense. Critical path tasks must be completed on time.

Basic Skills and Concepts

Scheduling a Paint Job.

11. The longest path between A and E passes along tasks a, e, and f.

13. The longest path through the entire network passes along tasks a, e, f, g, i, and k (vertices A, B, D, E, F, G, H). This is the critical path.

Building a Hotel.

15. Tasks a, d and e are on the critical path between A and E.

17. The longest path through the entire network passes along tasks a, d, e, g and h. This is the critical path for the entire project.

Start and Finish Times for a Paint Job.

19. a. The earliest time that task d can start is 1 hour. The earliest time that task f can start is 2.5 hours.

    b. The latest time that d can start is 2 hours; it is not on the critical path. The latest time that it f can start is 2.5 hours; it is on the critical path.

21. a. The earliest time that task d can finish is 1.5 hours. The earliest time that task f can finish is 4.5 hours.

    b. The latest time that d can finish is 2.5 hours; it is not on the critical path. The latest time that f can finish is 4.5 hours; it is on the critical path.

Start and Finish Times for Building a Hotel.

23. a. The earliest time that task d can start is 3 months. The earliest time that task f can start is 2 months

    b. The latest time that d can start is 3 months; it is on the critical path. The latest time that f can start is 12 months; it is not on the critical path.

25. a. The earliest time that task d can finish is 4 months. The earliest time that task f can finish is 5 months.

    b. The latest time that d can finish is 4 months; it is on the critical path. The latest time that f can finish is 15 months; it is not on the critical path.

Slack Time in a Paint Job.

27. Because task c is not on the critical path and has 1.5 hours of slack time, a one hour delay here will not delay the project.

29.

Task	EST	LST	EFT	LFT	Slack
a	0.0	0.0	2.0	2.0	0
b	0.0	1.0	1.0	2.0	1.0
c	0.0	1.5	1.0	2.5	1.5
d	1.0	2.0	1.5	2.5	1.0
e	2.0	2.0	2.5	2.5	0
f	2.5	2.5	4.5	4.5	0
g	4.5	4.5	7.5	7.5	0
h	4.5	5.5	6.5	7.5	1.0
i	7.5	7.5	9.5	9.5	0
j	9.5	10.0	10.0	10.5	0.5
k	9.5	9.5	10.5	10.5	0

Slack Time in Building a Hotel.

31. Because task d is on the critical path, a one month delay here will delay the project.

Further Applications

Doing the Laundry.

33. The slack time for a task is $LST - EST$ or $LFT - EFT$. For this job, the slack times are: a 0, b 0, c 10, d 0, e 15, f 30, g 0, h 0.

35. The critical path has length 150 minutes.

37.

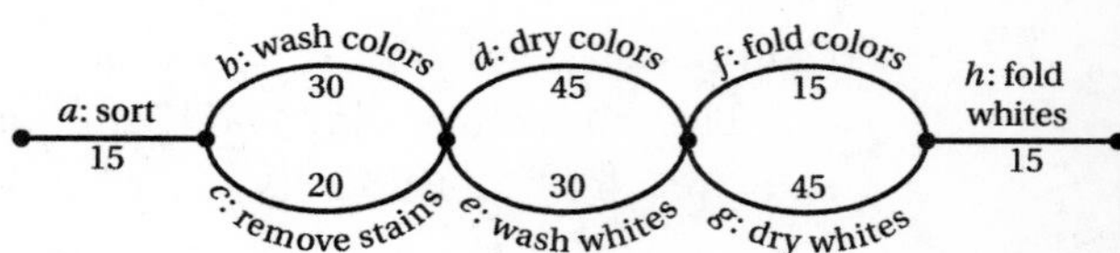

Cooking a Pasta Dinner.

39. The critical path passes through the tasks with no slack time. In this case the critical path is a, c, and f.

41. Tasks (a, b) and (c, d, e) take place at the same time. Task f must be done alone.